7770 5167

Uprising

Uprising

*Who the Hell Said You Can't
Ditch and Switch?*

The Awakening of
Diamond and Silk

REGNERY
PUBLISHING
A Division of Salem Media Group

Regnery® is a registered trademark of Salem Communications Holding Corporation

ISBN: 978-1-68451-007-8
eISBN: 978-1-68451-092-4
Library of Congress Control Number: 2020934519

Published in the United States by
Regnery Publishing
A Division of Salem Media Group
300 New Jersey Ave NW
Washington, DC 20001
www.Regnery.com

Manufactured in the United States of America

10 9 8 7 6 5 4 3 2 1

Books are available in quantity for promotional or premium use. For information on discounts and terms, please visit our website: www.Regnery.com.

Our book Uprising *is dedicated to GOD for blessing us with this opportunity. It could have been someone else, but he chose us, two black women from North Carolina, Diamond and Silk. God didn't make a mistake. He was so clever, and it was all in his plan, not ours.*

In 2008, I had a vision board in my office. It was one of those wooden framed bulletin boards. I would cut out pictures of whatever I wanted in life and pin it to my vision board. One day, I was looking to purchase an office chair and I came across this amazing red wine–colored chair. It was the big, elegant-looking chair that Donald Trump sat in when he starred on The Apprentice. *The chair looked so comfortable, but I couldn't afford it. So I cut out the picture of the chair with Donald Trump sitting in it and pinned it to my vision board. I said, "One day I will be able to afford to purchase this chair." Not realizing that I would be standing on the same stage with the man sitting in that chair seven years later. While I had my eyes on the chair, God had his eyes on something much bigger for me and my sister's life.*

If you think that's something, think about this: What are the odds that this same man who was sitting in that chair would be the forty-fifth President of the United States at the same time and in the same year that Diamond and Silk were both age forty-five? Some may call it luck, some may call it a coincidence, but we call it Divine Order.

Contents

From Mom and Dad

We are so proud of our daughters and excited about their success. We've raised them to believe in God and live by faith, no matter what. We've taught our daughters to be loyal to whatever cause they choose to embark upon and be the best at whatever they set out to do.

We've prayed for our daughters to make something out of themselves; we just didn't know that it would be anything like this. Looks like God heard our prayers.

We can remember back in 2014, Diamond came to us and stated these words: "I want to change the world." She said it with so much boldness, and she was direct. We are so thankful to God for empowering us with the knowledge to instill in our daughters, the powerful tools that equipped them for such a time as this.

—Elder and Evangelist Hardaway
Diamond and Silk's parents

Introduction

The roar of the crowd was deafening, but we could hear exactly what was being said. People leapt wildly for joy, arms flying in every direction, high-fiving and bear-hugging other people they didn't even know. Chants of "USA, USA, USA" were shouted from every angle of the room. Media cameras and cell phones flashed so constantly that they seemed to create their own blinding light in our eyes. American patriots who had fought hard to see this day come to pass were unified in hopes of seeing a great America, but the most visible patriotic symbols in the room were the red Make America Great Again hats.

It was November 8, 2016. Finally, it was official: Donald J. Trump had become the forty-fifth President of the United States of America.

We had been stumping for Donald J. Trump for more than a year. We understood the true heart of America because we saw it almost daily. We saw people who had a love for this country, people that had never voted before in their lives, getting registered to vote. We saw people switching their party from Democrat to Republican to vote for Trump.

Leading up to this extraordinary moment, we had worked very hard at mobilizing and energizing Americans to get out and vote. When the naysayers said that Donald Trump would never be president and that we were crazy for supporting him, we only felt liberated. People would come up to us crying, they were so afraid of what would happen to America if Donald Trump lost. Our response to that fear was always, "Y'all, we got this; we are going to win!" We were sure of it, without a shadow of a doubt. This was about much more than one man; it was about a movement to put a person who was willing and able to make changes and fight for the American people into the White House.

From our modest upbringing in the Tar Heel State of North Carolina to standing onstage with the President of the United States, it was like a rush of euphoria, a charge of excitement, and a sense of relief. We did it, and there wasn't anything that anybody could do about it.

Our critics—who claimed to be civilized and more enlightened than us deplorables—called us coons, Uncle Toms, and sellouts. They marginalized us, criticized us, stigmatized us, and when that failed, they tried to assassinate our characters and ruin our reputations. Through it all, no matter how they tried to hide us or get rid of us, Diamond and Silk weren't going anywhere. We were a force to be reckoned with.

So imagine how tickled pink we were when Donald Trump won; we knew that it was time for the Left and the left-wing media to start eating crow.

Y'all, I'm telling you, we had no plans for this.

You know, if you ever want to make God laugh, tell Him your plans. If you ever want to make God mad, try going against His plan. He will put a series of events into action that will wheel you around to what He wants you to do, not what you want to do.

We didn't have any plans. We were just going along with our lives as usual, then we were thrust into this political arena all because we dared to speak out and speak up for what we believed. It's like we've transitioned from one place to another place. Now, we are here. So let us take you back to how it all began.

Chapter 1

We Were Created for Such a Time as This: Where We Came From

When we started stumping for Trump, we needed no one's permission or validation. We couldn't have cared less about what anybody thought, including family. We weren't looking to score brownie points; we were looking to shed light on the naked, nasty truth!

As long as we can remember, we've never had any emotional attachment or connection to my father's side of the family. They've always treated us like we were the dirt under the bottom of their shoes.

Mm-hmm.

In their eyes, we were nothing, and we were never going to be anything. Our mother was treated like she was trash because she did not live up to their expectations, and, as children, we felt the brunt of it.

Oh, gurl, I can remember that so vividly. We weren't invited to a lot of the family reunions either; we only heard about them after they were over.

So when we started stumping for Trump and people told us we'd stop getting invited to the family reunions, we said, "Hell, we were never invited to the family reunions anyway."

3

Our mother's side of the family always told us we acted and talked like we were too proud. They would say we thought we were better than everybody else.

Yes, they would.

That was the furthest thing from the truth. Our parents raised us to keep our heads up, no matter our circumstances or struggles.

That's right.

Our mother taught us from a very young age about faith: if you believe it, you can achieve it! She wanted us to have more than what she had; she wanted us to have the best.

Oh, yes, she did! And I can remember Mother saying, "Faith is the substance of things hoped for and the evidence of things not seen."

That was followed up by our father saying, "Having faith as small as a grain of a mustard seed is all you need." He always demonstrated how tiny that grain of mustard seed was. It was like the tools for life: having the faith and working the faith.

Our mother was raised in Raeford, North Carolina. Her parents were sharecroppers. Sharecropping is a form of farming in which a landowner allows a tenant to work the land, tend crops, and develop a harvest. To pay for this use of the land, a share of the crops produced on the sharecropper's portion of land is given to the landowner.

In reality, sharecropping was just a form of undercover slavery and a way to exploit and take advantage of poor uneducated people, especially black people. Sharecropping was not about a fair and equal system, and it was not about giving black people a fair shake or making sure they received their forty acres and a mule.

Mm-hmm, it was a form of systemic racism.

But during the days of Jim Crow, it was the only sense of refuge and source of survival for black people. Back then our mother was not living the American dream; she was living in an American nightmare. Our mother grew up in extreme poverty. Being the oldest of five children, she had to drop out of school to help our grandmother and grandfather pick cotton and sucker tobacco.

That's right. Back in the day, harvesting tobacco was done by pulling individual leaves off the stalk as they ripened. As the plants grew, the tops of the tobacco flowers were removed—this is called "topping." At the same time, they would prune the leaves that were unproductive—this was called "suckering." This process helped ensure that most of the plant's energy focused on producing the large leaves that were harvested and sold.

Thank you, Silk.

You're welcome.

Mother would always tell us the story of how her family lived in a two-bedroom shack on Lentz Farm with no lights and no running water. They used an outside toilet, pumped their own water from a well, and cooked their food on a wooden stove.

They also heated their house, which was nothing more than a shed, with wood in the fireplace.

The floor of the house was made of wood planking with gaps or holes throughout. Mother could literally see the ground beneath the home. It was nothing for them to see chickens and snakes running up under the house. The roof of the house was made out of tin and wood. When it rained, it literally poured. They would have to put out buckets and pots to catch the rainwater.

That's right. Mother told us that when they would lay in their bedsteads, which were made of iron, the holes in the roof were big enough for them to see the stars.

She talked about how they would work all week long and how Grandfather was only given a little money by the farm owner. Grandfather was uneducated; he had dropped out of school in the first grade; he could not read or write; he signed his name with the letter X.

Wow. Yes, he did.

He took what they gave him, even though they were cheating him. There was nothing he could do about it back in those days; his only option was to continue working and hope for something better during a hopeless time.

According to our mother, he knew he was being swindled out of what he was supposed to get, but that was the life that he and other blacks were dealt. This was the only life they knew. The system was put in place by Democrats who thrived on cheap labor. At the time, Southern whites nearly all voted Democrat.

And guess what, Diamond?

What?

It looks like they are trying to put those same measures back in place.

When you think about it, Grandfather was probably just happy he and his family had a place to lay their heads. He took what they gave him, even if they were cheating him out of what he was supposed to get.

Yeah, I doubt that he was the only one; back then it was about survival or starvation.

Mother told us how at the end of the week they would only have enough money left to buy a bag of beans, a slab of fatback, and a jar of molasses.

Oh, and don't forget about having enough money to purchase flour to make hoecake bread to sop the molasses with.

In case you are wondering what hoecake bread is, it was nothing but flour, water, and lard mixed together and fried in a cast-iron skillet.

Mm-hmm.

Our mother grew up with nothing. They could not even afford the bare essentials like toilet paper; they used cotton from the cotton field. They washed their clothes with lye soap in a washpot. She tells the story about how Grandmother would build a fire under the washpot to heat the water. Once the water started boiling, she would put the soiled clothes in the pot, take a stick, and beat the clothes and stir them around to get the dirt out of them.

Then, using the stick, she would take the clothes out of the washpot, put them in another washtub, and use a scrubbing board to scrub them to make sure they were clean. Finally, she would take the clothes out of the washtub, put them in another washtub with clean water to rinse them, then wring them out and hang them on the clothesline to dry.

Around Christmastime, they were lucky if they got a little doll or even had food to eat. It was rough!

Yes, it was!

Our father grew up in Enterprise, Mississippi. He was the fourth child out of nine children. He often talked about how his mother didn't play. She was unique, peaceful, and she made the best bread pudding. She later passed away during childbirth. Our grandfather, who was a schoolteacher, was very firm and structured. He was always direct and to the point. He later remarried and continued to raise his children. Our father learned valuable lessons from his father, and he was able to pass those lessons down to us. He would tell how, back then, those were some hard days. With three older siblings, when things got down to him, he always got the least of what was left.

The thing that we admire about our father is his brilliance. He knows how to take nothing and make something out of it. Growing up, we would always hear our father say, "Use your head so that you can save your arms and legs."

Mm-hmm. Little did we know, that was the same thing that our grandfather used to say to Daddy.

Though his family was poor, he was not brought up in severe poverty. His grandfather, our great-grandfather, owned land, and they grew everything they needed right there on their land.

Mm-hmm. That's right.

Our great-grandfather, Will Hardaway, lived in Enterprise, Mississippi, through the days of the Great Depression. He would tell our father about how most days he went to bed hungry—so hungry that he could feel his backbone touching his ribs. He suffered!

Our great-grandfather was an ox tamer. An ox tamer is a person who tames and coaches oxen on how to pull and plow the fields. He even kept honeybees.

Mm-hmm.

He also had a smokehouse. His land was filled with corn, peanuts, vegetables, and potatoes. He had his own sugar mill where he made molasses. Back in those days, they didn't have deep freezers to keep things frozen, so he taught the older children how to can vegetables. Our great-grandfather had fruit trees on the land. He would always tell our daddy, "Don't ever plant a tree that doesn't have any value."

Wow. Look at all of that wisdom.

Mother worked as a sharecropper from age thirteen to sixteen. Her first real job was when she was hired to work at the five-and-ten-cent store on Main Street in Raeford, North Carolina. She also did domestic work, like babysitting, for a white family while they worked.

Our mother's father moved his family from Lentz Farm to Upchurch Farm, where they still didn't have any running water or lights; they lived on that farm while Granddaddy worked at Sandhills Furniture Factory in Aberdeen, North Carolina. When Mother turned eighteen years old, our grandfather got her a job working at the same factory.

Despite being poor, our mother always wanted the best for herself. After she started working at Sandhills Furniture Factory, she moved off the farm and out of the house that had no lights and no running water. She then rented a house in Raeford, North Carolina, where she had lights and running water.

Mm-hmm. That's right.

Our grandmother was very upset when Mother moved out. Perhaps she may have felt that our mother's focus should have been on helping the family instead of helping herself.

Perhaps.

But Mother was tired of being poor. She didn't want to be another black person with nothing. She didn't want to be another statistic or another hopeless cause. She saw a way that she could get on her feet and make her way without being dependent on the farm and stuck in the days of sharecropping.

She didn't want to be a victim.

Right. She wasn't looking for someone to pat her on the head and think that they were doing her a favor by giving her a place to lay her head. Mother was able to furnish her two-bedroom home because working at the furniture factory allowed her to get her furniture "on time."

In case you don't know what "on time" means, allow me to explain: It means that as long as you have good credit, you can obtain the item without paying for the item up-front. You had to pay off the balance of what you owed by making monthly payments until the balance was paid in full.

Like all young men of that time period, our father was drafted into the military when he turned eighteen. He was stationed at Fort Bragg, North Carolina, and he served in the Eighty-Second Airborne.

He met our mother in Raeford, North Carolina, while he was out with a friend who was dating my mother's sister. Once our parents met, they were inseparable. They were like a hand in a glove; Mother had the yin, and Father had the yang.

They balanced each other; Mother was always fiery, and Father was always calm.

Hahaha. Sound familiar?

They both wanted the same thing. Daddy had a home in Detroit, Michigan, and a new car; he admired our mother because she had no children at the time and she was renting a nice home filled with beautiful furniture. He was intrigued by her ambitious attitude. He knew that they could have something together, and they did.

Silk is the oldest of six children, born January of 1971, and I'm the second oldest, born on Thanksgiving Day 1971. We would often hear Mother and Father talk about how they had cooked up a lot of food on that Thanksgiving Day, only for Mother to go into labor and Father to rush her to the hospital.

Diamond wasn't waiting on nobody. She was actually born premature.

After Daddy got out of the military in 1972, he moved all of us to his home on the East Side of Detroit, Michigan. We lived in a small, brick home on Keystone Street with pea green siding. Silk and I shared a room, and our mother turned the third bedroom into a den, which was where we lounged and watched TV. Mother would not let us sit in the living room.

That's right; Momma didn't play that.

Another thing that our mother didn't allow: we could not run through the house and mess it up.

No, ma'am, we sure couldn't.

In 1973, Mother had two more children who were ten months apart: my brother, who is the third oldest, and my sister, who was the baby girl. All four of us are ten months apart.

Yes. We were considered stepladders. Eight years later, Mother and Father gave us another brother. He was the baby boy. About five years after that, Mother and Father adopted a girl, which gave us another sister. That made me the oldest of four girls and two boys.

When Silk turned five years old, she went to school while my brother, sister, and I stayed home with Mother. On that day, our father decided to cook oatmeal for everyone before Silk left for school. I never got the chance to eat any of the oatmeal because once I saw the expression on Silk's face, I didn't want to eat any of it. Silk is the reason I don't eat oatmeal to this day.

Hahaha . . . yes, you are right. I love to eat, but it has to have some flavor. When Daddy sat that bowl in front of me, I didn't know what it was, but one thing I did know is it didn't look good at all. It was lumpy and very thick. Everyone was waiting on me to taste the stuff before they would eat it. Finally, I braved up, opened my mouth, and tasted a little bit. Oh my, it was horrific. Was my daddy serious? How did he expect me to function in school with that awful gook in my stomach? My face had a sour look on it, and my sister knew that it was a big fat no to oatmeal.

That oatmeal had nasty all in it. It looked nasty and it definitely tasted nasty. I think Daddy may have forgotten to add some sugar or honey—something to sweeten it up. From that day until just a few years ago, I wouldn't dream of trying to stomach oatmeal. Now, I only eat instant oatmeal with raisins, dates, walnuts, berries, and sliced bananas.

Silk is also the reason why I don't have buckteeth today. As a baby, I sucked my thumb. When Silk was five and I was four, she said, "Don't suck your thumb; suck your baby finger." It was my saving grace. I still suck on my finger today, but I don't have buckteeth.

So I guess you can call me your dentist because I helped save your teeth. Hahaha.

Mother was a stay-at-home mom. She made sure the house was clean and food was cooked. I remember how, at the age of four, I would follow her around to try and help her clean. All I was doing was getting in her way. I remember one day Mother was sitting in the den, eating her Honey Graham crackers and watching the soap opera, I believe it was *The Edge of Night*. I was staring at her, and she said, "Why are you gazing at me? Do you want a cracker?"

I said, "Yes."

And she replied, "When you want something, you don't gaze at it; you ask for it."

I was four years old, and I'll never forget that. It was a defining moment.

When Daddy got home from work, all he had to do was wash up, have a seat, and eat.

Yes, he did. And I remember when Daddy would sometimes stop by the garage to drink him a beer. Out of respect, he made sure that he took his sip outside of the house. He would not drink inside of the home; Momma wasn't having that.

By this time, Momma had given her life to God, and she didn't want any drinking going on in front of her or her children.

So this one particular time, I remember jumping up in my father's lap to get a hug. The hug was a little, clever cover-up to see if I could smell alcohol on his breath. Sure enough, I did, and I yelled out, "Momma, he's been drinking again."

Daddy was so undone; it wouldn't surprise me if that was one of the reasons why he stopped drinking beer.

We had some memorable times when we lived on Keystone. I remember when our grandmother—our mother's mother—came to visit us in Detroit. This particular day, Grandmother had to babysit us because Mom had an appointment.

Yes.

So she allowed us to go outside to play, and while we were outside playing, a group of children came on our side of the street to start something.

Yes, I remember.

We went into the house and told our grandmother what was happening outside, and she was like, "Not my grandbabies."

She found a few wire coat hangers, opened them up like sticks, and sent us back outside. We went back out there like superheroes, and let's just say that it wasn't a good day for the other side. They didn't cross back over to our side of the street again.

Hahaha, yes. We showed them, didn't we?

We sure did.

Our father worked at Kroger Bakery, which was a factory that made bread. He made good money and got paid every week. It was nothing for him to bring home $600 or $700 a week, which was good because it was needed to take care of a family of six.

After staying at the house on Keystone for a few years, our family had outgrown our 898-square-foot home, so my father and mother purchased another house, on the West Side of Detroit, Michigan. I remember when he drove us to the house; it looked really huge. It was totally different from the three-bedroom home we had been living in. We had a living room, a dining room, a kitchen, and a kitchen nook. A slew of steps led to the four bedrooms and one bathroom upstairs. It was bigger than what we were used to living in, and it was beautiful.

Yes, gurl, I remember. It was the year 1976. The house was a 1,649-square-foot home, on a 4,792-square-foot lot, built in 1951. We thought we were the Jeffersons. We had moved on up, but it was to the West Side from the East Side.

It was totally different from the smaller home. Everything was bigger, including the backyard. A few years later, Daddy even put up a pool for us. And let's not forget the basement, where the washer and dryer were, down the stairs that led from the kitchen. The house even had a laundry chute: you could put dirty clothes in it from upstairs, and they would slide down the chute and drop into a wooden cage in the basement.

We had moved from a single-level home to a three-level home, and the change for the better was drastic.

The wallpaper was made of velvet and painted with designs; the house was carpeted all the way through; the gas stove was built into the counter; and the oven was built into the wall.

That's right.

Silk, my baby sister, and I slept in the pink room, with pink paisley wallpaper. Mother bought us all new bunk beds with beautiful linens. Silk had her own bed, I slept in the top bunk, and my baby sister slept in the bottom bunk.

Yep.

My brother slept in the blue room, where he had his own bed, and my parents had the master bedroom. The last bedroom was turned into a guest room.

Mother had the house decked out. She bought all-new furniture for the living room, dining room, and kitchen. She had everything in its place, nothing was out of order, and the house was so immaculate that she did not allow us to walk inside with our outside shoes on.

That's right. You had to take off your shoes at the door. Mother didn't care who you were.

Mother was so thrilled about her new home; she and Father were now proud homeowners. It was a big step up for Mother because it was a long way from living in the shack house with a wooden floor, the tin and wooden roof, and no lights or running water.

Daddy was still working at Kroger and, although he could work as many hours as he wanted, he wanted more for himself: he wanted his own business. He had never owned a business before. He and Mother did not know the ins and outs, but there's an old saying, "Nothing beats a failure but a try." So he was on the hunt for a business venture.

One day, in 1978, he was riding down Fenkell Road in Detroit, Michigan, when he saw an old-looking laundromat. It had all of the washing machines and dryers intact, but the place looked run-down. So he inquired about it.

After speaking to the rightful owner, he realized the place was being mismanaged and had become a drug den for addicts and dealers. Father asked the owner if he was willing to sell it, and the guy said yes.

Father was shocked and excited at the same time. The owner agreed to $7,000 for the equipment: $3,000 down and $200 a month until it was paid in full. Father also agreed to take over the lease and pay an additional $200 a month. The deal was done, and Mother and Father were the proud owners of a laundromat, which they named "Freeman's Neighborhood Laundromat."

Yes, that was the name.

I don't know about Silk, but I loved the laundromat.

Well . . . I didn't have a problem being at the laundromat, but there was no love lost here. But continue on . . .

It was interesting seeing people wash their clothing using quarters and needing dimes to dry them. I was infatuated with watching people put dimes in the dryer to start them. Hearing the dimes go into the slots and the knobs being turned was like listening to the sound of making money. The smell of Tide detergent and Downy fabric softener sheets bombarded my nose. The yellow dryers, which looked like machinery with windows, were lined up on both sides of the wall, and all of the washing machines were in the middle. The laundry tables, where customers were able to fold their clothing before leaving, were set on the sides of the washers.

Mother and Father also opened a pick-up store for dry cleaning inside the laundromat. Customers could drop off clothes to be dry-cleaned and then come back in three days to pick them up. Everything was convenient and at the customer's fingertips.

There were also snack and drink machines. The snack machine held up to nine items; all items were twenty-five cents. The snack machines back in those days were simple to operate, and we would get a kick out of putting our quarter through the slot, pulling the knob outward, and watching the candy be released. If we were good during the day, Daddy would let us get a snack and soda pop.

I can remember being outside and we were all playing behind the laundromat when, out of nowhere, this boy started picking on us. We didn't know who he was. Father came outside to check on us, and the boy continued to taunt us. My father told the boy to leave, and he wouldn't.

The next thing I knew, the boy threw something at us and took off running. Our father ran right after him; we didn't know Daddy could run that fast. The farther Daddy ran, the shorter Daddy looked. He brought that boy back to where we were, talked to him, then he let the boy go.

That day, our daddy was our hero.

After closing, Father would show us how to assist him with cleaning out the dryers and washing down the washing machines. We would help sweep the floors and wipe down the chairs. He would have us clean the windows on the dryers and take the lint out of the lint traps while he took care of the bathroom.

This is what it took to make sure the laundromat maintained a certain quality that was inviting to customers.

We would follow Daddy to every washer and dryer, watching him empty out the coin box—the box that catches the coins when they go through the slot—into a bucket. The coin box was always locked, and Father kept the master key. In order to get into the coin box, you had to unlock it with that key only.

I remember that funny-looking master key. It wasn't a regular key. It was flat at the top and round-shaped at the bottom, with a little, funny edge. The key only fit in that one lock.

The dimes would go into one bucket, and the quarters would go into another bucket. He would use coin rolls to roll the dimes and quarters, and sometimes he allowed us to help. Fifty dimes in a coin roll equaled five dollars, and forty quarters in a roll equaled ten dollars.

Mm-hmm. I bet you the average Millennial today would look at you as if you were crazy if you asked them to roll some coins. It's small learning curves like this that are missing from today's society.

Our mother and father taught us at an early age how to appreciate a business by showing us that cleanliness is next to godliness and to make sure to keep things clean.

Yes, they sure did.

Mother and Father didn't make a lot of money in the laundromat. It was a way for them to get their feet wet and experience being business owners. Though Father was always grateful for his job at Kroger, he was tired of working twelve-hour shifts and not being able to spend enough time with his family. He would pray to God to bless his business so that it could become his full-time job.

Be cautious about what you ask for because you just may get it.

You got that right.

It was 1979. The laundromat had been open for almost a year when Daddy received a phone call that made his heart drop and put him in panic mode.

Mm-hmm.

A friend from the job by the name of Hendrick called him to let him know that Kroger was closing for good and going out of business.

It seemed to our father that our lives flashed before his eyes: there was his new home, the new business that was not pulling in a lot of money, and now he was about to lose his biggest source of income—his full-time job.

There was nothing Father could do; he prayed that God would bless his business so that it could become his full-time job. God did one better: He fixed it where it would become his only job. Mother and Father had only one person to lean on—and that was God—and one thing to rely on—and that was faith.

Chapter 2

Defining Childhood Moments

We have to say, our upbringing had a lot to do with what we're able to handle today. We always felt a little bit separated from the crowd. Even though we all stood in the same line for the same Focus Hope cheese, other people thought we had more.

Our earliest memories, without a doubt, revolve around the holidays.
That's right.
We never missed Christmas, Thanksgiving, or Easter.
Mm-hmm.
Growing up, Mother and Father made sure we had beautiful Christmases . . .
Oh, yes, I do remember the beautiful Christmases: the tree, the lights, the snow. Yes, I do remember . . .
Father made sure we had a live Christmas tree every year; I can remember the fresh smell of pine. Once Father got the tree into the house, he would stand it up on the tree stand, then Mother would pull out the ornaments to decorate it.

Strings and strings of one-color Christmas lights would be bundled together, like a necklace with knots. Our job was to help Mother unravel the lights so that she could plug them in to see if they still worked from the year before.

Yes, she would. One string at a time, one bulb at a time. I remember plugging in the string of lights to see if they flickered. If they did, that meant that the string was live, but one bulb was loose. I would have to twist each bulb to make sure it was screwed in tight enough for the rest of the lights on the string to stay lit. Twist, next; twist, next, until the weakest link was found.

Of course, if I plugged the string of lights into the socket and got nothing, that usually meant one or more bulbs on the string needed to be changed. This was a bigger challenge for me, but, 99.99 percent of the time, I figured it out one string at a time.

After the lights were sorted and put on the tree, Mother would allow us to help her hang the ornaments. Afterwards, she would place garlands around the tree and then put the star on top.

And, just like that, the tree decorations were complete.

Christmas was always a great time. Leading up to the big day, Mother would demand that we be good because Santa Claus was coming. If we didn't behave, Santa would pass right over our house.

Mm-hmm.

We would start practicing how we would get up on Christmas morning and sneak down the stairs to see what Santa had brought us.

We sure would.

We would go to our bedrooms, and Silk would practice how she would wake me up, then I was supposed to wake my baby sister up. Slowly and quietly, we would move to the blue room and wake my brother. We all snuck down the stairs by sitting on them one at a time and lifting ourselves onto the next stair without causing any squeaks or making any noises. After the practice run, we had our routine perfected, and we were ready.

Yes, we were.

On Christmas Eve, we would start preparing for the arrival of Santa Claus. Father would make cookies.

Oh, my . . . I do remember the sweet smell of those cookies.

He would bake cookies for us and Santa.

Mm-hmm. He'd tell us Santa was going to be eating them too, so we would sit there and watch him make them.

Smelling the cinnamon settling in the air made us so giddy, we couldn't contain our little selves. We were always overexcited. We would take our baths while the cookies were baking—I think Father made that rule to calm us down.

After our baths, Father would let us taste the cookies, which were always baked to perfection so that they would melt in your mouth.

After our snack, it was time for bed.

We didn't want to go to bed.

We never wanted to go to sleep.

We were so eager for Christmas morning to arrive that we were too anxious to go to sleep.

Don't forget about the thought of Santa coming down the chimney. And, guess what? We had a fireplace with a chimney.

And that's how Santa was going to bring our presents. We had it all figured out. Of course, it never dawned on us how Santa got a bicycle down the chimney. We just prayed that the chimney was big enough for him to fit in without getting stuck.

Remember the time we woke up, and you told me that Santa had kissed you on the cheek?

Gurl, yes. He kissed me on my right cheek. I woke up just slightly and saw his white beard and red suit.

You were so excited about that kiss, you made me excited too. So, you can imagine the disappointment we felt when we found out there was no Santa. Didn't matter to Silk. She still believed that was Santa who kissed her on the cheek.

Of course, years later we found out it was really Mother and Father, but just thinking about that moment now, I guess that started the dreaming process for me. You know, being able to dream, being in the magic of it all, I realize it all started with Santa.

As sure as the sky is blue, there we'd be in the wee hours of the morning, just as we practiced, sneaking downstairs to see what Santa had brought us.

Mm-hmm.

After getting down the stairs, we'd all stare in unison over to the right where the Christmas tree was. All of the toys that Santa had brought us were there: baby dolls, bikes, you name it, we had it.

Finally, Mother and Father would come down and watch us open our gifts.

Wow. Those were the days. Mother and Father outdid themselves every year.

On days like Christmas and Thanksgiving, food was always plentiful: turkey and dressing, candied yams, ham, chitterlings, collard greens, macaroni and cheese, baked beans, sweet potato pies.

And don't forget the banana pudding. Just thinking about it right now, makes me want to eat.

Yes. And it was all about family and love. We were a close-knit family because, even at a young age, we knew all we had was each other.

That's right.

The spirit of believing in Santa also brought in the faith aspect.

The faith, yes . . .

Because we were preparing for what we wanted, we felt happy. We were feeling as if it was going to happen, as if it had happened. Then when we walked down the stairs with our little selves in the morning, there it was.

Yes. We felt it, we knew it, and it happened.

I can even remember when we were little, in order to complete our chores, we would compartmentalize. If we were doing laundry and putting clothes away, we would play cleaners; when we had to do dishes, we played restaurant; when we had to do homework, we played school. We were the schoolteachers, and we had imaginary students that we had to teach our homework to. We literally wrote on the wall with chalk to teach our imaginary students. One day, Mother told us to stop washing the walls with Ajax. Little did she know, it wasn't Ajax; we were writing on her walls with chalk!

We also made up imaginary friends who were rich. One of them, Jackie-Ackie-Fackie, was getting married. Silk was the flower shop owner and made the flowers out of toilet tissue. Our job was to bring him these flowers. He lived out of town, so we had to make plane reservations.

We would actually call the airport and make reservations, using our imaginary names.

The upstairs steps served as the airplane taking us to our destination. We would pack our little bags, go sit on the steps, and pretend to travel.

We never realized that was preparing us for what we do today.

* * *

It was in elementary school that I remember getting my feelings badly hurt for the very first time. I was in the second grade, and my favorite teacher, Ms. Jones, yelled at me. I was a very sensitive child and always clung to my mother. Mother babied me, and she never hurt my feelings, so I didn't understand why Ms. Jones had hurt my feelings.

But why did she yell at you?

She was sore with me because I wasn't moving fast enough for her. I guess I had worked her last nerve, and she yelled in such a loud tone, "Hurry up, Hardaway." The pitch of her voice scared me to the point that I became embarrassed.

I call it a defining moment because that was when I learned, in one hard shot, to stay in my place and do what I'm told. If I didn't, people would get ugly.

Hmm.

Now, in fairness to Ms. Jones, she may have been having a bad day, but as a little girl I didn't understand that; all I saw was that she didn't like me anymore because she had yelled at me.

So, now, thinking back to that stage and age in my life, I would say that one of my defining moments was being in class and having to solve math problems.

The teacher's name was Mr. Williams. He was kind of a heavyset guy, and he didn't like to stand up a lot. I can see him, always leaning back in his chair.

This one day, he wanted the entire class to play this game. To me, it was more like a challenge. I had to go head to head with another student to see who could give the teacher the correct answer to the math problem first. Mr. Williams was clever in the way he got us to learn. He would pull out money, like pennies, nickels, and dimes . . .

Wow . . .

And he would tell us that if we answered the problem right, we would get this nickel or dime.

When the game was over, I was the winner. I won the challenge. Though I was giddy about winning, I was more excited about being able to be in a challenge to see what I could do.

Silk has always been the competitive one.

I don't know if I want to call it competitiveness. I think that it was just the thrill from the challenge of competing against my own self and saying to myself: I know this; I got this; I can win this.

Today, I really don't like being in competition with other people because I feel like everybody should have an equal playing field. You do you, and I do me—with the same tools.

But the one thing I notice about you is that if there is a problem, you're going to get to the very bottom of it, even if it takes you all night.

Oh, yes.

At times, I'll get annoyed with you, but that's how you are, and that is the gift that God gave you.

You're right, because I've got to do my research. I've got to dig in and see what this is; I've got to see what that is; I've got to make sure that it's right. I feel like there is a science to everything, and the challenge is to find the key ingredient that makes everything work.

That's Silk. You can call her Inspector Gadget and me the Mouth of the South.

Gurl, yes, I've got to figure it out.

∗ ∗ ∗

By the time I got to the third grade and Silk got to the fourth grade, Mother and Father were on to another venture. The lease was up on the laundromat, and the building owner, a man by the name of Goodson, wanted to raise the rent.

Mother and Father didn't have a problem with him going up on the lease; they had a problem with him tripling the rent.

Sometimes building owners will raise the rent every year or every two years, but they shouldn't go up so high that it feels like they are darn near price gouging.

Because Goodson saw a steady flow of customers and that Freeman's Neighborhood Laundromat was being patronized by the community, he thought that the business must be raking in the money—but that was not the case.

By the time you figured in the lights, water, and gas to heat the place, Mother and Father were barely breaking even. So when the landlord raised the rent so high, Father had no choice but to move out the machines and close down the laundromat. It was a sad day for the community because the laundromat was leaving, and they would have to find somewhere else to do their laundry.

But it was really a good day for Mother and Father. They may have been down, but they weren't out. When one door closes, a big old window will open, but this time my parents had to leap through it by faith!

Yes. So, one day, Father was driving in the heart of Detroit when he saw a man setting out dry cleaning equipment. He pulled over, got out of the car, and asked the man why he was setting out the equipment.

The gentleman turned to him and said he could not pay his lease, and he had only so many days to move the equipment out.

Mm-hmm.

My father asked if he would like to sell it, and the man said yes. My father offered him $500, and the man accepted. Father gave him $100 down and agreed to pay him $100 a month until it was paid for in full.

The man looked at Father as if he were crazy. The equipment weighed about 3,000 pounds, and he couldn't figure out how Father was going to move it.

Oh, but what that man didn't know is that our father had a plan. He called a friend by the name of Elder Vie, an elder at a church we often visited. Elder Vie was experienced in moving heavy equipment. He and Father moved all of that heavy equipment to our garage, where it sat until Mother and Father found a building.

We knew it was just a matter of time before God opened up another door for Mother and Father, and that door was about to swing wide.

Mm-hmm.

It wasn't long before Father was out riding down Plymouth Road, in Detroit, Michigan, when he saw a building up for sale. He said, "Hmm . . . that would be a good spot for a dry cleaner."

He whipped his car around in the middle of the street and landed in front of the building in order to look it over. After giving it a good inspection, he hightailed it home to let Mother know what he had seen.

Father was so excited. When he walked through the door, he rushed up to Mother to tell her what he had found.

Mother said to him, "How are you going to pay for it?"

When Mother said that, Father was crushed—but his spirit was still intact.

Yes. That's when he walked upstairs and disappeared into his bedroom. We didn't know what to think.

Here's what happened when he locked himself in that room, as he tells the story: He sat on the edge of the bed and began to pray. He said to God, "If this building is for us, touch my wife's heart and let her see the vision that I see."

Mother finished cooking dinner, and Father came downstairs to eat. After dinner, Mother looked at my father and said to him, "Let's go and see that building you were talking about."

Father says that his heart almost jumped out of his chest. He couldn't believe his ears. He had just prayed to God, and the sun hadn't even gone down. Mother was showing some interest in his vision.

They immediately jumped in the car and drove to the building. Thereafter, our parents were the proud owners of Hardaway's Dry Cleaners.

Diamond and I had an opportunity to visit the building back in 2018. It was abandoned, but here's the crazy thing: On the sun-damaged, faded-out green awning, you can see remnants of wording from when our parents owned it—and also the word "Silk" left over from the services the next set of tenants had offered.

That felt like a boomerang moment.

* * *

Mother got tired of us being in the public school system. Because she hadn't been able to finish school, she wanted us to have the best education possible, so she put us in a private Catholic school.

Right!

I was in the fourth grade and Silk was in the fifth grade in our first year at St. Casimir, where Father Gene and Sister Leonard ran the school.

That's right.

Another significant and defining moment came from my fourth grade teacher, Ms. Jeffries, who was a black teacher. Now, I'm going to be honest, I just was not applying myself. But instead of pulling out what was in there with encouragement and recognition, this teacher's answer was to divide the class into sections based on how smart we were. The smart kids sat in the front sections; the ones that may have been a little smart were next, in their own section; then came the next group, who were just a tad less smart; and then came the kids who just did not grasp it, and they were put in the back. I was one of the girls that sat in the back.

Hmm.

The teacher may not have thought that I knew how I was being labeled. But I did, and I was an impressionable young person. I may not have caught on to her teaching methods, but I had enough intelligence and instinct to see what she was doing.

This is when I totally checked out of the fourth grade. If I was going to be labeled "dumb" and be put in the back, why should I apply myself?

Mm-hmm.

If she felt like I was not applying myself, then it was her job as the teacher to find out why.

Right.

From that day, all the way through high school, I felt separated from my classmates.

But back to St. Casimir: My second year there brought me to the fifth grade. And it was in that year that there was a defining moment that actually altered me and propelled me into my calling.

My teacher's name was Ms. Mosley, and her classroom assistant's name was Ms. Houston. Ms. Mosley was skinny and had a caramel complexion. Every day she wore pantsuits; we never saw her in a dress.

My fifth grade year was great all the way up to the time Ms. Mosley and Ms. Houston decided to have a fruit party for the class.

For reasons of her own, my mom didn't buy fruit for me to take to school that day. So while the fruit party was going on, one boy and I couldn't participate because we had not brought any fruit. We were told to put our heads down.

Why was this such a significant event? Because as my head was down on the desk, it was down in shame because I didn't have what was needed to participate. This is why today, as an adult, I'm so passionate about advocating for people that don't have. During that time when my head was down, though I felt ashamed, I decided—you know what?—I want to advocate for people that don't have.

I have such a big heart for those in need, and this defining moment is one of the reasons why. I don't ever want anyone to feel ashamed because they don't have something. I've been in grocery stores and have paid for the person's groceries in front of me if they didn't have enough money to pay for them. I've helped people that needed to eat who didn't have the money. I've helped people who were homeless to try to give them a fresh start.

If I know of someone in need, I'll see if I can figure out how to help them. Because I don't want—now I'm about to cry—that was embarrassing and that was humiliating, and you should never do that to a child.

That was a defining moment.

Wow, sis. That was so profound. As you were telling the story, it was as if you were reliving it all over again, with such emotion. You're passionate about people who don't have, and your response is always, "Let me see how I can help you."

I am like that; I'll give my last.

Because at times you could be standing in a line, and if somebody has a problem, you would get involved.

Because every time I think about it, I feel that same humiliation I felt back then. No one should ever do that to a child, make them feel like they can't participate. Because maybe the parent forgot, or maybe the parent couldn't afford to buy fruit for thirty students.

Right, right, right. Well, unfortunately, that's how it was back then. It's important to see how that defining moment prepared you for today.

Right.

Just like that time when we were standing in line at a restaurant waiting to give our order, and a supervisor was scolding his employee in front of everybody. It was you that stepped up and got that supervisor straight. You didn't know the girl or the supervisor. You just knew that there is a right way and a wrong way to talk to a human being, even if you are their supervisor.

That is why I advocate for people who don't have and speak for people who can't speak. They're telling you that you can't have; I'm telling you that you *can* have; I'm telling you that you *can* come up, and you *can* be more.

Right. Hmm . . . that was a huge defining moment, it surely was.

As moments like that go, I vividly remember one time when I was sitting in class, looking at the teacher writing on the chalkboard. The words looked like a lot of letters scrambled together, and none of it made sense to me. I sat there and tried to figure it out because I was too scared to ask questions, in fear that the rest of the class would pick on me.

When we would have to do an assignment, I would just put down any old answer and turn in my paper. Yup, I got my big fat "F," written in red ink. No worries. I thought the teacher was the one who had the problem.

Now, it's at the end of the quarter, and it's time for parent–teacher conferences. No shame in my game; it was the teacher who didn't know how to figure out a way for me to understand what she was talking about.

Well during the conference the principal of the school told my parents that I would never be able to learn and that it would always be hard for me to comprehend, and that was something they would have to accept. Again, no worries. I let it roll right off of me. I didn't get offended at all because I knew that something was definitely wrong with the teacher, not me. Hell, I wasn't getting paid to teach her, she was getting paid to teach me.

As I continued to pass to each next grade by learning how to teach myself, I saw things in a different manner and from a very different perspective. I heard things a particular way that didn't make sense to anyone else but me. I had to learn how to remember, go and get a book, read it, and compare what I read to things that I could relate to or to things that were very simple.

I had to actually develop my own system of how to comprehend things myself, especially before I took a test. Now, did I cheat? You bet your bottom dollar I did. It was better to cheat than to repeat.

If I really had to explain my methods to someone else, they wouldn't get it. I can't learn it their way, so I'll learn it my own way because my way is the right way for me.

Here's an important life lesson from this particular defining moment: I understood that someone was trying to label me, but I didn't agree with them. The teacher was the adult; I was the child. She was supposed to be there to teach me, and if I wasn't getting it that meant that she wasn't doing a very good job at teaching.

To this day I still use all of the skills that I developed for myself. In fact, my dog-on-bone research has become a very important part of what we do. I find it fairly easy to break down the most complex issues by using a level of common sense that resonates with our everyday life.

Now comes our third year at St. Casimir. I move into the sixth grade, and Silk is in the seventh grade. While everyone was going back to school happy about their summer vacation, I was returning with my skin all broke out because I was coming into puberty. I looked like a hot mess; my hair was falling out; I was really stressed out.

So, now, this was the perfect opportunity to get picked on and bullied because my hair was not long enough; my skin was not good enough. So I felt insecure. I didn't feel confident at all, not in the sixth grade, and this made the bullying all that much worse because I believed the things my tormentors were saying.

Now let me point out one thing: it was not white children bullying me; I was harassed by people with the same skin color as me.

Right!

What my classmates didn't know was all of the stress we were experiencing at home. Our homelife had become so stressful that my hair started falling out in patches. It got so bad, Mother went and bought me a small wig.

So, after the Easter holiday break, I returned to school wearing a wig, not because I wanted to but because I had no other choice. Of course, the bullying got worse; I was bullied relentlessly.

Yes, I remember.

Chapter 3

Preacher's Kids

As we speak our truth regarding religion, it's not to disparage or disrespect its sanctity. Remember, we were taught faith at an early age and understood God was good. However, we were inundated with the doctrine of denomination, and we came to understand some harsh realities about the church, especially the black church.

Religion and God have always been an integral part of the black community and the black family. Conservative values and faith in God were the glue that sealed our hope and etched it into our very being, all going back to the days of slavery.

Since the days of slavery, most black people have felt out of place or uncertain of their place. With that said, everyone, especially black people, wants to belong or to become affiliated with something higher than themselves. Because of the atrocities of slavery, black people needed something to sustain and uplift them.

Ancestrally, from the very beginning of slavery, black people were told and even coerced into believing they were not good or not good enough. This is nowhere in scripture, yet this belief was instilled in our ancestors and has been passed down from one generation to the next generation.

Slavery started in the U.S. in 1619, and it took almost three centuries for parts of the country to view slavery as extreme cruelty. During those days, black people didn't have rights. They were considered property, not human beings, and religion was used to keep black people in bondage and oppression, thinking that that's where God intended them to be—instead of speaking what scripture really says, which is that we are all designed by God to be equal and free.

Slaves were used to pick cotton, plant and harvest other crops, build railroads, wash clothes, cook, and clean. They did this from sunup to sundown. Slaves were beaten, lynched, and maimed to keep them in line. Slaves were intentionally set against one another to cause strife and dishonesty.

Back in the day, the slave masters were so cruel, they would sell off the children of the adult slaves to other slave masters, causing family separation.

Mm-hmm.

Ever since I can remember, I've always hated being a preacher's kid. I could never live up to the expectation of being perfect. In my eyes, "being perfect" meant having no flaws. Not only did I have flaws, but there were also secrets lurking in the crevices.

There is a difference between God and religion. God is the source, the supplier, the creator and ruler of the universe. Religion is doctrine, theology, and persuasion. We don't serve religion; we serve God.

Yes. For me, God lives in me. Religion is something that was being indoctrinated into me.

I love God, and I will never stop loving God, but I loathe religion.

Mm-hmm, the indoctrination of religion.

You may ask me what I mean by that.

Yes, please explain.

I hated the construct and dogma of an ideology that made some appear more superior than others. Religion has always had people pointing the finger at each other as to who is right and who is wrong. Religion was used by some to keep people in line. It was a means of controlling people. That's not God's love; that's conveniently applied abuse.

Yeah, sis; I'm with you on that.

Well, we grew up in a very religious family. I can't count the number of churches we attended. We became members of some, and others we didn't. I remember being in church all day on Sundays, and I used to dread it. First, there was Sunday school, then morning worship. Afterward, you went home, ate, and then came back for evening service. On Tuesday nights, it was prayer service; on Thursday night, it was Bible class. After all of that, there would usually be Saturday choir rehearsal or someone's usher board meeting to attend—and God forbid if you didn't show up.

Mm-hmm. You're taking us way back.

Services were always so long and drawn out. I was always irritated by it.

The first church we went to was the Church of Our Lord & Savior Jesus Christ of the Apostolic Faith. I was five, and Silk was six years old. We were baptized in that church. I will never forget it because it was a big church, and the children went to mini-church.

The church teachings were strict. I remember having to wear patty-cakes, which were called chapel scarves, on our heads. All the women in the church, even down to the children, had to have their heads covered.

Mm-hmm. Yes, I remember.

Mother would get us up early on Sunday morning and get us ready for Sunday school. We would have on our pretty little dresses with matching shoes, our little purses, and we were ready.

Don't forget the matching hair bows.

That's right. Sunday school classes used to be in the basement of the church. I remember sitting there listening to the stories and being ready for it to be over. After Sunday school, there was a children's church, but most of the time Mother had us in the sanctuary in the front row. The one thing about Mother, she didn't play. She would sit us in the front row and let Silk hold the switch in her lap to keep the rest of us in line while Mother sang in the choir.

Yes, she sure did. I was the oldest, so I had to keep everyone else in line.

Living the apostolic faith was very rigid and strict. Anything that defiled the temple—meaning your body—was forbidden, like wearing pants or makeup, drinking alcohol, or smoking cigarettes.

There was no listening to the radio because that music was worldly. Any music other than gospel music was prohibited. Many times, I had to sneak and listen to some secular music to keep up with the trends.

You see, being in school around my peers and not knowing about a new rap song or a new singing group could make me seem lame. So when Mom and Dad would leave the house, we would blast the radio, the record player, and the tape recorder.

But we had to make sure that we were on the lookout. When that Thunderbird or Cadillac Seville drove into the driveway, everyone knew what to do: go turn it back to the gospel stations, just like Momma had it, or you were going to get it. We even had our own chant, "Momma is here. Momma is here. Momma-Is-Here!"

We had been to several different churches by the time we were in middle school, and Mother and Father just did not agree with the majority of them. Throughout the years, we went through this span of churches. Mother had become an ordained evangelist and Father an ordained minister. Then they opened their own church.

Being a preacher's kid meant we had to set, and be, an example, but we had no clue how to be the example. We were in middle school, about to approach high school. We wanted to be normal, like everyone else.

Because our parents became so ingrained in religion, they missed all of the telltale signs of ill treatment and abuse. Once they started the church, nothing was ever as it appeared, in my opinion.

Yeah. Sitting here now, looking back, it was like we had to put on a mask to appear a certain way when we were out in public.

From the eyes of a preacher's kid, it seemed that the brunt of building the church fell on our little shoulders. We had to illustrate how to lead a godly life and go out to win souls. Having to set the example and be the example was far too much of a burden to bear.

Remember, my hair was falling out; I was coming into puberty, so my skin was breaking out; I didn't want to be an example. Heck, I didn't even want to be seen.

By the time I had gotten to the eighth grade and Silk had gotten to the ninth grade, Mother sat us down and told us that we could not wear pants anymore, and we weren't allowed to wear makeup. She said we needed to present our bodies as a living sacrifice, holy and acceptable before God.

Gasp. Now, that was a real blow for me. What was I going to tell my friends when they asked me why I always wore a dress? How was I going to participate in gym? I was thirteen years old, just starting the ninth grade with people that had seen me wearing pants. I had my favorite pants that I loved to wear. Now, all of a sudden, I would have to go to school looking and feeling like I was in some kind of cult. I literally went into a state of depression and rebellion all at the same time.

Yes; we were ticked off. We could not understand why, in the prime of our young lives, right in front of our peers, it was God's will for us to go to school looking different from everyone else. A drastic change of this magnitude made it easy for us to be bullied and harassed. It was an embarrassing time, so humiliating that I just checked out.

I remember feeling that our lives were ruined, all because of religion. What other children were allowed to do, Mother would not let us do. I started to rebel; I hated school, and I hated my life.

Yes, the way to godliness was presented as total strictness and restrictions.

When parents go into extreme thinking, they will push children to the edge, or over the edge, and the children will have nowhere to go but down. Mother never gave us any wiggle room. It was just, "Do what I say, or else."

In our opinions, looking back over those days, maybe Mother saw that we were growing up and developing and was afraid that men would start looking at us in a sexual way. What Mother didn't realize is that we were already being abused. In my opinion, making us wear dresses gave easy access for the abuser to abuse us even more.

I spiraled out of control. I remember getting into trouble, then pulling Silk into it so she could be in trouble with me. It was nothing for my parents to get a call from the principal's office, saying they were kicking Silk and me out of school because of the mess that I had gotten into.

By the time I got into the ninth grade, I was already skipping school. I got tired of going to school and being the laughingstock. Day in and day out, schoolmates made derogatory remarks, just to humiliate me. On the days that I went to school, I was always in trouble for sassing back to a teacher or something else. I had gotten so bad that I was kicked out of school for half of my ninth grade year.

After I was kicked out of school, Mother made me get up in the mornings and go to the cleaners with her and Father and work during the day.

Silk was so upset about our new life of restrictions that she took pills to try to end her life! Thank God, Silk is still here to tell the story.

That's right. Because I'm still here, I will tell the story: Being young, not knowing or understanding, all bundled up with a feeling of worthlessness, made me blank out. I didn't want to be here. I couldn't do anything. I lost a lot of weight because I was too depressed to even eat. I didn't have another lie to tell my friends. I didn't want to go through life like this.

By this time, our parents had a church. As it happened, we had a small fire at our home, and while the house was being renovated, the family moved into the Sunday school part of the church. Well, we were in really close quarters. One day, after coming in from school, I decided to just go to my zone. I wanted to scream, but I couldn't. I felt so alone, and no one understood or cared about the emotional pain that was wreaking havoc on my body. I was literally motionless. I wanted to die. I remember saying to myself, "If I have to live like this, I may as well be dead."

I can't remember what I took, but it was a handful of pills. I swallowed them down with a cup of water. I walked downstairs into the sanctuary part of the church and lay on the pulpit and fell asleep. I can't remember how long I was there for. All I remember was my mother and father calling my name and trying to get me to drink milk to throw up whatever I had swallowed. I was so weak. I couldn't walk; my words were very sluggish, and I was in and out of consciousness.

Finally, I came to. My parents asked me why I had tried to take my life. I was honest in telling them the exact reason why. I hadn't done this for attention. I did it because I hadn't wanted to live like that.

Looking back on that moment, I believe that may have been a small wake-up moment for my parents. Mother slacked off just an eency-weency bit. We still couldn't wear pants, though.

The church was connected to my parent's second dry cleaners. Occasionally, my sister and I would work at the cleaners after school. When we were there by ourselves, I would search through the bags of clothes for any orders that had been there longer than a year. If there were any pants that I could fit in, I would put the pants in my book bag, change into them when I got to school the next day, and change back when it was time to go home from school. I learned how to cope.

About two years later, our aunts, uncles, and cousins from Mother's side of the family were visiting for the summer. Mother saw my cousins with their pants on, and she later sat us down while they were there and told us that we could start wearing our pants again. We were so happy, we jumped up and down like typical teenagers. We didn't want our cousins poking fun at us.

I was just finishing eleventh grade, about to go into the twelfth grade. I would save up my little money and have my father drive me to the clothing store on Grand River Boulevard to purchase my pants, all in different colors.

The summer of my tenth-grade year, I had to go to summer school because, throughout the school year, I just didn't apply myself. During summer school I got into a fight with a girl who thought her boyfriend liked me. That was the furthest thing from the truth. We fought, she won, and a few years later the boy ended up getting killed.

Mother was so annoyed with me for always getting into trouble or being in some type of confrontation. She was tired of being in a big city, always being afraid for our safety. She started contemplating moving us all back to North Carolina.

After enjoying a great weekend with our cousins and aunts—along with getting into a fight with some girls at Stoepel Park because they accused my cousin of touching their stuff—we came home to another chaotic event in the front yard of the house. After this chain of events, my parents said it was enough and that we were moving.

Mother and Father sent my brother to North Carolina to stay with my aunts and cousins. Then, a few weeks later, my father drove me to North Carolina. While I was there, I lived with my aunt and her three children in a small three-bedroom house. Living with my aunt was different from living with my parents. Mother and Father had rules; my aunt was relaxed. No, she didn't let us do whatever we wanted, but she didn't try to control what we did—and she allowed us to be ourselves.

She was considered the fun aunt; she was not strict or strenuous. Though we did go to church, we could wear whatever we wanted to wear. Our living conditions had changed; they were not what we were used to. My aunt didn't live in a big house, there was no swimming pool in the backyard, and there was no dry cleaners to clean your clothes. There was just a washer and dryer, and if you wanted something pressed, you had to iron it.

The house was heated with a kerosene heater, and Auntie wouldn't allow us to take showers in the morning because she thought we might catch a cold. It was life made simple.

As for me, Mother and Father kept me in Detroit with them so that I could continue with school and help with their new janitorial business while the family was transitioning from Detroit, Michigan, to North Carolina. At that time I was four months pregnant. A month before, I actually went with another friend to the clinic to see if she was pregnant.

To keep her from feeling alone, we both took the test. After she took the test, the nurse told her that it had come back negative. Then the nurse asked me to go into another room. While I was sitting there, she told me that my test had come back positive. I gasped and said, "Are you saying that I'm pregnant?"

She was very straightforward, yet reserved, as she said, "Yes."

I instantly got hot all over, and my mouth got very dry. I had to stay calm because I had to drive back home. I was sixteen years old, and my parents were pastors. Lord, how was I going to tell my mother this? It's one thing to be a preacher's kid, but it's another thing to be a pregnant preacher's kid. So I kept it a secret between myself and my sisters.

I remember standing in front of the mirror and seeing this little pouch in the lower part of my belly. It felt strange. I wasn't bloated, and this wasn't gas. I was carrying a little human being inside of me.

Well, a few weeks later, one of my aunts found out. During this time I was going to summer school. After school I would go home and sleep for the rest of the day. All I wanted to do was sleep. Then one evening I was at the kitchen sink washing the dishes. Out of nowhere, I heard my mother gasp loudly. I acted like I heard nothing, even though I knew that she had figured it out in that moment.

Later we went out to do the janitorial business. We would go in after business hours and work late into the night to clean up office buildings. On that particular night I was walking through to another office, and I walked in on my father consoling my mother. That was my confirmation that she knew I was pregnant. They never saw me, and I don't recall ever telling them what I had seen that night. I continued working and contemplating in my head how I was going to tell them.

Finally we got home, and my mother asked me to come into the kitchen. My heart dropped, but I had to suck it up. "Come in and have a seat," she said. "Do you want some ice cream?"

I replied, "Yes."

She placed the bowl in front of me. I held my head down and began eating very slowly. The tension was so thick that a knife with a super sharp blade would have been too dull to cut through it. My mother asked me if I was pregnant.

I replied, "Yes."

She asked me how far along I was.

I replied that I didn't know for sure.

Y'all, I thought my mother was taking it hard, but then I looked up at my father's face and saw the disappointment. I looked back down and continued eating the rest of my ice cream. My father asked me why I didn't use protection.

I replied that I didn't have access to protection. You see, back then, in the eighties, teenagers didn't have easy access to certain forms of birth control. You had to have parental consent. And going to my parents, who are pastors, to ask them for their consent to get birth control so that I wouldn't get pregnant at the age of sixteen would have been like jumping in the middle of an ocean without a life jacket, knowing damn well that I didn't know how to swim.

Then, my mother said that she was taking me to the doctor the next day. I said "Okay," and I got up and got ready for bed. While I was sleeping, I woke up to my mother's hand on my stomach. I lay still with my eyes closed until she walked out of my bedroom.

The next day, my mother drove me to the doctor to get an exam and to get on prenatal vitamins. I could tell that the doctor's office was used to seeing teenage pregnancy because while the receptionist was in deep conversation with my mother, the doctor was asking me a lot of personal questions while doing my examination. After the doctor's appointment, we went back home.

I was five months pregnant, about to enter my twelfth-grade year. My parents took me to the high school to speak with the principal about doing half of the year in night school and the other half during the regular school hours after my baby was born. I decided to go to night school so that I could still get my credits without all of the hassle of going from class to class during the day. I was still able to work at the janitorial business every day after I got out of night school. Then, during the end of my seventh month, I went in for my bi-weekly checkup. During the examination, with the monitor on me to check for the baby's heartbeat, something seemed strange.

The doctor asked, "Do you feel that?"

I said, "Feel what?"

She said that the monitor was showing that I was having contractions.

I told her that I wasn't feeling any type of pain.

Well, they continued to monitor me and began to talk to me about a possible caesarean section. I had to call my parents to let them know what was happening. They wanted me to keep the baby inside of me as long as I could. They wanted me to rest. They allowed me to go to night school, but they didn't want me to go to work. They wanted me off of my feet as much as possible. I stayed on bed rest for the rest of my pregnancy. My mother did her best to get me whatever I was craving, especially when I craved fried okra with ketchup on top from Church's Chicken, or extra-crunchy peanut butter right out of the jar.

My daughter came about one week before her due date. I had just eaten five extra-crunchy peanut butter and jelly sandwiches. Oh, they were so good. I lay down, and, out of nowhere, I felt this light but sharp shooting pain. Then it happened again. I thought it was gas, so I lay there a little longer. All of a sudden, the same pain got harder and sharper. The pains started happening five minutes apart.

My younger sister called my mother to let her know that I was in pain. My mother rushed home from work while my father finished cleaning the buildings, and she drove me to the hospital. My baby girl was born at 1:11 that next morning, 7 pounds, 5 ounces, just four days before my birthday.

I had messed up in my ninth and tenth grade years; I even failed summer school the summer of tenth grade. By the time I got into the eleventh grade, I had to hunker down and play catch-up. Luckily, things in North Carolina were not moving as fast as the city life. I was able to calm down and focus on my studies.

Mother flew down to visit us around my sixteenth birthday. She bought me a birthstone ring, and she bought my brother a motorbike. She was also there so that she could start looking for a place for the family to stay once everyone moved to North Carolina.

When Mother arrived in North Carolina, she was surprised at how much I had grown. Then she got upset when she saw how my auntie had pierced my ears, allowing me to have a second hole in my ear. I remember Mother ranting and raving and telling me that I could not wear a second earring in my ear.

Finally, the eleventh grade was over, and it was summer. My brother and I were going back home to Detroit for the summer, and we were excited. I was so happy to be home. I had missed Mother and Father immensely, and finally I could satisfy my cravings for White Castle and Coney Island.

Gurl, you didn't say, "White Castle and Coney Island."

Gurl, yes, this was the kind of food that you could not get in North Carolina.

Mother seemed a lot more relaxed and not so rigid. I spent my summer helping to pack up the house because it was happening—we were all moving back to North Carolina for good.

Mother and Father had finally found a home in North Carolina, and right before my twelfth grade year, Mother and the rest of our siblings started the move. Father stayed in Detroit for another month or so to tie up loose ends. Silk and I stayed with him.

Mother and Father sold the church and the dry cleaners; they also had a janitorial service that they gave up. We were going to miss Detroit, but even though we did not want to leave the big city we knew deep in our hearts it was probably for the best. Once things were in order, Father loaded us up in his small, red, stick-shift car and drove us all the way to North Carolina.

Yes, he sure did.

Living back home under my parents' roof always meant that things were going to be structured and strict. Despite Mother allowing us to wear makeup and pants, she had other ways of being controlling and domineering in our lives.

Yes, she sure did.

When we moved back to North Carolina, she opened a church, and, yes, again I hated it.

But we were still able to wear pants.

I was just going into the twelfth grade. My parents had moved to North Carolina, and for some reason people thought we were rich. That was the furthest thing from the truth. We stayed uptown in a house that looked regular to us, but others got the impression that we were rich.

I remember one time, my sister's schoolteacher saw her walking in the neighborhood, and he assumed that she was doing something mischievous. He asked her what she was doing in that neighborhood, and she replied that she was walking home from school. He was shocked to learn that we lived down the street from him.

Coming from the city, our view of things was a little different from the attitudes in the South. People automatically assumed that my parents were supposed to work in manufacturing because that was what most parents in that area of North Carolina did. My parents were entrepreneurs, however. They opened up a store and turned it into a health food store.

Yes, they sure did.

Moving back to North Carolina to a small town, we felt the envy and jealousy. When my brother and I lived with my aunt, another one of my mother's sisters would always let us know that we weren't anything special. Some of my mom's family members felt disdain for her and us because, I guess, in their minds they were like, "Who in the hell do you think you are?" What they failed to realize was that my parents thought differently. They didn't do the norms; they always went against the norm.

Things really changed when Mother and Father starting buying airtime on television to promote the church and their health food store. The health food store grew, the church grew, but we, the children, got sucked back into setting the example again. I wanted to shut down and get away. I hated all the attention, I hated being on television, and I hated being photographed. I didn't want to be a part of anything that brought attention to me in any way.

Hahaha. Now, that's very funny because we are on TV, we are photographed all the time, and we get a lot of love, attention, and affection from our fans.

As for me, I was the choir director, the secretary, and I worked one of the cameras that was used to film the church services for the televised program. Every Sunday, I made sure that I gave 10 percent of my earnings. I was faithful, and I learned how to establish my own personal relationship with God.

Mother was very outspoken and dominating. I was in my thirties, still being told what to do and how to do it, with the fear that something would happen if I tried to do it on my own. Things had gotten so out of control that it was time for us to stand up for ourselves and start making our own decisions. I wanted change; we needed change, and that was the spark that gave us the guts to leave my mother's church and utilize our faith to guide us the rest of the way. It was such a scary time, but we made it!

Yes, it was scary, but we had to step out on faith. If we hadn't made a move, we would have been stagnated, at a standstill.

That experience prepared us for this day. We awakened to what we wanted in life. In order to get what you want, you have to say no to what you don't want. When we got sick and tired of being sick and tired, we walked out of that church, then off of the Democrat Plantation.

We left and never looked back.

Chapter 4

Overcoming Obstacles

I was seventeen years old, in the twelfth grade, and had gotten pregnant—but I was not about to let this ruin the rest of my life.

When my mother found out I was pregnant, she was adamant about me going to find a job. Her exact words were, "I'm not signing no papers for you to go and get on welfare." I got a job working at Shoney's Restaurant in Aberdeen, North Carolina, as a waitress and hostess–cashier. When I got hired, I told no one, not even the manager who hired me, that I was pregnant.

Every day after school, I would go home, do whatever homework I had, eat, and get ready for work. During the week, I would work from 4:00 p.m. to 8:00 p.m., and on the weekends I would work longer hours. Some days I would greet the customers, and on other days I would wait tables. For some odd reason, I absolutely loved it. The benefit of having a job was having my own money so I could buy my own clothes. I loved not being dependent on my parents for the little things.

My supervisor, a white woman by the name of Barbara, taught me how to run the register and correctly count change back to the customer. I remember one day a customer was checking out and paying his bill, which came to $11.51. The customer gave Barbara, who was hostessing at the time, $20 and a penny. For the life of me, I could not understand why he was giving her a penny if he had given her a $20 bill.

After the transaction, I mustered up the courage to ask her, "Why did he give a penny if he had already given $20?"

She turned to me, without judgment, and explained in simple terms that he gave the penny to keep from getting pennies back. She went on to say he gave me the penny so that he could get 50 cents back instead of 49 cents.

Wow, this seemed like simple math. I had been in school for twelve years, confined to the four corners of the public or the private school system, and no one had ever taught me this simple trick. Today, most Millennials don't know this simple math. If you don't believe me, test them by giving them a penny if you ever have a bill that totals up to the change being an odd number.

I learned a lot from Barbara. She taught me how to meet and greet customers, how to run hourly reports to see if sales were up or down from the previous year, and then record them. She showed me how to keep the menus and the front of the store clean, even down to the bathrooms. She would say, "Customers can tell how clean the restaurant's kitchen is by checking the bathrooms. If the bathrooms are dirty, then the kitchen is dirty." A lot of these tasks were easy for me because Father had taught me the importance of such things when he owned the laundromat.

When I worked on the weekends, I was able to wait tables. As a waitress, if the supervisor saw you just standing around, she would say, "If you got time to lean, you got time to clean." It was a good day if you were able to make $60 in tips. Most days when I was waitressing, I would make just that.

The one thing I loved about my supervisor, Barbara, was that she never made me feel inferior or less than. If I didn't understand something, she would explain it; if I needed something and she had it, she would give it. She did everything within her power to help me, and I trusted her wholeheartedly. And one day, after I was going into four months of being pregnant, she came right out and asked me directly, "Are you pregnant?"

Almost too embarrassed to admit it, I told her, "Yes."

She never looked at me differently. She congratulated me and said she hoped it was a boy.

I worked the whole nine months of my pregnancy. Some mornings, I would have morning sickness because certain smells would make me sick. I would always push through and continue to go to school because my number one goal was to graduate on time from high school. I refused to be added to the statistics as a dropout, and I refused to let morning sickness or any sickness having to do with my pregnancy keep me from working. I kept going, and finally I was graduating.

After graduating from high school, I continued working at Shoney's, and I was able to obtain more hours. Though I was getting bigger, I still went to work every day, and the people that I worked with had become my work family. They looked out for me because I was pregnant.

I remember wanting a baby shower, and Mother said that she was not throwing me a baby shower because I was having a baby out of wedlock. Things were a lot different back in those days. Being pregnant without being married was looked down upon, not celebrated. I wasn't saddened by it; it was what it was. My colleagues at work took it upon themselves and gave me a beautiful baby shower. My parents did not attend because of their beliefs.

During my pregnancy, I went from 110 pounds to 180 pounds. There were days when I just didn't feel well, but I kept pushing it. One day, while at a doctor's appointment, the doctor looked at me and said, "You look like you are holding too much fluid." She admitted me to the hospital to induce labor because my baby was not budging. Though it was time for him to come out, he was not ready.

When they admitted me into the hospital, they began giving me medicine through an IV to induce my labor, which had me experiencing contractions. The contractions were so painful, the doctors ended up giving me an epidural.

An epidural is an injection of a local anesthetic into the space around the dura mater of the spinal cord in the lower back region to produce loss of sensation, especially in the abdomen or pelvic region.

After that, I remember falling off into a deep sleep. The strangest thing is, I could hear my surroundings, but I was asleep. I remember hearing the TV show *Dallas* going off when my mother must have gone to get the nurse. She said she could see the baby's head. After that, they were waking me up, ready for me to push. A little after 11:00 p.m., my son was born. It was official, I was a mother.

After about a week of being home with a newborn baby, I was ready to return back to work, and that's exactly what I did. Mother thought I should stay in the house for six weeks, but I felt fine. Thank God for Mother because, while I worked, she took care of my son. Then, after a long day of work, I would have to come home and pick up the slack.

My son's father was about to join the military. His mother called me and told me that he would give me fifty dollars a month in child support, and I should go get on food stamps. Damn that! I wasn't interested in getting on any form of welfare, and I wasn't just going to accept fifty measly dollars a month. So I sued him for child support. Once my son's father joined the military, my son was able to receive an allotment. When he got out of the military, my son was able to receive child support.

I thank God for my parents during this journey in my life because they were able to stand in the gap when my son or I needed anything.

After my son's father got out of the military, things started rekindling again. It was like old times but with a son. As we were dating, though, I started noticing his manipulative and controlling ways. He always had a problem with me being around my sisters; he would say they were coercing me into doing things he didn't like. He was trying to keep me in this box where I could have no outside contact with anyone but him. One day, he saw empty beer bottles in Silk's car and made it his business to go and tell my mom about it. Silk and I were livid.

The next thing he did was leave a note on my parents' car, informing them that he and I were having sex. When I got off of work, Mother and

Father called me into Mother's office and sat me down to question me about it. I was pissed off and petrified at the same time. My mother looked at me and said, "If you're going to be having sex, then you need to be married. We are pastors. How is this going to make us look when you're out there having sex, and you're not married!" She demanded that I get married.

I felt powerless and like I was being forced into something that I did not want to do. Though I was sleeping with my son's father, I did not love him, and I had already stopped liking him because of his manipulative ways. But I did what I was told to do, and it was the worst mistake I ever made in my life.

I don't blame my mother; I blame myself for not speaking up on my own behalf and for not using my voice, which was my power, to say "No" to what I didn't want. I went along to get along, and, in the end, I ended up all alone.

The marriage ended in divorce, and the experience left me so empty, I never wanted to be married again. In the end, life was giving me a crucial assignment that I had to keep repeating until I passed the test and learned the lesson.

Some may ask why I didn't go to college. I could have gone to college; hell, I tried to go to college, but when I walked in that classroom and saw the teacher writing all of that stuff on the board, I didn't know what it was, so I got my little book bag and walked right out. I watched my cousins go to college because their parents told them to get it on the wall. One cousin went to school to be a foot doctor, and we found out years later that she's no more a doctor than Dr. Pepper.

Years later we also found out she couldn't even pass the medical boards. All that money was wasted.

I was working at Shoney's, but I still wanted to make more money, so I got a second job at McDonald's. I started off there happy to work, ready to do my part. Only trouble was, McDonald's wanted to have me work on the fry machine, but I had a Jheri curl.

Oh, God. We did have the Jheri curls with the activator and mois-turizer, hahaha.

I did not want that grease popping in my hair and, all of a sudden, now we have a fire.

Hahaha. This wasn't around the time when Michael Jackson's hair caught on fire from his Jheri curl, was it?

I can't remember, but it probably was.

So I had two jobs: I had to make the salads for the next day, and then I would have to get on the fry machine. All was well until I noticed that when the supervisor hired for the cashier positions, he always hired white girls.

So this one particular day, I asked him if I could move to the register or do something else because I didn't want my hair catching on fire from the fry machine.

He said when the next cashier position opened up, then I could take that position. No worries.

I kept doing my job, showing up on time, giving it all I've got. I was happy because the only part I didn't like about the job would end soon.

Shortly after this, another cashier position opened up. I'm thinking, okay, good, I'll get that position, and my time on the fryer will be over with.

Would you believe, y'all, the supervisor hired another white girl for the position?

Wow.

That was my last day working on the fry machines, though, because I went off on that manager, gave him his little apron, and I quit. That was my first time quitting a job, but I felt justified in walking out. He had told me the next cashier's position would be mine, then he turned right around and gave it to someone else. It wasn't even about the girl being white. It was about him lying to me, telling me one thing and doing another.

Was your supervisor a white supervisor, a black supervisor, or Hispanic?

He was a white supervisor. Remember now, this was in the late eighties. I quit because he promised me something but didn't deliver on what he promised.

Mm-hmm.

So, after I quit, I only had my job at Shoney's. What about you, Silk? Where did you work?

I remember working at Kolcraft. I was eighteen years old when I started there. Kolcraft makes baby furniture, and they are still a pretty big deal in Aberdeen, North Carolina, today, employing about 245 people.

My job was making the small components that connect car seat handles to the actual seats.

My trainer's name was Martha, and she was a good trainer. In fact, she trained me so well that I became the lead on that particular line. When the line got moving along, everyone started scrambling, but that's when I rested a bit because I had produced so much work that the line had to catch up with me.

You were a fast, strategic worker.

Exactly. I went ahead and did what I had to do, but I did it in a particular way, and the method worked. The way I saw things, there was no point in being on the line if what you were doing wasn't working. Why bother being there?

About six months later, I got my second job, at Burlington Industries, in Raeford, North Carolina. I hated to do it, but I had to go back to Kolcraft to let them know I was quitting. I'm not going to lie, they put up quite a fuss. The supervisors wanted to know if there was anything that they could do to make me stay. They told me that if it didn't work out at Burlington, I would always have a job there at Kolcraft.

Oh, my . . .

I remember that, gurl, and it meant a lot to me.

Whenever I'm traveling back and forth to the airport, I pass Kolcraft, and I often look over there and remember what those supervisors told me. That left a vivid impression on me—then I thank God that He delivered me, hahaha.

Hahaha, I know that's right.

So I got hired at Burlington when I was nineteen. It seemed like everybody in Raeford wanted to get on at Burlington. It was a long, exhausting process, and people would park their cars at two or three o'clock in the morning just to get in line.

The reason everybody wanted to get on at Burlington was because they were a manufacturer. Back in the late eighties and nineties, people could raise families, send their children to college, and pay their bills with a good job like that.

That's right.

So, staying in a small town such as Raeford, if you were able to bring home $30, 40, 50,000 a year, that was really good money for the average family.

That's right.

That's why people were lined up; they wanted those jobs.

Exactly right.

So, I got in line, and I put in my application like everybody else. However, what I did differently is almost every other day I called and spoke with someone to ask if they had received my application. I also let them know how hard a worker I was and that they would not regret hiring me. It was like I was doing my own interview over the phone, almost every day.

I talked to whoever happened to answer the phone in human resources. It got to the point where they knew my name when I called. Finally, the day came when I was receiving the call back from them. They wanted me to start on third shift that same night.

So there I was that same night, starting my new job at Burlington Industries in the winding department. I had a wonderful supervisor, Betty K.—light-skinned, beautiful lady—and Mary R. was my instructor. She taught me how to drop the bobbins to create the yarn so that they could be processed to go to the next department.

So with Silk being at Burlington Industries making all kinds of money, of course I wanted to work there too. Not long after Silk started there, they needed workers for the cloth room. I didn't know a thing about cloth, but they were hiring for that position. So I put in an application.

Mm-hmm.

Just about a week or two later, I got a phone call for an interview. I was thrilled; this would provide the kind of money needed to make a good life, so I thought. I think I had to do a drug test, and all that kind of stuff came back good, so I was hired.

Mm-hmm.

Once I got hired, there were a few weeks of training. They were upfront about it: if we couldn't pass the training, we wouldn't get the job. Myrtle was our trainer, and she showed us how to thread up a needle, how to look at the cloth, how to read the cloth to determine whether there was a missed reed or a wrong draw or if we had to stitch it somewhere to fill in that missed reed. Whatever the error was, we only had so many minutes to fix it.

Mm-hmm.

Once that cloth started rolling on the roller, we had to inspect it to make sure no damaged cloth was delivered to the customers. We were the last department before the cloth shipped out, so after it went through all of the other departments, it came to the cloth room.

If there was a missed reed—when the yarn didn't stitch all the way through—or a wrong draw or something that just didn't look right, we would have to either fix it or mark that it was unable to be repaired.

The stress of those few weeks in training was almost overwhelming. Luckily, I was able to complete each and every task that they gave me. Not everyone made it through training because it was challenging, it really was. I remember one of the other girls, she was a Caucasian girl, she could not thread her needle up fast, and she was not fast enough sewing in the little spaces that needed to be mended.

Mm-hmm.

So they were giving her one more day to catch on, and we were all rooting for her, but she couldn't get it right, so they had to let her go.

Oh, no . . .

After moving up from training, I was officially a cloth inspector on third shift. I had to inspect that cloth to make sure that no damage had been done to it and there were no missed reeds or wrong draws. We had to be on our game because after we inspected it, it went to another inspector to make sure we did our job. If we didn't do our job accurately, they would send all that cloth back for us to inspect it again.

That's right. Wow.

In the winding department, we had to make sure that the bobbin colors didn't get mixed up because the shades and hues were so close. If we didn't read all of the item lines off to make sure that we had the correct color bobbins, we could easily be working with the wrong yarn. I became especially intrigued with counting my numbers at the end of my shift to see how many bobbins I had actually dropped.

One time, I had just come back from lunch, and when I got to the two machines I worked on, all the bobbins in my tray were gone. Everything was empty; my machines were stopped; everything was lit up red.

Well, I felt like I turned into Wonder Woman.

Hahaha.

All of a sudden, gurl, here I go: I started from one end and worked my way to the next, getting those machines back up and running. I was working at high speed; that's just something that I excelled at. I didn't bother anybody, and no one bothered me. I didn't look up to see if anyone noticed me; I just kept dropping those bobbins.

I went down one row, came back up on the other side, and completed row after row in that way. When I was just about done with the last row, I noticed this distinguished-looking white gentleman standing there.

I remember that gentleman. He was a department head, and he looked like Richard Gere when he was fine.

Hahaha. Yes, that's exactly who he looked like.

So he was standing there at the end of my machine, and he said, "I just stood here and watched you drop all of these bobbins and just get your job back up to running smoothly." And he said, "Have you ever thought about working in the weave room?"

Now, y'all, the weave room is where you made the big bucks because you're really making the actual cloth that's about to be distributed to the other departments in order to make quality clothes.

Right.

So I was excited about this possibility, and I'm sure my eyes were wide and the surprise was all over my face as I responded, "I want to work in the weave room, but I'm blind in one eye."

When I was born, my optic nerve did not develop properly, so I am legally blind in one of my eyes. I can see some light, but everything is blurry. I refused to go on disability, though, because I didn't want my blind eye to "dis my ability" to be able to work. Does that make sense?

Yes, it sure does.

It never stopped me, and no one ever knew about it unless I told them. Since I've gotten older, my eye has gotten a lot lazier. I've received several emails from some good-hearted folks offering to correct my eye free of charge.

Wow.

Although those offers were kind and considerate, I decided not to tamper with it. I've been living with this eye like this for all of these years, I'll just leave well enough alone. Some may call it a cockeye, but I call it my super eye, hahaha.

Hahaha.

My super eye has the capability to look at you and around you at the same time. I feel like the chosen one because I have something the average person doesn't have. I turned my negative into positive. I've embraced and replaced my flaws with peace, and I always ask God to lead and guide me in the right direction.

That's the right way to look at it too.

So, anyhoo, I told the supervisor that I am blind in one eye, and that's been my deterrent. He gave me his name anyhow. Turns out he wasn't just a supervisor; he was head honcho over the whole department.

So he told me what time to come in the next day and where to go and to tell the people up front that he referred me. I did just what he said because I wanted that job.

Mm-hmm.

As part of that application process, I had to go back through another eye exam. I was so nervous, I even told the examiner, "Ma'am, I can't see out of this eye."

She said, "Oh, don't worry about it."

I thought they were testing to see if I was going to work out okay. I found out later that this supervisor wanted me in the weave room so bad that the testing was just a formality. I already had the position. The next day, I was in training. It happened just that fast.

Wow.

So here's the craziest thing, y'all: By the time Silk left the winding department and was in the weave room, where the big bucks were at, they were getting ready to lay off people in the cloth room. So my job was being threatened by layoffs.

That's right.

I actually thought I was going to be laid off, but instead they moved me to the winding department. I believe they trained me on second shift, and my supervisor's name was Charlie D. Then I was pushed to third shift, and my supervisor was also Betty K.

So, now I'm in the winding department, and Silk is in the weave department, both of us working midnight to 8:00 a.m.

Mm-hmm.

Well, on one of my shifts, at about 7:00 a.m., I had to get a crate of yarn. So I went through this whole procedure of taking the main bobbin out and making sure to match it to what was on the machine so I was sure to be running the right bobbin. I was focused on my task, not paying attention to anything else around me, really, when the department head comes through—the one who looked like Richard Gere.

Well, he saw me following the right protocol, doing something that the others weren't doing, and while their yarn was getting mixed up, mine wasn't.

So he came over and complimented me on following the rules, and then he asked me if I would like to be in the weave room.

I'm staring at him in shock and I said something like, "Well, my sister works back there; it sounds good to me."

And, so, I don't even think I had to put in another application. It was like, "Training starts on this day." And that's just the way it was.

Mm-hmm.

Let me add this, y'all: I know sometimes black Americans feel like all white people are racist; that's not true. Even though I had experienced racism in the workplace, if I had let that be my story for every job I went to, I might not have accepted that this individual—a white man—was looking out for me. He wanted me to have this job, just like he wanted Silk to have the job, because he felt that we could do the job.

He couldn't have cared less about Silk being blind in one eye.

Hahaha. That's right.

Hell, he didn't care if she could see at all, as long as she kept those machines in that weave room running, hahaha.

Hahaha, yes.

I didn't fit the criteria for employment in the weave room. They wanted us to have high-functioning vision to work with the fine details of the cloth. He wanted me back there for my work ethic.

Right.

So, I'm working back there, and now my sister is back there. You've got your tool belt and I've got mine, and we're making good money and doing our thing.

Mm-hmm.

Betty M. was the only trainer at the time, and they needed another, so the position of instructor opened up, and I decided to apply. I was ecstatic when I got the job.

The individuals whom I trained, after finishing training and getting out there on the floor, were outstanding in their positions, and they stayed there a long time. I actually began making more money than the instructor who trained me because of how effective I was.

Wow.

For me, y'all, I was back there in that weave room, trying to keep the machines going, but I just woke up one day and I felt like I wanted to be a supervisor.

Mm-hmm.

Of course, when I went to talk to the department manager about it, he looked at me like I was crazy.

Yes, he did.

He didn't think I was ready to be a supervisor, and maybe I wasn't ready; but, hell, at least I tried.

Yeah. Nothing beats a failure but a try.

That's right. I never became a supervisor. So, instead, I focused all of my energy on keeping those weave machines going so that the cloth would weave because we had to produce that cloth and move it out of there.

The machines, which were called looms, were huge and dominated ten feet of space all around.

That's right. Yes.

We had to wear our tool belts with our scissors and our weave hooks ready.

Yes. We tied weaver's knots.

Yes. We had to tie weaver's knots, and we had to tie them in so many seconds.

Yes.

We had to be able to inspect the cloth to make sure that we didn't have a wrong draw. A wrong draw happened when one of the threads broke. We had to get a matching thread, tie a knot, pull the string through the heddle eye with a weaver's hook, then take a reed hook and thread it through the reeds, and then start the machine.

Mm-hmm.

Now, the pattern had to match the other pattern. If it didn't match, it could have been a wrong draw or a missed reed.

Mm-hmm.

You did not want your cloth going far with a wrong draw because you could get written up or even get fired, because it's a total loss to the company.

That's right. Imagine purchasing a coat, and you see a yellow line that's not supposed to be there going down the back of the coat.

Absolutely. Even when I shop for clothes today, I can pretty much spot if there is a missed reed or a wrong draw in the fabric because I'll take a look at the pattern.

Mm-hmm.

A wrong draw was easy to have happen because sometimes the pattern looked the same. They would have to take a little magnifying glass out and put it on the cloth to see if the pattern was wrong.

Right. Sometimes you were using two or three different colors that looked the same. You had to know how to look at the yarn, to twist it, to see if it was double or single yarn.

Wrong draws were not something that Diamond or I did often.

Right.

But every now and then, something could get crossed up. Dust would sometimes get into the machines and put a knot in the yarn, causing one of the threads to break. Before you knew it, things were crossed up, and it was up to you to uncross it. That's why we had to do an inspection every hour on the hour. I even remember my inspection number, it was 212.

Right.

We'd have to go over there and unmat it; remember that?

Oh, gurl, I remember it.

So, whenever that happened, our supervisor, Mr. Williams, was there to really shield us because he loved the Hardaway girls' work ethic.

Yes, he did. I don't even know if Mr. Williams is still alive, but he was a really good supervisor. I really enjoyed working for him.

Yes.

We've really always been proactive and involved on the job.

That's right.

If we learned that somebody was upset about a new rule, we had no problem going to the department head, department manager, or a supervisor to get it all straightened out.

That's right.

I specifically remember a meeting that was supposed to last no more than fifteen minutes; we stayed up there for almost an hour.

Mm-hmm. I remember they wanted us to do some extra jobs. At that time, they had a crew of workers who blew the dust from under the machines. During the meeting, they told us they wanted to add that to our list of job duties.

Whoa, whoa, whoa! We shut that meeting down. This was not part of our job description, and we weren't supposed to do this. They already had workers to go through there and blow the lint out from under the machines.

Right. We weren't going to do additional tasks that were outside of our job description without getting paid for it. They had a crew to clean out all of the lint. Don't put that on us to do.

We shut down a few meetings when we didn't like something. There were times I may have even gone too far, but they put up with us because it wasn't about starting trouble just to start trouble. It was about having a high-quality work environment for everyone. The flip side to that was we were responsible to produce excellent work. We did that, and we constantly picked up shifts and worked overtime.

That's why they weren't going to fire us.

I remember working twenty-four hours straight. Each shift needed somebody to work, and they came to us. Because one thing they knew about us Hardaway girls, we didn't have a problem with work. We would work, and we were going to get the job done.

Mm-hmm. Thank God for our mother. She would have food cooked up.

Yes.

Sometimes somebody would have to bring us a plate out there for dinner.

Yes. I remember that. They allowed us to have whatever we needed so we would be happy.

Yes, they did. And back in those days, it was common for us to bring home $1,000 every two weeks. Now, that may not sound like a lot of money today, but back then that was very good money.

Right. It sure was.

You could pay your house payment, your car payment, buy a few extras, save some money. I mean, those were the days back then.

Mm-hmm, yes.

Do you remember that supervisor who was so highly educated that he knew nothing about the machinery? He knew nothing about the looms—he didn't even know how to start them—and he didn't know how to tie a weaver's knot.

Gurl, I remember this one time when that man was walking the weave room floor, I had my machine running good, y'all, and he was trying to show me how to do something. I'm looking at him like, get off my job, I know what I'm doing, you're making me miss out on money while my machine is stopped.

He went ahead and got off my job.

Hahaha, I'll bet he did.

So we really enjoyed our work, and we used to work overtime whenever we could.

We didn't just work over in the weave room. Sometimes we'd be walking through the winding department, going home, and a supervisor would stop us to see if we could work over in that department too.

Yes, that's right. That highly educated supervisor saw how much overtime we were getting—sometimes we were bringing home more money than the supervisors—and he didn't like it.

That's right. By working over in both departments, we were making more money than he was, and he was supposed to be the top-notch supervisor.

He was like, "You're making that type of money? Oh, no, you don't. You're making more money than me."

This one particular night, we wanted to work over because they needed people.

Yes.

Well, the supervisor with all that education was running that shift and didn't want us to work over in anybody's department.

Yes. He was the one who didn't want us to work over, but another supervisor was the one who went running around telling other department heads not to let us work over.

Okay. So the one with the fancy-pants education was like, "Well, y'all can't work over on my shifts anymore."

Right. But the other supervisor was the main person who brought us our checks. He would look at our checks and be like, "There's no way these girls are making this kind of money." Then he'd give them to us and we'd keep on going, but we knew he was jealous.

That's right. So just thinking about it, who in the hell did he think he was?

Yes. Who in the hell did he think he was?

He went over to other departments and told them that the Hardaway girls couldn't work over in their departments. They're the ones that wanted to be supervisors; all we were doing was the weaving. We made the money because we put in the time.

So, now the supervisor with all the education needed people for overtime work, but there was such a fuss going on about how our paychecks looked, he didn't want to give us the opportunity to work over in his department.

So you know what? We went on home. No problem. You may not pay what you owe, but you will reap what you sow.

That's right.

Well, that next night, y'all, he needed some people to work over, and all of his little friends that he gathered the night before weren't going to help him out the next night.

Mm-hmm.

So here he comes, looking at us, coming to us wondering if we could work over. And we were like, oh hell, no.

We said the words, "Hell, no."

We said, "Hell, no." We knew he needed people, but it wasn't going to be us two people.

Yes.

Oh, yes, we let him have it. We said, "You figure out how you're going to run all of these looms because we won't be running them. Not tonight."

Yes, we sure did. I remember this vividly, yes.

Production was down that night. He had no one to work over, so he had sections of machine lights lit up in that weave room like a Christmas tree, hahaha.

Hahaha. Yes.

Lights on every machine were on because there wasn't anybody keeping them running, so they had stopped.

See, we were the reliable people that worked over, and he wasn't allowing us to take advantage of an opportunity. He allowed all of these other folks to work. They promised him they'd be there, then let him down. Now, here he was running to us.

Mm-hmm, that's right.

Never, ever, let anybody do that to you. First of all, when you know that you're good at something and somebody tries to make you think you're not good, it's only because they're envious of you: the money you might be bringing home, your potential, the possible success that might come your way.

They told us no, but when they needed workers, they came back and told us yes.

Mm-hmm.

That's when we simply looked at them and told them, "Hell, no."

"Hell, no."

What I'm saying is, don't let people use you.

Mm-hmm.

He was trying to use us for his own gain. When we wanted to help him, he didn't want that.

No, he didn't. We wanted to work over, and he wouldn't let us.

He wasn't going to use us when it was convenient. He better be glad that, at nineteen years of age, I didn't have the words or the empowerment to say what should have been said. If I was treated that way today, I'd have to take him down.

Hahaha. That's right.

Those supervisors should have lost their jobs, first of all, for meddling and going to other departments and discussing our pay, then conspiring with other supervisors to keep us from working and making our money.

Exactly right. That situation got out of hand, and we got it back in hand by not allowing them to use their other hand to stop us.

Don't get us wrong, the company was good to us and a good place to work. I specifically recall one perk: they would have nice steak dinners for the different departments that met certain quotas.

Mm-hmm.

Well, we couldn't attend this one particular steak dinner because we found out we had chicken pox.

That's right. We had the chicken pox. It was Silk, y'all, that broke out first. At that time, I was living with Silk, so living in the same household, I broke out too.

See, the chicken pox vaccine was added to the childhood immunization schedule in 1995, which means we probably weren't vaccinated for it. In fact, back then, it was a normal childhood experience to get the chicken pox. Well, sometimes people got them later in life, and they were generally more severe in adults. So there we were, with the chicken pox.

Yes. We both got them together. So, on the night of the dinner, they said, "Send somebody up here to get your food."

They had our steaks and all the fixings packed up for us to come up there, and they brought them out to the car for us.

Right. That's what they did.

We didn't even go in the building.

Right. We had the chicken pox; we couldn't go into the building with it because we didn't want to spread it to anybody, but they still made sure we got our steak dinners.

That's right.

That was fun. You know, working in the weave room was really a fun experience.

Yes, it was.

We got to see the machines, how cloth was made, and how the process developed. It was a good experience for us to know how certain things were done.

Then, all of a sudden, around mid-1993, it seems as though things started dwindling down.

Mm-hmm.

They began doing something called "short time." So instead of working forty hours a week, you might work thirty-two hours a week, or somebody would be rotated out. The person that was rotated out had to draw unemployment for that week.

That's right. Temporary unemployment.

We didn't know what was going on, but we knew something wasn't quite right when we started seeing things like that.

Mm-hmm. That's when NAFTA came into play.

Right. All of a sudden, Bill Clinton started talking about NAFTA. Now, in case y'all don't know what NAFTA is, it stands for North American Free Trade Agreement. Sounds nice, doesn't it? However, in a nutshell, this was an agreement to ship American jobs overseas.

Mm-hmm.

Now that I'm older, and I look back on all of this, it wouldn't surprise me if old Bill Clinton didn't get a kickback-paddy-whack for sending jobs overseas.

Mm-hmm.

I can remember hearing talk about it, then Silk started asking, "How is this going to benefit us?"

Right.

This was going to kill our jobs.

What I couldn't understand for the life of me was how our jobs were being sent overseas for somebody else to work; the products would then come back here; then the American people were expected to have money to be able to pay for the products, but we didn't have the jobs to make the money.

I'm like, y'all don't see what's about to happen here? It didn't make sense to me from the start. Then, as time progressed, you see how it turned out because a lot of people lost their jobs.

Yes. A lot of people started getting laid off.

Right. There were three parts to this that we saw: American jobs were going overseas; illegal aliens came here and were trained by Americans for the jobs that were left; after they were trained, the Americans that had trained these people were laid off, and the jobs were given to illegal aliens for lower wages.

That's right. In reality, if an illegal alien wasn't taking your job, your job was going overseas.

That's right.

And they started really laying off people in droves. For those who kept their jobs, companies cut the work week down, so people were working four days a week instead of five days or six days.

Right.

Folks were used to rocking a seven-day workweek. Suddenly, they wouldn't work for three days straight, and they'd have to draw unemployment. So it started getting really, really scarce when Bill Clinton put NAFTA in place.

Now, let me make sure that we specify this: the illegal aliens that we saw were working at the turkey plants and hog plants.

Right. We didn't know that they were illegal aliens; we thought they were just Mexican folks.

Right.

Companies were laying off regular Americans, especially black Americans who had worked there faithfully for ten or twenty years, and they brought in these illegal aliens for cheap labor.

We didn't know that at the time, but that's why they were brought in: for cheap labor.

You know, when you look at all of the American people, white people thrive on having something they build or whatever they have; Hispanic people, they do the same; Asian people, they do the same; but black people, we are always left at the bottom of the totem pole. I've always wondered why that is.

In this case, though, it didn't matter whether you were black or white, you couldn't get some of those jobs anymore. It was like they were bussing in illegal aliens, and they were taking over.

That's right.

Those illegal aliens were able to come in and take these jobs; they also built Spanish-speaking communities; they built businesses all while they were taking American jobs.

And then you even had, in some instances, almost twenty to thirty of them in one home, living together, without paying any taxes. I would think about this and wonder how other Americans weren't seeing this.

So when I would see American people without a job, on the corner, losing their homes, losing their cars, it did not make sense to me, and no one was doing anything about it.

It needs to be said, too, that even though they were living thirty to a house and not paying taxes, they were still taken advantage of because landlords would charge them outrageous rates, by the head, to stay there.

Yes. So, when you hear us talk about illegal immigration—or, excuse me, let me rephrase that: they're called illegal aliens, and we talk with such passion because we actually saw how it destroyed a lot of families, American families, people that did it the right way.

They broke into the house of America. When you break into the house, you are an illegal alien, not a guest.

Yes.

When you get in line, wait your turn, and do it the right way, you are a legal immigrant.

Mm-hmm. At Burlington, we saw, firsthand, a lot of jobs going overseas because of NAFTA.

Here in the South, manufacturing was pretty much everywhere. It wasn't like you had to go get a college degree. You could still raise your children and provide for your family from working at one of the mills, in manufacturing.

That's right.

After NAFTA, most of the manufacturing buildings were closed.

They were closed, and they sat empty.

They were. They were empty because of NAFTA. Anything that's coming back now is because of President Donald J. Trump.

That's right. Donald J. Trump.

So, especially in the South, manufacturing was one of the keys to survival. It was very important when it came down to the economics in the South because people worked in manufacturing to take care of their families.

Yes. Also, what I found interesting is that when the other jobs did go overseas, they coerced folks to go back to school.

Mm-hmm.

Well, you had no other choice. If you needed a job, you had to go back to school and take more training to do other jobs.

That's right.

And all these older people were getting into more debt. Now, they had to use their Social Security to continue to pay off that school debt. And, really, they didn't get any further ahead than when they had the first job, working in manufacturing.

Yes. That's right.

I'll tell you, it devastated the American people, and it left people destitute, with nothing, absolutely nothing.

Exactly. I clearly see that it was a Democrat that signed NAFTA into law, causing jobs to go away; then Democrats told us how we needed to go back to school to become qualified for new positions.

I don't know what it is about Democrats: They don't want us to work and have the opportunity to obtain things on our own without getting involved in it and twisting it up. It seems like when they see that you're doing something and it's working well, Democrats find a way to put some red tape there to block you or stop you.

I call them left-leaning liberals, and you're absolutely right. They don't want the people to thrive; they don't want the people to prosper; they don't want the people to be successful.

Instead of Bill Clinton having somebody whack him up under the desk, if you know what I mean, he should have been thinking this: Wait a minute, if I sign NAFTA into law, how many millions of people will be out of work?

That's right.

Because it destroyed whole communities. Companies were doing what they could to keep things going, but it was a hopeless time. At Burlington, they didn't completely close down, but they closed certain departments, like the weave room, like the cloth room.

Mm-hmm.

They outsourced those tasks, and they sent those jobs overseas.

That's right.

So those kinds of good jobs were gone.

Let me touch on another thing: When you say manufacturing jobs kept the whole town going, that goes for the grocery stores, small service businesses, the entertainment that was going on in those towns. When the manufacturing businesses were thriving, people were able to open up a business within those communities because people had money to be able to go out and spend.

That's right.

You see, restaurants, theaters, even beauty salons and specialty shops whittled down and went away.

It affected everything, and it affected everybody.

Yes.

That was one of the great devastations that we will never, ever forget.

You know, speaking of jobs, I remember when you were interested in being a teacher.

Hahaha. Yes. Back in the day, when my son was younger, I used to volunteer in his classroom, and I remember thinking I wanted to be a teacher. So the first thing I did to get my feet wet was volunteer.

Mm-hmm.

So, this one day, I volunteered at my son's school, but the principal, for some unknown reason, had issues with me.

So this particular day, a teacher had an emergency and had to leave, so the principal needed somebody to volunteer for a class for about an hour until school let out, and he couldn't find anybody to do it.

So I said, "I'll do it."

Well, he wouldn't let me, and he didn't want me to do it. I don't know who he ended up finding, but I ended up not doing it, and that sort of deterred me from even wanting to help or volunteer in anyone's school. Maybe he thought I was going to take his job.

Mm-hmm. Maybe.

Sometimes people may try to break your spirit or stop your flow because either they have a problem with you or they don't like something about you. This just means they have a problem with themselves.

However, when you know you are good at what you do, you have to just keep it moving.

Now, did I ever become a teacher at a school? No. We became teachers that teach all across the world. Because we don't just teach thirty students in a classroom. Now, we can teach millions of people in the United States and around the world.

That's right.
That just proves how good God is.

Chapter 5

Your Emotions Can
Kill—or Heal

While we had been working at Burlington, Silk and I both started beauty school. We had a vision of being in business together, offering a service, having our own freedom. We had worked at Burlington for about four or five years before the NAFTA nightmare became so bad that Burlington slowed to a crawl.

We knew it was time to make a move, before the doors of Burlington closed and we found ourselves without a job or a career. I remember being so elated about it that we told a coworker by the name of Roger A. what we were planning. We confided in him about our aspirations and what we wanted to be. He looked us square in our eyes and told us we weren't going to be sh—t!

He sure did.

Wow! What discouragement. It may have dampened our mood, but it didn't break our spirits. Besides, he was right: we weren't going to be sh—t; we were going to be better than sh—t.

You got that right.

We both enrolled in Paul Mitchell beauty school in Fayetteville. We went to class during the day and worked second shift at night. It was our second week in school when something unfortunate and unexpected happened to Silk.

Yes. I was on second shift in the weave room one night, doing my inspection in the back of the looms, checking for lint balls that could potentially cause damage to the cloth. As I was checking the cloth, a worker I did not know was pushing the steel comb cart and ran into me, hitting me in the back. The guy pushing the cart claimed that he did not see me.

I had enjoyed working for Burlington for five years; the challenge of exceeding my previous quota excited me. We were loved by many there, but when this accident happened, people showed their true colors.

They tried to make the accident look like something I set up, as if I walked backwards into the steel cart that was being pushed forward. Why would I do that? Retaliation against the coworker pushing the cart? Absolutely not. I didn't know the guy who ran into me, and I certainly had no vendetta against him. I had no reason to set something up that would cause me so much pain. At times, that area can still get agitated.

I had to drop out of beauty college. Burlington wanted me to do light-duty work until I was able to come back to full-time work. Because of my injuries, even light-duty work was painful. There were times that the supervisor would call me into his office and taunt me. They began telling lies to me and about me. It got so bad that I had to go purchase a tape recorder to keep on me for my own protection so that no one could say that I had said this or that.

I was so upset with Burlington and human resources about how they treated my sister. All the times we worked hard, worked over when and where they needed us, and they couldn't have cared less about Silk being injured. What if she had been paralyzed? No one cared. They only cared about how many man-hours they were going to lose because of an accident.

I finally had to stop work and go on workers' compensation because of the injury.

While going back and forth with Burlington about my case, I still had to take care of my responsibilities. I remember going to social services to apply for food stamps so that I would at least be able to feed my daughter. I was honest and turned in the requested information. After processing the application, the lady looked at me and said these words: "You make one dollar too much to qualify for food stamps."

What? I couldn't believe my ears. One dollar too much? How was I going to feed my daughter? What was I going to do? I immediately broke down and started crying, right there in the social services office. I couldn't understand how I had worked hard for years, paid into the system every pay period, and when I needed it the most, I made one dollar too much!

The money that I was receiving from workers' comp was barely enough to keep the lights on. I was literally living workers' compensation check to workers' compensation check.

Thank God for my parents. They helped me out along the way.

After settling everything with Burlington and becoming functional again, I was able to go back to beauty college full time. This time I enrolled in Fayetteville Beauty College.

A month after graduation, I was fortunate enough to open my own beauty salon, Creations of Elegance.

After Silk left Burlington, I immediately started looking for another job. A company that didn't care about their employees' wellbeing wasn't a company I'd invest my energy into anymore.

I knew I was an experienced weaver operator. I immediately started calling around to the different factories to see if they were seeking applications. When I called WestPoint Stevens, in Wagram, North Carolina, I was told that they were looking for weaver operators and to come in and put in an application. I went in, put in the application, and was hired on the spot. I was told to be back the next week on Monday morning to start the training process.

I do remember going into work at Burlington that night, on second shift. I walked in, said goodbye to a couple of coworkers I'd become close with, and walked right out. I never told Burlington that I was quitting, and I never told them I had another job. I just quit without any notice, and it felt good.

WestPoint Stevens made towels. I started my training that Monday morning. Training was a breeze because I was already familiar with tying weaver knots and inspecting cloth. The difference was, I was now performing these tasks on cloth for towels.

After training, I was added to the twelve-hour shift: three days on and four days off, then four days on and three days off the next week. I worked from 7:00 p.m. until 7:00 a.m.

Weaving towels was different from weaving cloth. When weaving towels, you needed to keep the machines running all the time. If there was a missed reed or a wrong draw, it didn't matter: fix it, then start the machine. The goal was to make sure the machines were running at all times.

I was a hard worker, but the worst thing about working at West-Point Stevens was the big water bugs and the mice. They were everywhere. Rarely would I bring food from home; I was always afraid a rodent would get in it and eat it. Lint and cotton were always all over everything, either from blowers blowing from under the machines or just from the towels. I always had to wear a bonnet on my head if I wanted to save my hairdo.

I love to work, and I believe what the Bible says in 2 Thessalonians 3:10, "If any would not work, neither should he eat." Because of my rigorous schedule, I dropped out of beauty school to work my twelve-hour days at WestPoint Stevens. Once the Christmas holiday rolled around, I picked up a part-time job working at a catalog call center called Daymark.

I would work from 7:00 p.m. to 7:00 a.m., go home, rest until 11:00 a.m., get up, eat, and get ready to be at Daymark from 1:00 p.m. until 4:30 p.m. Then, I'd go home and do it all again the next day. Back in those days, I remember working so hard I was about to go crazy—but I did it.

Father saw how hard I was working, and he would tell me that I was working too hard. He did not want us spending the rest of our lives in the factory, looking broken-down. He wanted us to find something else to do.

I heard him, but I continued to work. After two years of working at WestPoint Stevens, I started feeling tired.

* * *

When you don't listen to your body, your body will start to speak loudly.

I didn't think anything was wrong when I saw the bruises on my feet. I thought it was because of the type of work shoes I was wearing, so I ignored it. A few days later, while brushing my teeth, I saw little red dots on the roof of my mouth. I didn't know what that was about, so I called the dentist to make an appointment.

They didn't know what was going on either, but they told me my teeth were fine, not to worry about it, that it should go away.

A few days later, I knew something was wrong when I woke up spitting up blood, not knowing where the blood was coming from. I thought I had coughed it up, but it was coming from my bleeding gums. I remember the morning it happened, I drove to Mother's house, crying the whole way. I told her what had happened, and she immediately responded according to her faith. She prayed for me and told me that I would be fine. She was right; the bleeding stopped, and I was fine—so I thought.

I was still working both my jobs, but my strength to keep up the pace was disappearing. I was getting so tired, and my menstrual cycles were getting very heavy. Finally, I scheduled an appointment with the doctor to get checked out. She thought my heavy periods were causing me to become severely anemic, which explained the fatigue. She also ran a complete blood count to check my red blood cells, white blood cells, and platelet count. When the numbers came back showing that my platelet count was dangerously low, she immediately admitted me into the hospital.

That was the first time I had been admitted into the hospital since I had my son. It was a scary experience because I didn't know what was wrong with me, why my platelet count was so low, or what to expect. I remember a hematologist coming to my room to talk to me, and she diagnosed me with idiopathic thrombocytopenic purpura (ITP).

According to Johns Hopkins Medicine, "ITP is a blood disorder characterized by a decrease in the number of platelets in the blood. Platelets are cells in the blood that help stop bleeding. A decrease in platelets can cause easy bruising, bleeding gums, and internal bleeding. This disease is caused by an immune reaction against one's own platelets."

Platelets are responsible for clotting the blood. My immune system was attacking my platelets and making them look foreign, as if they were not part of my body. This was described to me as an autoimmune disorder.

The doctors needed to know why my body was attacking my platelets. They started running all kinds of tests to get to the bottom of what was causing my body to overreact. I even remember them doing a bone marrow aspiration by sticking a needle through my breastbone and drawing out the fluid to do a biopsy and test it for leukemia.

It was such a scary time. One doctor suggested that I have a splenectomy, but it wasn't a guarantee that my immune system would stop destroying my platelets. In my mind, I was like, why would I have an organ taken out of my body on a maybe and not a guarantee? I needed assurance that a splenectomy was going to make this all go away.

I never got the splenectomy. What I did get was a firsthand look at how doctors try to coerce patients into having surgeries that may not help them—the medical system ripping off the people they're supposed to be taking care of.

They finally ended up releasing me from the hospital and sending me home with a prescription for sixty milligrams of prednisone a day. I was to follow up with a primary physician and a hematologist. Still not knowing what was wrong with me, I tried to do exactly what the doctors told me to do.

Because of my sickness, Mother and Father stood in the gap, making sure I had whatever I needed. I remember Mother being so concerned that she even suggested I leave my jobs. I ended up being out of work for six months. My platelet count was less than 5K, which was in the danger zone. It needed to be 20K or better. I kept believing that it would come back to a safe range, and I could return to work.

Mother prayed for me, fussed over me, and spoiled me, but it was time to get back to some normalcy.

Finally I was able to go back to work. The doctor wasn't really for it, but I begged her to please let me go back to work; it would do me some good. Yes, I was still anemic, but my platelet count had come up to almost 20K.

My body was destroying the very cells that produced what my body needed in order to live: blood.

None of my doctors could explain why I was sick. They just kept telling me it was autoimmune and how I was very anemic.

In the meantime, I was so happy to be back at work. Being self-sufficient and having myself back in the game was a great feeling. I was starting to feel like an adult again. Remember, I loved to work, and I loved making my own money.

Things were going well, and though my platelet count was not at 100K, it was hovering around 20K. That kept me out of the danger zone.

Every two weeks I would go to my doctor. She would inform me that my platelet count was still low, but it was out of the danger zone. However, I was still severely anemic.

One day, I went to the doctor, and she told me she wanted me to go straight to the hospital to get a blood transfusion. I said I would, but I didn't go that day. That was a workday, and I had to go to work. I remember being so tired, but I worked my twelve-hour shift. That night, the supervisor put me on a set of looms in the back of the weave room, close to the entryway, just in case I needed to run to the bathroom.

Finally, I got through the shift. It was about 6:30 a.m. when another weaver relieved me from my job and told me to go up front to see the nurse. I didn't think anything of it because periodically the nurses would call us in to do breathing tests and hearing tests. That's what I thought this was. Come to find out, she wanted to check my hemoglobin. When she checked it, it was so low that she told me I needed to go home, and I could not return to work as long as it was low. She informed me that as long as my hemoglobin was low, I could fall, hit my head, and get seriously hurt, and they would be liable. She told me I needed to get my things and leave. She said I wasn't fired, but I could not come back until my hemoglobin was up.

I suspect my doctor may have called to let them know it was dangerous for me to be working, being severely anemic. I broke down and started crying. I've always tried to do the right thing, and I felt like I was being punished and kicked aside. I didn't know what I was going to do.

When you can't do anything about anything, then do nothing, and get still.

That's right. Just like the lyrics of the gospel song, "After you've done all you can, you just stand."

The next day, I remember feeling so down as I was getting ready to go in for my part-time job. Once I got there, I remember sitting in a cubicle and feeling like I wanted to burst into tears. By then, things had started slowing down there, and people were getting laid off. Though I still had a part-time job, it was not a secure job. That was my last day at Daymark—I quit. Then I contacted my sister, who contacted the Fayetteville Beauty College—the school that she graduated from—and talked to the owner about me getting a grant to go back to beauty school. I had accumulated a few hours but not enough to graduate. I was told to go in and complete the paperwork. I did, and I was able to receive a grant.

I restarted beauty school while I was sick. It was strenuous, but I did the best I could. Sometimes when the instructor could see how weak I was, she would put me in the supply room to hand out supplies. I only needed fifteen hundred hours to graduate.

One morning, I went to get up to start my day and couldn't; I was just too tired. I started bleeding, and I just couldn't stop. I was so tired and so weak; I couldn't even lift my head. Mother knew I wasn't feeling well, so she and my other sister came by the house to check on me. By this time, I was covered in blood. It was like someone was butchering me, and the bleeding would not stop.

The last thing I remember was passing in and out of consciousness. Mother was shaking me, trying to keep me awake. The inevitable was happening; I was leaving this earth.

Silk was now working as a hairstylist. After work, she came by my house to check on me . . .

Immediately, when I walked into Diamond's house, I saw my sister lying in a pool of blood. Everybody was praying, but nobody was doing anything. My sister kept going in and out of consciousness. My mother was crying, praying, and screaming for my sister to come back to us. My father was standing helpless, unable to make it all go away. It was like death had entered the room to take my sister. We were all emotionally distraught.

Just thinking about this moment is making me emotional right now. My sister was dying, and nobody was able to do anything. Yes, I believe in God; yes, I have the faith; yes, I believe in the power of prayer; and, yes, I believe that prayer changes things; but I also believe that God gave wisdom and vision to man so that he would be able to save his fellow man's life.

I hollered out, "She needs to go to the hospital. We've got to get her to the hospital." My father and I jumped into action. My sister was gone—still breathing, but gone. We literally had to lift her up to put her in the car. She was like deadweight. Strength came out of nowhere, and my father got her in the car. After taking off, I decided that it would be best to call the EMS. They could get her to the hospital faster, plus they have the proper equipment.

As luck would have it, we were passing my parents' home en route to the hospital. We stopped there and I called the EMS. In no time, they were there. Diamond's vitals were all in the danger zone.

I remember being too weak to open my eyes, but I could still hear what was going on around me. I was taken by EMS to Moore Regional Hospital.

I was in such critical condition that a medical team had to helicopter me to UNC Medical Center, in Chapel Hill, North Carolina. I ended up in intensive care. The medical team did not expect me to make it.

I was praying for you to live, but, before they flew you to UNC, Chapel Hill, they told the family that you might not make it. I went home, went into my bedroom, and I prayed like I've never prayed before.

By the time they got me into intensive care, my blood count was 0.1. The first thing they did was give me a blood and platelet transfusion. I remember the next morning, a team of doctors were around my bed, asking me a lot of questions: "Do you know what day it is? What is your name? When is your birthday?" I had lost so much blood, they feared that not enough oxygen had been in the body to get nutrients to my brain.

That next morning, I called the hospital. I told them that I was calling to see if my sister had passed. I was literally weak, sickened, and crying. After I gave my sister's name, the nurse put me on hold, came back to the phone and said, "No, your sister is alive. She's up and eating."

I couldn't believe it. Her vitals were good. The day before had been so gruesome; now, it was as if nothing major had happened. I started thanking God. I got dressed and headed to UNC Medical Center.

Once my body was pumped with blood and platelets, I felt like I was new again.

Someone from the air medical team came by just to check on me; they thought I had died. I was told not even an animal could live with a 0.1 blood count. I was supposed to be dead, but God said . . . Not so, and not right now!

Doctors didn't know what to do. They were giving me rounds of blood transfusions, along with platelets and high amounts of prednisone. I stayed in the hospital for three days.

And I was there for all of those days. I even spent the night.

Yes, you did, gurl.

Once they got my platelet count up to a safe zone and my hemo-globin was also up, I was released.

The doctor told my mother that I could not drive a car or do any-thing that could cause me to get into an accident or have an injury. Just a minor cut could cause me to bleed to death. I moved out of my house and moved in with my mother and father. They were my sole providers. I felt like a child, and they treated me like a child.

They sure did.

Mother meant well, but she was so domineering and controlling. She wanted me to do everything her way, or it was no way. Most of the time, I was irritated with everything and the way my life was going. I hated being sick, and, though I enjoyed being spoiled, I hated being treated like a helpless child.

Although I thank God for my parents, I also thank God for all of my siblings, especially Silk. She was there for me, even when I just didn't have the strength to be there for myself.

While on prednisone, I was having mood swings and started gain-ing weight. I felt like I was losing control of my very existence. I was used to being self-sufficient; now, I was dependent on Mother and Father to take care of me and pay my bills. I was always in tears and always depressed. I wanted a normal life, like everyone else.

I didn't want to be anyone's charity case. Mother was babying me so much that, truth be told, she turned me into a spoiled child. Mother and Father allowed me to behave like a little kid because I was sick. My siblings started doing everything for me. Mother would say, "Lynn can't do it; you know she's sick," and I fell into the helpless trap. I didn't want to be sick nor did I ask to be sick, but my body was rebelling against itself, and there was nothing I could do about it but accept the fact that I was sick.

I eventually ended up completing beauty school and moving out of my parents' house, back into a house of my own.

About three or four years after this trauma, I had a second near-death experience; a blood clot was lodged in my lungs. If I had waited and assumed the pain was gas, I would have died. My first instinct was to get to a hospital, and it saved my life. To this day, I'm still under a doctor's care for both of these life-threatening conditions.

Chapter 6

Walking through the Fear of the Unknown: How It All Began

The questions we hear most are, "How did all of this get started? When did this start? Why did it get started?"

Well, here is what happened: In November 2014, Wendy Williams was on the top of her game, right?

Mm-hmm.

Well, she was making this movie about Aaliyah and her life. Everybody was eager to watch the movie because Wendy Williams had promoted it so good.

Mm-hmm.

So that night, when the movie was about to premiere, we're hanging on to our seats, me probably eating a bag of popcorn. I watched the movie, and I was disgusted in the end because the movie just didn't turn out the way we thought it was supposed to.

Right.

So the next morning, Wendy Williams was very, very quiet about her movie, yet she was on her show talking about everything everybody else had done. Not one time did she utter any words about the horribly scripted movie she put out.

Mm-hmm. No, she sure didn't.

So, I felt like I wanted to create a platform to call people like Wendy Williams out when they can't admit they're wrong and when they can't admit they've messed up.

Right. I remember you coming to me about that, saying those exact words: We need a no-judgment zone, where people will be able to speak what they really feel, say what they want to say without being criticized or ostracized. We would be able to call out people like Wendy Williams—or anybody else.

Right. Not only did I call Silk, but I also called my other sister.

Mm-hmm.

I wanted to get her in on the action as well. So, we all put our heads together and decided we didn't want to be seen on the Internet, but we did want to be heard.

Mm-hmm.

So we decided to start up a podcast.

Yes, we did.

To create a podcast, I thought we needed a microphone, headphones, and a computer.

That's right.

I got busy, and I ordered everything we needed, then everybody paid me back for their share.

Mm-hmm.

Once everything came in, I started setting up for us to do a podcast.

Right.

Once I had everything set up, I called everybody over to my house.

Yes, and once we got there, we did the podcast, and it was so much fun. I felt liberated just to be able to vent.

It was liberating.

Yes.

Now, Silk and I loved the podcast; we didn't see anything wrong with it.

No, we didn't.

But our other sister felt like we were being so mean, and she felt we shouldn't put that out there like that.

That's right.

So that was the first and the last podcast we all did together. We never went back to doing podcasts together.

No, we didn't. After that, we created our Facebook page, on November 17, 2014, and we named the Facebook page "The Viewers." On that particular page, we began posting articles and posing questions to get people's opinions. We were basically calling it, "The no-judgment zone."

We wanted to hear what people had to say. We wanted to provide a place for people to really just be able to vent without being criticized.

Right. I remember, once you created that page, Silk, I looked at you and asked, "Will we ever get a million people on this page?"

And I looked at you and said, "Yes, we will get a million people on this page, and, once we get one million, we'll get two million.

After that, we didn't think anything of it; we started the page, and we started posting.

That's right.

And throughout our busy lives, the deal was, we all had to post on the page: Silk, my other sister, and myself.

Mm-hmm.

Silk and I were comfortable with what we were supposed to do, but my other sister just couldn't see the vision, I guess, so she really didn't post. Finally, when we came to her about posting on the page, she sucked it up and posted one post.

Mm-hmm.

After that, she never posted again.

Right. We continued to post, and then you did a video with no sound.

Mm-hmm. I did a video with no sound. During that time, y'all, everything was in an uproar.

Mm-hmm. It sure was.

You had people out in the street, burning down their communities, arguing and fighting. You had Black Lives Matter shouting, "Black lives matter!"

Mm-hmm.

Then, when somebody would ask, "Well, what about other lives?" they made it seem like no other lives mattered.

Yeah, they shouted them down.

So I went back and we put together a video with no sound that showed all of the atrocities that happened to black people up to that current day.

Mm-hmm.

Then, at the end of that video, it said, "Black lives matter, and all lives matter."

That's right. That's what it said.

Before I even got into the political arena, I had enough sense to understand that, yes, black lives matter, but all of our lives matter, no matter what color your skin is.

That's right.

When I'm in the grocery store, I don't just see black people. I see black people, white people, and all of sorts of people.

Right.

I thought it was offensive to say only one group of people's lives matter and not everybody's lives.

Right. That's right.

So that was the first video that was posted on our YouTube channel.

Right. At that time, Black Lives Matter was not as divisive or political as they are today.

That's right, they weren't. People asked us if we were part of the Black Lives Matter movement. We were never part of the Black Lives Matter movement. We saw the movement, we understood what they were trying to do, but when they invoked hatred and implied that only black lives matter and no other lives matter, that's where we had the problem.

That's right.

Then, everything fell apart when they started chanting at police, "Pigs in a blanket, fry 'em like bacon." The original intent of their ideas was polluted with such hatred that their message came to a screeching halt.

That's when they got political—very political.

We couldn't go along with or agree with that. If an accident happened or a crime took place in my home, right now, I can't pick up the phone and call Black Lives Matter for help. I can, however, pick up the phone and dial 911, and they'll send an officer out to protect and serve.

That's right. So when you made the silent video, that's around the same time that I created the YouTube channel. That video was posted on January 2, 2015.

Right.

After that, no more videos were posted on our YouTube channel until June 15. That's when you were talking about Rachel Dolezal.

Oh, Lord . . . Rachel Dolezal. Y'all might remember, Rachel Dolezal worked for the NAACP as a black civil rights activist. Basically, her parents outed her because she wasn't really black; she was white.

So I remember putting a video out about that. I didn't see anything wrong with her wanting to be black.

Me neither.

If she wanted to act black, let her act black. If we can have someone like Bruce Jenner live his life as a man for over sixty years, become a husband and father, then all of a sudden change and say he's a woman, why can't she identify as black? If it was okay for Bruce Jenner to identify as a woman, then it should have been okay for Rachel Dolezal to identify as black if she wanted to.

I really didn't have a problem with it, so I made a video about it.

Yes. Why was it a big scandal for her to identify as black, when Bruce Jenner was applauded for identifying as a woman?

That's right.

* * *

So while Donald Trump was announcing that he was running for president, I was watching it on CNN. Right after his announcement, it seemed like the media slid into the hate speech they spew today.

So, anyway, I was watching it on CNN, and I sat straight up because Donald Trump was talking about illegal aliens. I'm listening, like, oh my God; he's right!

Now, we saw the influx of foreign workers moving into our small town and taking jobs. Like we said before, we didn't know they were in the U.S. illegally. We just thought they were Mexicans.

I was lying across my bed watching with excitement, and I immediately stood up, went over to my dresser, picked up my cell phone, and dialed my sister's number. I was impressed. He wasn't playing; he wasn't wavering; he wasn't backing down. Everything he said, he meant, and I loved it.

Mm-hmm.

When she answered the phone, I said, "Gurl, cut on your TV. Donald Trump is announcing that he's running for president."

I stopped what I was doing, and I cut on the TV. Even though I know it's supposed to be "turned on," I cut it on.

That's what she did.

Mm-hmm.

Then we hung up, y'all, and I'm looking at this man on my flat-screen TV, like, oh, my goodness.

It wasn't even a good two minutes later that Silk called me back, halfway through Donald Trump's speech. This is what she said: "Gurl, this is going to be the next President of the United States."

That's right. I felt that as he was talking. All we'd seen and heard since NAFTA were problems, and here Donald Trump was talking about solutions he wanted to implement to help the different communities within this country.

Everything that had been ailing the communities—especially the black communities—he had the solution for.

Mm-hmm.

When Donald Trump started speaking about it, I was like, wait a minute . . . He's going to be the next president. He did not have a scared bone in his body, he was speaking words that were almost forbidden, and he wanted to face down the swamp.

Yes! He didn't sound scripted, which was inviting and enticing because it was like a breath of fresh air. It was like, finally, I understand exactly what this man is saying. He's not using these big words. He's just saying it, and we, the American people, all could understand it.

Right.

I was so mesmerized by this man speaking out about how he was going to fix this country.

That's right.

Remember, we had eight years under the Obama administration. Of all those eight years, the last two years were especially rough. It seemed like Obama waited for a time when he was secure in his presidency to really let his true intentions show. We got tired of seeing people in the streets fighting and bickering and arguing. We got tired of people killing each other. We didn't want to see that. We wanted all communities to come up, including black communities.

So when he said he was going to secure the border, the first thing we thought was, well, that's a no-brainer. Don't you secure your house?

Don't you?

Ain't the White House secure?

Ain't it?

Then the house of America should be secure.

That's right.

Now, my heart's racing because it felt like someone was throwing the American people a lifeline that we badly needed. I agreed with Donald Trump, and he continued, saying he was going to bring back jobs.

Mm-hmm.

See, we remember the jobs that were here, and we remember the NAFTA bill that was signed into law by Bill Clinton that took those jobs away.

Yes, we remember that.

Also, we used to work in manufacturing. We watched our jobs gouged piece by piece, while different people—yes, foreigners—were being bussed in to take them. We didn't realize those people were in our country illegally.

To see Americans out of work, losing their homes, losing their vehicles, with no hope at all, it made us start asking, "What's going on here, and why are these people coming in? How is it that they're able to come in and work, but Americans can't?"

We didn't understand what was really going on until Donald Trump started exposing it, right there on live TV. Then it all started making sense. Nobody had the answers for us to these questions, but when Donald Trump started talking, it confirmed our thoughts and feelings about the devastation we'd seen in our communities. It was like an unexplained secret, and he was explaining it.

Remember, Obama ran on "Hope and Change." We were hoping that something was going to change, but it didn't change, and that's the truth.

Yes. It got worse!

Here, you have this billionaire businessman letting all Americans know what was really going on; here's what we can do about it; here's how we can fix it.

Right!

When he talked about our jobs being outsourced, our first thought was, why would leaders outsource our jobs to leave the American people with no jobs? Who does that? If you're ruling over a nation, why would you want to see people in distress, depressed, oppressed, with no job because you've outsourced them to other countries? I would have to assume it was because you were getting a kickback. No other explanation makes sense.

Yes. It was like Trump was outing the government, exposing their dirty little secrets. He changed the narrative from, "Oh, what a noble program NAFTA is" to "How does this make any sense?"

It didn't make sense, but you know who did make sense? Donald Trump.

Donald Trump made sense, and we finally understood what had been going on and why it had been going on. Nobody else was man enough to stand there and say what he said. He was calling out illegals and the un-American values that were being forced on Americans. That was refreshing by itself, but he also had true answers and solutions to solve the problems. I knew that he was the man for the job.

That's right.

So after that, y'all, Donald Trump said he wanted to bring back spirit. With everything that had been going on in our country, we needed spirit. We needed a different kind of man. We didn't need another career politician; we really needed a businessman.

The first thing that came to my mind was, if you really want to know what's going on with the body of people, check the head.

That's right. Check the head.

If the head is prosperous and successful, then it's going to trickle down to the body of people, and the body of people will be prosperous and successful.

That's right.

So, from day one, he had me hooked.

Yes. We were both hooked.

We were hanging on to his every word.

That's right; we were.

I noticed that after Donald Trump announced he was running for president, he stayed in the news every day, all day. They vilified him, demeaned him, disparaged him, and disrespected him, day in and day out.

That's right. They sure did.

Nobody wanted to speak up for him. Everybody acted like they were afraid to speak out, even though they felt he might be on to something.

Mm-hmm, that's right.

I didn't like it, so I decided to speak out about it.

Now, most of the time, I would just record from Silk's cell phone. This time, I remembered that Silk had gotten me an iPad for one of my birthdays. Well, I looked at the iPad, and I noticed that there was a camera on it.

Mm-hmm.

So I got the iPad down, took a coaster holder—one of those little things you put drinks on to preserve your furniture—I took the coasters out, put the iPad in between the prongs, then took a towel and stuffed it in the back to keep it upright.

Hahaha. So you could angle the iPad wherever you needed it to be without it falling over.

Absolutely right. Then I clicked on "Record," and it recorded me.

Mm-hmm.

Honey, that's when I went in, all the way, in favor of Donald Trump. I said, "I think I'm stumping for the Trump. I think I want to switch my party." I was finally paying attention because I was so mad.

I wasn't just going along to get along. We were doing something that was not normal. No matter how sassy you think you are, you don't go that far outside the box unless you are convinced that it's necessary. I was thinking way outside of the box.

Mm-hmm.

I wanted something different, and I saw something different in Donald Trump. It was unfair that they weren't giving him a fair shot.

That's right; they sure weren't.

And so that was the first video that I made regarding the election and my support for Donald Trump.

That was on July 5, 2015.

Right. I did a lot of cussing because I was pissed off.

Mm-hmm.

I was mad at the way things were. I was mad at the system. I was mad at the media, how they were trying to destroy somebody before he even got started. I thought it was totally unfair, and I spoke out about how I felt.

Right.

So after I did the video, I didn't know how to upload it to YouTube, so Silk had to step in and help, hahaha.

Hahaha, yes, I did.

Silk uploaded the video to YouTube, and it started garnering attention to where HLN emailed because they wanted to interview me.

Right. Now, at the time, we didn't really understand all of this Internet and email and so forth, hahaha. That particular email was not set up for us to receive a notification, so we didn't know that HLN wanted Diamond on for an interview.

Mm-hmm.

By the time we got the message, it was too late. I looked at Diamond, and I told her, "You don't ever have to worry about missing another interview request because I'm setting this up to make sure I get all notifications. So if any one of these stations want you for an interview, we'll be able to respond in time."

Keep in mind, I was not doing the videos with Diamond at this particular time.

See, that's what I love about my sister: she takes care of all the little things, so I don't have to worry about them.

A lot of other things started happening in the country, and I would make videos on these issues. I was creating videos on any topic that I felt I wanted to address.

That's right.

Well, some news was coming down the pipeline about Bill Cosby, and I wanted to shy away from it.

Right.

I didn't really want to talk about it, but Silk did.

Yes, I did. I had an opinion, and I told Diamond I really wanted to talk about Bill Cosby. Diamond didn't think we should do it, so I didn't force it.

Then, one night, I was taking a shower, and I had this epiphany in my gut. It hit me so strongly that I really wanted to talk about what was going on with Bill Cosby.

The name of our platform was the same as our Facebook page, The Viewers. We talked about anything and everything.

That's right.

And that was something that I wanted to talk about.

Right.

So I called Diamond, and I said, "Gurl, I was just in the shower, and this thing hit me in my gut. I really want to talk about Bill Cosby."

She said, "Well, I just got finished taking my shower too, and something came over me."

That's right. I decided we needed to talk about him. Now, remember, it was supposed to be a podcast with three people when all of this first started.

Mm-hmm.

We recorded that first podcast and never did another one.

We never even went public with that podcast.

It doesn't exist anywhere.

No, it doesn't.

So I knew Silk was coming to my house so that we could discuss Bill Cosby, but I also reached out to my other sister to see if she wanted to come and be a part of the discussion. She wasn't interested at all.

Here's the deal: every time I would do something on video, she would always discourage me and say, "No one's looking at that; no one is watching you; no one is going to see it."

So the last time I invited her was when we got ready to do this Bill Cosby video, and she was busy and couldn't do it.

That's right.

No problem. Silk and I went ahead and did it.

We did it. I had my notes, and I did my little thing, and I'm so glad that I did. It brought me to where I am today.

That's right.

At that time, all I know is that we were venting—period.

We were venting and speaking our minds about what we thought.

Now, let me make something clear: What we think about Bill Cosby today is really nobody's business. The point is, that was when Silk joined the conversation and chimed in with me, sitting right there in my dining room.

That's right.

We were both there. The few followers that we had on YouTube and Facebook, they loved it because they loved our interaction.

Hahaha.

Now, we couldn't see our interaction.

Right.

People were telling us that we were so funny, and we couldn't see it until we went back and looked at it.

Right. A lot of people thought that what we were doing was scripted, but it wasn't. This is how we act all the time.

It's just our personalities.

Yes.

You can see us anywhere, and this is how we act. We're never going to change the way we act.

Yes.

So, after that, we started putting out videos together.

Mm-hmm.

Well, the thing that was in the news all the time, every day, all day, twenty-four hours a day, was Donald J. Trump.

That's right. He became the topic of discussion at the watercooler, around the dinner table—everywhere.

So that's what we discussed, politics.

That's right.

I remember sitting in my office one night, probably at about 9:00 p.m., and Megyn Kelly was on Fox News.

Mm-hmm.

That was the time Megyn Kelly accused Donald Trump of something so hideous, I won't even repeat it.

Mm-hmm.

Michael Cohen was mixed up in the discussion, and we did a video defending him.

That's right.

We didn't think anything of it. I want you to understand, we didn't know Michael Cohen from Adam or Eve.

That's right.

We hadn't met him at that time; we didn't know who he was; we just didn't like the fact that they were accusing Donald Trump of salacious BS. We felt like they were tying Michael Cohen to it in order to demonize a presidential candidate.

Mm-hmm.

So we made a video. We didn't know Michael Cohen was going to see it.

No, we didn't.

So rumor has it that Lynne Patton was the one who saw the video first and took it to Michael Cohen.

Right.

When Michael Cohen saw it, he immediately reached out to us via email. He thanked us for supporting Donald Trump, the candidate, and he thanked us for taking up for them.

He sure did.

He wanted to send us some T-shirts and some campaign gear, and he asked where he could send it to.

Mm-hmm. We gave him our address so he could send it.

That was the end of it. We didn't think anything else of it. We continued making our videos, speaking about things, and letting people know how we felt.

That's right.

A lot of people ask us how we knew that Trump was the one. For me, I knew that Donald Trump was the one because he was not like the others. He was not politically correct. He was correct! He was firm, to the point, and he was real.

Right.

And because he was speaking the truth and talking about solving the issues that were plaguing the country, I knew this man was the one. I had no doubt. There's an old saying that if you doubt, you may as well do without. We weren't going to do without. I did not want this country to do without whatever this man had to offer. The reason why I say that is because I heard the common sense in his words, and it resonated profoundly with my very existence.

A lot of people are watching the news, and the media is telling you what they want you to hear, and they're spinning the narrative. Donald Trump didn't have to do any of that.

Mm-hmm.

He just told it like it was. He said what he meant and meant what he said and didn't care who liked it or not. He was fearless, not fearful. He didn't have a problem with calling a spade a spade and being vocal about it. I knew we needed someone like that in this country, instead of what we had become accustomed to having.

Right. So we were making these videos, and one night I just got this inkling in my gut to Google us.

Mm-hmm.

Y'all, we were in so many blogs, it scared the living daylights out of me.

Mm-hmm. Literally.

So that night, I called Silk, and I said, "Gurl, Google us."

Yeah. When I Googled us, I saw us everywhere.

In so many blogs.

There were so many blogs and places where people were talking about us, I could not believe it—I just could not believe it.

We were shocked, we really were. We only had about ten people on that YouTube channel.

That's right. Only ten folks.

We had no clue at all that we were making this much noise and people were hearing it. We didn't realize it until people started telling us, "You said everything that we've been wanting to say, but if we say it, we'll be labeled racist."

Yeah. That's right.

Just after this video, Donald Trump was going to the border to assess things.

Yes, he was.

So when I went to my sister's house, I didn't know what she was going to say in that particular video. She just started ranting.

What happened was, I was still watching all of the news, and I noticed how people like Montel Williams and Rick Perry were saying the most nasty, salacious things about candidate Trump.

Mm-hmm.

Now, we don't script our videos.

No, we don't.

We just go off the cuff about how we feel.

Mm-hmm.

So I said, "Silk, come on over, we're going to make a video because this is getting ridiculous, and I need to speak out." By that time, candidate Trump had started on his way to the border because he was adamant about putting up the wall.

That's right.

Now, back then, we thought it was a fence. Later, we realized that it was a wall.

Hahaha. That's right.

Well, honey, I talked about Rick Perry, I talked about Montel Williams, and a lot of other ones. Then we got to talking about the border because candidate Trump had been there.

Then, I said, "Let me tell you why he went to that border."

And I said, "Tell me why."

"He went down to that border to take measurements because he's going to put that damn fence up." Like I said, back then, I thought it was a fence.

That's because there were already fences up—falling down, rickety old things, with big holes for illegal aliens to walk right through—but that's what we assumed would be put up.

After that video, y'all were so tickled. That's when we found out we were in all of these blogs because of that one video saying Donald Trump went down to the border to take measurements.

Yes, that was the video. When I looked online at the different blogs, people were referring to that particular video because we had just dropped that video.

Right.

So, that morning, when I got up, I went into a separate room, and I just turned my face into the corner of the wall and thanked God.

We didn't know any of it was going to be heard, and we weren't trying to make anything happen. All we could do was go with the flow. Like I've said, if you ever want to make God laugh, tell Him your plans. We didn't have any plan for any of this. We were speaking sincerely, from the heart.

Mm-hmm. We sure were.

We spoke how we felt about everything. We didn't know we were resonating with other average Americans.

Nope. We were just venting because it felt good, hahaha.

Hahaha. It sure did; it felt real good.

We were new to politics. Even though we were lifelong Democrats, I don't ever remember watching a presidential debate or even being interested in whatever was being debated. So the first Republican Party presidential debate I watched was held on August 6, 2015, and hosted by Fox News. Candidate Donald Trump had qualified to participate in the prime time–tier debate because he was polling as one of the top ten candidates.

These were the top ten candidates: real estate mogul Donald Trump, former Florida governor Jeb Bush, Wisconsin governor Scott Walker, Florida senator Marco Rubio, New Jersey governor Chris Christie, retired neurosurgeon Ben Carson, Kentucky senator Rand Paul, Texas senator Ted Cruz, former Arkansas senator Mike Huckabee, and Ohio governor John Kasich. The moderators were Bret Baier, Megyn Kelly, and Chris Wallace. We didn't know what to expect, but we were excited that our man, Donald Trump, was on the stage.

We sure were. Now, one of Megyn Kelly's first questions was, "Mr. Trump, one of the things people love about you is you speak your mind, and you don't use a politician's filter. However, that is not without its downside, in particular, when it comes to women. You've called women you don't like 'fat pigs,' 'dogs,' 'slobs,' and 'disgusting animals.'"

Then Donald Trump responded, "Only Rosie O'Donnell."

Y'all, I was fit to be tied. Something inside of me started boiling over. I couldn't believe what had just come out of Megyn Kelly's mouth. I was watching *The View* when Rosie O'Donnell started that whole thing. She didn't care about Donald Trump's feelings when she was mocking him, so why should he care about her feelings? If she was woman enough to dish it, she should have been woman enough to take Donald Trump's reply. As the moderator, why would Megyn Kelly ask that question anyhow? She should have asked a question of substance, not an ignorant question.

How is asking an ignorant question going to bring back jobs and help the economy grow?

When I woke up that next morning, I was still ticked off at Megyn Kelly. I didn't like the way she had treated Donald Trump. With this being my first time actually watching a debate, I felt like Megyn Kelly deliberately asked Donald Trump certain questions to try to paint him in a negative light. I picked up the phone and called Silk. I told her to get dressed, come to my house, and we were going to do a rant video about what happened at the debates.

I was like, "Okay," and I was at her house within the hour.

Silk didn't know what I was going to say, but she was ready. I went off the cuff, and she followed along without missing a beat.

Yes, I sure did. Y'all, Diamond was pissed. We pressed "Record," and Diamond went off. I had no idea what she was going to say, but she said it the way she felt it. I still laugh today when I see that specific video. Diamond said, "Leave my man, Donald Trump, the hell alone. If you got something to say, you got something you want to tell him, run it by us first, and I'll let you know if you have permission to come for him. Don't come for him unless he invites your ass." I tried to keep from laughing, but it was so hard.

Yes, Silk, I felt it all in my bones. It kept coming to me, word after word. I had to get Megyn Kelly straight. After we finished the video, I had to add the intro and the outro to it. Silk had to then load it to our YouTube account. Instantly, the video started blowing up. The viewership skyrocketed. We couldn't believe the response that we were getting. Y'all loved it.

We started getting requests for interviews. People were happy that we did this rebuttal to Megyn Kelly.

One day, we were actually sitting in a restaurant eating dessert . . .

And I was in the middle of eating my apple pie à la mode.

Now, don't judge us, we love to eat. So we got a phone call letting us know that the video had gone viral. At that time, we didn't know what "viral" meant. So we replied that we didn't have a virus or a cold, hahaha.

Hahaha. So when you have a video that gets a certain amount of views in a short amount of time, it's considered "viral."

Later on that same day, we received another phone call letting us know that we had made Drudge. We had no idea what the frantic-sounding person on the other end of the phone was talking about, so we replied that we were not on drugs; we don't do drugs nor do we sell drugs.

Hahaha.

What we didn't know was that the Drudge Report was a huge news outlet. We found out later that it was the first time that a video sat at the top of the Drudge Report page.

Chapter 7

The Opportunists

If you didn't make it, you have no right to take it.

We've found that anytime you are doing something that could garner attention, there is always an opportunist lurking in the shadows like a dark cloud looking to come and rain on your parade. They come as if they mean you good, but every compliment, smile, and intention is for themselves. We've had several experiences with these types of narcissistic sociopaths. We call them "opportunists."

An opportunist is a person who takes advantage of people and their circumstances with no regard for morals and integrity. They come off as being very friendly, kind, and concerned. They come into your life as though they have the sole purpose of being involved in your life to make it better.

Yeah. They act like they are in your corner and truly by your side—in order to benefit themselves.

They want to gain something from you. They use you as a stepping-stone for their own illusion, stepping all over you and your innocence just to fulfill their fantasy. They have their own agenda, like a devil in disguise.

Sis, you got that right. Describing opportunists as "devils in disguise" is an insult to the devil!

Opportunists are nothing new. During the days of slavery, our ancestors invented things that revolutionized and transformed America. However, they were unable to take the credit for any invention because they were the property of slave owners. Being the property of a slave owner meant the slaves had no rights, and they could be bought, managed, and sold at any time.

After slavery, when black people would come up with ideas, an opportunist would take the idea and run with it if it was a good idea. *Mm-hmm.*

The invention of the cotton scraper is one example. A black man named Ned invented the scraper, and the patent was refused because a black man invented it. Then Ned's owner, Oscar Stewart, made a significant amount of money selling the non-patented tool.

White people often ask, "Why are black people so angry?" One of the things that make black people angry is when they've worked hard through their sweat and tears to build something and opportunists, who didn't contribute one thing to their success, think they are entitled to take credit for it.

In our case, let me be clear about how we got started: We were stumping for Trump and making videos, and it was real and genuine. Nothing was rehearsed; all of our ideas were authentic and our own original thoughts. We never sat down and discussed a strategy for what we were doing or how we were going to do it. We never viewed other videos to give us examples. We just did and said what we thought. It was our truth.

I made the first video by myself, entitled, "Dump the Rest of Those Chumps, and Vote for Donald Trump." Shortly after, Silk came onboard.

Y'all, it didn't take long before the opportunists started showing up. They tried to use us to help raise their profile. We talked to one over the phone. This person wasn't concerned about our aspirations; this person ranted and ranted about himself and how he stays so busy. This person went around and around in a circle with words, like a rat chasing its own tail. This person was only concerned about making himself appear a certain way, as if he had all of this power to make things happen for us.

Hahaha. How could he make something happen for us if it wasn't already happening for him? He was able to talk the talk, but he couldn't walk the walk. After talking to him for a few days, we realized he literally sounded like the epitome of a racist. He began speaking to us in a tone like he was superior to us and we were less than inferior to him.

I can remember when this one opportunist asked us if we were serious about stumping for Donald Trump. Are you kidding? I wasn't sure if I'd heard right. This person wanted to know if we would take a look at Ted Cruz and get behind him.

My whole body started to fill with rage, and it seemed like I could taste blood, not from my ITP but because I was mad as hell. I couldn't believe people were asking us a question like that. We told everybody, straight out of the gate, that we supported Donald J. Trump only.

We found that when people are out to use you, they only have one agenda, and that's their agenda. Sometimes people may think that we are standoffish, but we're not. Experiences like this are the reasons why we don't have any managers controlling us.

Most of the time, when you are in the middle of a situation, you can't clearly see the details or why they are important. When the experience is over, you have to learn from it.

In all honesty, we've been victimized and taken advantage of by many narcissistic opportunists who thought they could verbally and emotionally abuse us to get us to bend to their will. People thought they could use and exploit us, then exploit Donald Trump. Well, that wasn't going to happen on our watch.

Oh, no, it wasn't.

We spoke out because we were tired of career politicians, and we needed something new. From day one, everything that we've done has always been authentic.

We were created by God for such a time as this. We took nothing and made something, and we are still building.

The only ones who get credit for our success are God, who created us; our parents, who raised us; us, Diamond and Silk, who created our own platform; and Donald John Trump, who allowed us to speak on his stage. That's when we became famous.

Chapter 8

Ditch and Switch

There is a swamp, and it's filled with Democrats, some Republicans, elitists, the Deep State, and people who wanted to change the rules in the middle of the game to ensure that Donald J. Trump couldn't win the 2016 election.

First of all, when Donald Trump announced he was running for president, the news media made a big spectacle, trying to mock him, trying to make him look like a racist, and it was day after day of attacks on him. Everything seemed set up to destroy one candidate.

That's exactly what it seemed like. All of a sudden, they came up with all of these creative rule changes.

Rule changes or stories? If they couldn't damage him with a story, then they would try to change the rules in the middle of the game.

Right.

So one night, I'm sitting in my office watching Fox News, and Megyn Kelly was on. She used to host *The Kelly File* weeknights at 9:00 p.m. As I was watching, the screen flashes with this sudden, breaking news. It was another negative news story about Donald Trump.

I'm watching it, and I'm upset about it. I knew blatant lies were being told about this man to keep him from succeeding in the presidential race.

Mm-hmm.

Now, about this time, we learned that some Democrat voters could not vote for Trump in their primaries.

That's right. Different states had different requirements when it came to voting in a primary election, and some states required that in order to vote Republican you had to be registered as a Republican. If you were a Democrat, you couldn't vote for a Republican in some primary elections.

Mm-hmm.

Because we were Democrats in North Carolina and we wanted to vote in the primaries for a Republican candidate, we had to switch our party from Democrat to Republican in order to vote in the primary election. So in September 2015, we put out a video to show people how we went to the Board of Elections, dressed in our Make America Great Again hats and T-shirts, to switch our party from Democrat to Republican.

As we were educating ourselves at that time, we knew the general public was unaware of some of these rules.

Absolutely.

The average voters believed they could vote for whoever they wanted, regardless of how they were registered. However, this wasn't a general election; this was a primary election, and the rules were different. A lot of people were not aware of the election rules.

Well, I was so disturbed about the fact that a lot of people didn't know how a lot of this worked, so I picked up the phone and called Silk. We were fired up, and one topic led to another, and I said, "Gurl, we need to do something. We need to start some type of movement to educate people about switching their party to Republican so that they can vote for Donald J. Trump."

That's right.

So we sat on the phone, and we brainstormed all sorts of names until we knew we'd nailed it: "Ditch and Switch Now."

At first, we wanted "Ditch and Switch," but Silk did her research, and she found out that T-Mobile already owned the slogan Ditch and Switch. Anytime that I propose an idea and we debate it out, Silk always researches it to make sure we have the domain and so forth.

Exactly. After doing my research, I went to Diamond's home, and, while standing in her office, I had to deliver the bad news that we couldn't use Ditch and Switch. So we were trying to either add something to it or switch it around so it would work.

Mm-hmm.

We kept throwing out all of these different added-on words, and, out of nowhere, I said, "Now, we want them to ditch and switch and do it now, so why not 'Ditch and Switch Now'?"

I was like, "That'll work."

So I said, "Let me check to make sure that domain name is available." And, sure enough, it was, so Ditch and Switch Now was born.

It sure was born. If you key "Ditch and Switch Now" into Google or Bing, Diamond and Silk pages will come up right along with it.

So, we made a YouTube video on September 28, 2015. We look at it now, and we can't believe how young we were! I was wearing yellow and Silk wore a tannish-looking color. Now, we'll be the first to admit that we may not have known everything, but we knew enough to garner up this enthusiasm that made people want to switch their party from Democrat to Republican in order to vote for Donald J. Trump.

We felt we had to do this because the stories in the media were wild, and we really felt they were doing everything they could to try to stop the voter from connecting with a certain candidate.

Mm-hmm.

So Silk did the research on it and put the website together with all of the states' information for those who could not go to the Board of Elections.

And Ditch and Switch Now took off.

We got credit for Ditch and Switch Now in Philadelphia, four states away. This was in a March 15, 2016, article put out by renegadefinancialplanner.com: "Thanks to the Ditch and Switch Now movement started by the two North Carolina sisters, Diamond and Silk, nearly 46,000 Pennsylvania Democrats have switched to Republicans since the beginning of the year. The paper says in Massachusetts, as many as 20,000 Democrats have gone from blue to red this year, with Trump cited as a primary reason."

Right. I remember hearing about this older lady that had heard a Diamond and Silk video, and she went to her Board of Elections and told them that she was there to ditch and switch, hahaha. They didn't know what she was talking about. She kept insisting, and they finally figured out that she wanted to ditch the Democrats and switch to Republican because she wanted to vote for Donald J. Trump.

We started that movement by pumping it out there using Facebook, YouTube, and Twitter. As a matter of fact, Dan Scavino even tweeted something about Ditch and Switch Now, and that also garnered up more enthusiasm.

We wanted people to leave what we call that "Democrat Plantation."

Yes. We wanted people to leave the Democrat Plantation, and we didn't want them to miss out on the opportunity to vote for Donald Trump because of the different rules that had been implemented by these different states.

See, Alabama, Arkansas, Colorado, Georgia, Indiana, Massachusetts, Minnesota, and Mississippi have what's called "open primaries." Registered Democrats in these states who wanted to vote for Trump would be fine because voters didn't have to be affiliated with a political party in order to vote for a partisan candidate. In other words, if they were registered Democrats, they could still vote for Trump in the primary elections.

Alaska, Arizona, California, Illinois, Iowa, Kansas, New Hampshire, New Jersey, North Carolina, Ohio, Oregon, Rhode Island,

Utah, and West Virginia have "semi-closed primaries," where previously unaffiliated voters may participate in the partisan primary of their choice, but voters who are already affiliated with a political party can only vote in that party's primary.

Now, these states do allow voters to register or change party preference on Election Day, but we didn't want anything to go wrong; better to take care of the ditch and make the switch beforehand.

Here's where it gets tricky: Connecticut, Delaware, Florida, Kansas, Kentucky, Louisiana, Maine, Maryland, the District of Columbia, Nebraska, New Mexico, New York, Pennsylvania, and Wyoming have "closed primaries." For states with closed primaries, voters have to vote the party they are registered with, and you have to have that in place prior to Election Day. People may vote in a party's primary only if they are registered members of that party prior to Election Day.

So these Americans couldn't show up to a primary election as a Democrat and vote Republican, and they had no ability to change their party on Election Day. We absolutely knew there were millions of Americans that didn't know this.

Mm-hmm.

That's why we had to put that web page together. It was Diamond's brilliant idea.

Hahaha. Thank you, Silk. I can come up with the idea, but I don't have a clue how to implement it, hahaha.

Hahaha.

Silk comes up with the way to make it happen.

Right; I figure it out: Strategy A, B, and C is how we're going to make that happen.

We really do complement each other in that way.

That's right. It's like when two people sing on different notes to harmonize the whole song. I feel like that's what's missing, even in this country. Everybody wants to sing the loudest instead of allowing people to use their different gifts to harmonize and make a melody.

That's right. You sing your part; I'll sing mine. You stay in your own lane, doing your thing; I'll stay in my own lane, doing my thing. Together, it's harmony and balance.

That's right, and that's what creates the music.

So our Ditch and Switch Now slogan became a movement. And thank God we did our research. We knew that it was important. We didn't just sit back and wait for our fate. We had to be Republicans to vote for Donald J. Trump in the primaries, and we made sure we were. We didn't want to go to the polls in the primary as Democrats and find out we couldn't vote for our preferred candidate. Donald J. Trump is the reason we switched our party to Republican.

Exactly. We often say that it's not about the party, it's about the person. So let me just explain that for a moment: it's not about the party, it's about the person, but because of the different rules we still had to play a smart game. We still had to go along and follow the rules of the election process.

That's exactly right. And it just galvanized a whole group of people who understood our message and what we were saying. They also believed in candidate Trump and what he was saying. Something propelled them to get up and go switch their party.

That's right. Now, because there were so many different rules for all of the different states, we just told everybody to ditch and switch; that way they wouldn't run the risk of losing their vote.

I want our readers to understand that we weren't being paid any money for this.

And no one told us or forced us or coerced us to do this. You have to remember, this started from an idea Diamond had. Nobody told us to do it; nobody paid us to do it; we just discovered some truths and decided we needed to educate everyone else as to what we found out, and that's why we did it.

About a month after the Ditch and Switch Now movement started, in October 2015, we happened to be looking through our Twitter page and discovered that Donald Trump had started following us on Twitter.

Mm-hmm, yes.

I called Diamond because I was going through our Twitter feed.

Yes. Because I really didn't know how that Twitter stuff worked.

Right. We had just learned how Twitter really worked anyway. So I called you to tell you what was going on. By the time we figured it out, he had been following Diamond and Silk for three days.

I'll tell you, we were very humbled by it all. We did not get the big head because somebody very powerful was following us on Twitter.

No, we did not.

We were very excited yet discreet. Other people always brought it up and made a big deal out of it.

Yes. People figured it out, but it was really authentic, y'all; this was authentic. We didn't ask for it, and we didn't know it was going to happen. Like I said, we didn't even know for three days, hahaha.

That's exactly how it happened.

Mm-hmm.

So after October, when he started following us on Twitter, comes November . . .

I don't remember if we were doing interviews or what that day, but it was the end of a long day, and I remember checking Twitter, and that's when we saw a tweet from Dan Scavino. The Trump team was inviting Diamond and Silk to the GOP debate in Wisconsin.

That's right.

We replied with a picture.

It was one of our animated pictures because we were shocked, hahaha.

Hahaha.

We weren't expecting it; we didn't know it was going to happen, and we were over the moon because this was going to be the first time we'd ever been to a debate. I mean, yeah, we saw debates on television, but we'd never been to a live debate, much less been invited by the Trump team. We were so excited.

Yes, we were.

Now, the debate was in just a few days. So Silk was booking flights and arranging a hotel; it was happening just that quick.

Yeah, it really happened fast.

Anyhoo, the debates were the following night, so when we got to Wisconsin we had to call an Uber. That was the very first time we ever used an Uber.

Hahaha. Yes, it was.

The first car that came was so dirty, we refused to get in the car.

Gurl . . . yes it was. We were dressed up really nice, and the car had a lot of salt on it because it had snowed there. It was dingy, nasty, and dirty. We actually had to order another Uber.

So we got to the event; we were feeling good, wearing our blue pantsuits.

Yes.

I'm not going to lie; it was nerve-wracking in an exciting way. We didn't know what was supposed to happen. When we walked into the venue, there were people who knew us from our videos. They kept asking us if we were the two girls.

We were like, "Yes. We're Diamond and Silk."

So just as we're feeling sharp and a part of things, we locate an usher, and he escorts us up to our seats. We thought we were going to be right in the middle of the action; after all, the Trump team invited us. Y'all, they had us in the nosebleeds. In case you don't know what the nosebleed section is, it's all the way at the top of the auditorium.

Hahaha. Yes. The altitude is so high, it threatens to cause nosebleeds.

Hahaha. It was so far to the top that everybody looked like little ants at the bottom. Even Donald Trump looked like a tiny image of himself, and he's 6'3".

You just took the words out of my mouth. That's exactly what I was about to say.

The advantage we had in this section was that we were able to see everything unfold. It was very exciting to be present at this debate and see it all go down.

Especially because we were new to politics. We may have heard about debates, we may have seen a little flash come across the news talking about a debate, but to actually sit there and be in that energy at that time, it was spectacular. That was an emotional moment that still stays with me because I never imagined myself having such an experience. We weren't looking for that to happen, but it happened.

So right before the debate ended, Dan Scavino and another member of his team came over to greet us. Unfortunately, we didn't get to meet candidate Donald J. Trump that night. We were all able to take photos, but not with the candidate.

We were not disappointed that we didn't meet him that night. We were just excited to have the opportunity to be there and actually watch the debate happen.

To have the Trump team invite us to a debate that so many people probably wanted to attend, I'm still boggled by it all.

You know, I've learned some hard-fought lessons in my time, and I've learned not to try to make things happen. Just let them happen. Oftentimes, people want to force a flame to ignite. What happens when you force a flame is you end up with a forest fire that you can't put out. Now it's a mess.

Exactly right, a hot mess.

Always let things happen. That's sort of a policy we live by, we pretty much always let it happen.

Let it happen, let it unfold, go with the flow. So that's exactly what we did.

Right. Turns out it was the best thing because there were some things in the works that we didn't know about, and eventually we were going to meet our man.

Chapter 9

Your Haters Make
You Greater

So after the experience at the Wisconsin debate, we came home and made a video talking about what a great experience it was to see the debates and watch candidate Donald Trump dominate. Because that's all he did, dominate the stage.

Dominate, yes, he did.

Less than a month later, we found out that candidate Trump was going to be in North Carolina.

Right.

And there was no way he was going to be there without us being there.

No way.

So it was arranged for us to be right there in Raleigh at the rally.

Mm-hmm. Raleigh, North Carolina.

Well, we live about two hours away from Raleigh, so we drove there the night before and stayed in a hotel because we didn't want to contend with the traffic in Raleigh.

That's right.

This was our very first rally, and we wanted to get there without any hassles.

Right. This was the very first rally that we'd been to with Donald Trump and our very first presidential rally.

That's right. So we got to the hotel, we settled in, and we anxiously waited for the next morning. Now, the next day, I was all over the place. Y'all know Diamond doesn't know how to contain herself, and I was walking back and forth because I was so excited about seeing candidate Donald J. Trump live.

Mm-hmm.

I was excited about meeting him because we had been stumping for him since June 2015. They were even calling us the Stump for Trump Girls.

Exactly. But while Diamond was all over the place, I was calm, cool, and collected.

Hahaha. We were trying to play it smart and get something to eat beforehand, and I was so excited about going to this rally that I really couldn't even eat.

For me, I didn't have a problem eating, including the cheesecake, hahaha.

Okay, so we got ourselves ready. I was still overanxious, but I was okay. Finally, a driver comes to pick us up from the hotel. He had us get in the back seat. No problem. I know that Rosa Parks may have had a problem sitting in the back of the bus, but we didn't have a problem sitting in that back seat because Raleigh is huge.

That's right.

So with all of that traffic, I was just happy I didn't have to drive through it.

That's right.

So they get us to the venue, and they rush us around back. I looked over at Silk, and I said, "Listen, I thought those days were over with. Why are we being driven around to the back? Why can't we go in through the front door?" Little did I know, that's what they do for famous people: they are taken to the back.

Mm-hmm.

We didn't realize that we were famous. We felt completely normal. So a gentleman by the name of George came out and greeted us. George was the facilitator for most of the Trump rallies.

That's right.

So he brought us inside and whisked us up to a room, and he put us inside of this room. Once we were in there, we were separated from the action, and I looked at Silk and said, "Why do we have to sit here in this room? We don't have the plague."

Well, little did we know that was the greenroom.

That's right.

Well, they should have painted it green.

Hahaha. Sounds reasonable.

Finally, a member of the Trump team came and got us out of the room and he said, "Listen, I want you girls to stand right there because Donald Trump is going to be walking through those doors, and you'll be able to take a picture with him."

Yes, that's right.

So I'm there all antsy in my little brown suit, just fidgeting back and forth. Guess who is calm, cool, and collected? Silk.

Yes. I was standing where I was asked to stand so that I could see this happen because, remember, in Wisconsin we didn't get to meet him. So now they've got us standing in a place where we would get to see him come in the door.

Right. So, finally, y'all, the doors open. It was like, lights, camera, action.

Like at the Academy Awards.

All you hear are cameras flickering.

Yes. Click, click, click, click.

Lights were exploding around us, and in walks Donald J. Trump. It was like this man sucked all of the air and oxygen right out of the room.

Yes, it was just like that.

It was mesmerizing. He has this ability to shine, and he doesn't try to. He wasn't overexerting his power; he wasn't acting arrogant; he was being himself; but people were mesmerized by his mere presence.

We're watching this whole thing happen in front of us. So he did a few interviews, and then he stepped to the front of the line for those who wanted a picture with him.

Mm-hmm. People were everywhere, y'all, and he was snapping photo after photo. Finally, he just sort of looked into the crowd, and the first person he noticed was Silk.

Yes, he did.

So he used his left hand, and he pointed to her. Then he looked and saw me, and he said, "Get up here, get up here."

Mm-hmm.

So now we're in the front of this line, and we are about to take pictures with Donald J. Trump.

Wow.

First of all, he was so happy to see us. The first thing that he did was hug and kiss us.

He hugged me and kissed me on my right cheek.

Yeah. And this hug was a genuine, caring hug. The emotion that came from the hug was like we were family.

Yes. It was very affectionate.

This was the first time in our lives ever meeting Donald J. Trump.

Right. And his first time ever meeting us. It was like he was excited to see us, and we were excited to see him.

Mm-hmm.

So after we took pictures, we started having a conversation. The one thing I noticed that made me admire him even more was when he started talking to us, he immediately tuned everything else out. Lights are glaring at us, cameras were clicking nonstop, people were everywhere, and he was paying attention to Diamond and Silk and our conversation.

Crooked Hillary didn't win because she didn't know how to pay attention. Maybe she was banking on that hot sauce, but that wasn't going to do it. Candidate Donald J. Trump knew exactly how to pay attention.

That's right.

He gave his undivided attention. He listened without being distracted. So, y'all, we shot the breeze with candidate Trump. We talked about what he was going to do for this country. We talked about how we wanted him to be president, how he was going to make a good president, and we were behind him all the way.

Yes. And he thanked us for supporting him. It was like this man was family. It was interesting how he interacted with everybody, but especially us because he only knew us from what he saw on our videos.

Right. It's important for me to say this: no one made Diamond and Silk support candidate Trump. We heard what he was saying and decided for ourselves that he just made sense.

That's right.

He actually learned about us through his wife. Trump told the story about how First Lady Melania saw us on a video and showed it to him. He was intrigued by it, and the rest is history. Any other stories that you might hear are hype. Stop believing it.

That's right. Nothing but lies.

So we had our conversation, and they whisked us down to the auditorium and had us take our seats. So we're sitting there, y'all, and when the crowd noticed us, they started yelling our names, "Diamond and Silk, Diamond and Silk!"

We were like, "How do these people know us?"

Yes. They started chanting it. I was blown away.

I was blown away too. I couldn't believe how these people knew us. Now, remember, we left our houses the day before just like anyone else attending this rally. We lived normal lives. We didn't know anything about being famous.

Well, we're sitting there, and these very serious-looking men are surrounding us, and they wouldn't let anybody get close to us. This is how brand new we were at all of this, y'all: I'm wondering what's wrong with them. Why don't they want anybody coming over here to talk to us? I didn't realize that was security.

That's right. Hahaha.

I thought they were trying to be funny.

Yes. Because people were actually coming to us, wanting to shake our hands, wanting to say hi, but these guys were blocking them. We were like, why are they doing that?

So now the rally had begun; candidate Donald J. Trump was onstage. At this particular rally, the audience members were able to ask him questions. So somebody turned to us and said, "Girls, do you want to ask him a question?"

We said, "Yeah, we want to ask him a question." So we're standing on the stairs next to the platform, ready to ask candidate Donald J. Trump a question. He turned around and saw it was us, and he says, "Get up here."

Yes, that's just how he said it.

So now he's telling us to get up there on his stage.

That's right.

Truth is, I wasn't nervous at all. It was like I was meant for that moment.

That's right.

So we went up onstage, and candidate Trump started telling his story about how he saw our videos. He said something that I know the world heard: "I hope you've monetized this."

Yes. That's what he said.

Now, in case you don't know what monetizing means, it means to earn revenue from.

Mm-hmm.

So when candidate Trump said, "I hope you've monetized this," he meant, "I hope you are earning revenue from what you are doing."

That's right.

A lot of times we get criticized by the Left because we monetize.

Mm-hmm.

If there are tools out there for you to monetize your platform, monetize your brand, I don't see anything wrong with monetization. I don't see anything wrong with candidate Trump, the billionaire, telling us, hey, "I hope you've monetized this."

Yes. That's right.

The Left tries to put millionaires down, calls them white racists. What about black millionaires? I believe Donald Trump would be the happiest if we all reached our fullest potential and became as rich as we could be. By the way, do you see the difference? The Left seems to want to emphasize our differences, keep it rich against poor, black against white, gay against straight. No. All Americans can rise to their full and happiest productivity.

So he wanted us to be successful—financially successful—even if we couldn't even see the possibilities before us.

Exactly. And with him being a billionaire and making that statement to us—I thought it was awesome, and it reflected a sincere desire to see others prosper. Meaning, he doesn't have a problem saying to you: Make it. I want you to be prosperous. I want prosperity to fall on you.

When you look at the fact that he said, "I see two of my friends in the audience, and they've become very famous and very rich," he was speaking prosperity on us.

Prosperity and success. Just like Romans 4:17 says, he was "calling those things that were not as though they were." And that's how we felt in that moment.

You know, oftentimes, especially in the black community, the churches have taught us that there's something wrong with having money; there's something wrong with being prosperous.

Right.

If you're doing anything half-assed, some in the black community and some left-leaning white liberals are happy with that. When you have your stuff together, your ducks are in a row, and everything is going accordingly, they criticize your progress.

They sure do.

And when this white man, who happened to be a billionaire, who didn't know us from Adam or Eve, looked at us and said on national television, "I hope you've monetized this . . ."

In front of the whole world.

That says to us, "I'm not jealous; I'm not envious. I want you to be successful; I want you to be prosperous."

Yes.

Let me repeat this truth: if you ever want to know what's wrong with a body of people, check the head.

Mm-hmm.

If the head is successful, then the body of people are going to be successful.

So with candidate Trump telling us that, that let me know he wanted us to experience success, gain wealth, become prosperous, and be all that we could be. It wasn't going to bother him; he'd just sit back and be tickled pink by it.

That was a great description. When I look within our communities, I see how ingrained the mentality is that it's okay to be poor, broken, and in poverty. Many on the Left want to make sure we're put back in that place. I wonder how we allowed a party to make us believe it's okay to be less than.

Right. What people have to understand is that when the Democrat Party created and enforced the Jim Crow laws, the real objective was to intimidate, manipulate, keep the black population stuck, and stifle their reach.

Exactly right. It was a disgusting list of rules that suppressed the black communities. Systemic racism is what I call it. A system full of rules used to keep you down.

Then, to compensate for the crisis they created, the Democrats started giving away free food, free housing, and other "perks."

Sound familiar?

Mm-hmm. This entrenched the American black man even further into dependency. Black men fell for the con that if they didn't take what was free, their families would starve.

Now, all of this was orchestrated under the Democrat Party, and they sure wanted to keep it going. That's why we call the Democrat Party the party of slavery.

Yes, we do.

They did not want it to end because they wanted to enslave people to do their work without paying them.

That's right. They wanted free labor.

The way to get that free labor was through control, manipulation, and cruelty.

So when you really sit back and think about it, at the end of the day, do you want free stuff, or do you want freedom? Because if you remember, it was the Republican Party that freed the slaves.

What people don't understand is, all of this was designed to keep the black man stuck. And now that I'm older and I'm looking at everything, it seems designed for the black man to have a poverty mentality, a low mindset—just barely getting by, no motivation to have more. Then the Democrats and the Left implement things in the community for black men's mindsets to stay that way.

Now, that's the truth.

They do what the slave masters did to our black ancestors: They got their slaves to appoint one black man as the leader of all, and then indoctrinated him with religion, telling him he had to serve and obey his master if he wanted to have a clean soul before God. Truth is, they didn't give a damn about the black man's soul; they just wanted to keep their slaves in line.

That's right.

There was never indoctrination about being independent, prosperous, and successful—which are the true principles of God. If you look at the black leaders today, we have the same thing going on. In our opinion, black leaders like Al Sharpton, Jesse Jackson, and Maxine Waters are rich and comfortable from the exploitation of their black constituents, who don't have a damn thing.

Barely getting by. Living paycheck to paycheck.

Some on the Left got very upset with us because candidate Trump said, "I hope you've monetized this."

Yes. They would even ask us questions about the statement he made about us being very rich, like it's suspicious.

Exactly. Like there's something wrong with black women being rich.

Well, if Madam C. J. Walker can invent hair products and become rich, then Diamond and Silk can become rich too. If Oprah Winfrey can go from being a millionaire to being a billionaire, then there is nothing wrong with Diamond and Silk becoming millionaires or billionaires too.

That's right. Madam C. J. Walker made her fortune by developing and marketing a line of cosmetics and hair care products for black women.

Mm-hmm. The reason the Left has a problem with Diamond and Silk is that we don't do what the Left wants us to do. They want to control what we do. I promise you this, if we had been onstage with a black man, he never would have said, "I hope you've monetized this." He'd be telling us to get back in line.

That's right.

Another one of the evil categories that the "tolerant Left" wants to throw conservative black folks into is the "dishonest swindler" category, or the grifter. They'd rather categorize us as con artists than entrepreneurs or people who are obtaining the American dream.

You know who calls us grifters? It's these left-leaning white liberals—and then black people fall in line with it.

Mm-hmm.

They always talk about racism; they want to keep that before you. Those are called dog whistles. They use it to keep you in line on what we call the Democrat Plantation. Now, I'm not talking about people being physically on a plantation. I'm talking about your mindset still being stuck in the era of somebody having you in bondage and pain.

Yes. Wow.

It's rooted so deep in you that you can't even pull yourself up a little bit to get out of that type of mentality and that type of stinking thinking.

Mm-hmm. That's right.

The Left had average citizens terrified of some kind of white supremacist takeover where the freedoms of the minority groups would be trampled. That's not true at all. When Donald Trump said, "Make America Great Again," it was not an invitation to white people to take over. It was an invitation for all Americans—all—to dream something big in your life, go after it with hard work, and be as great as you can be. That's the American dream. And that goes for black, white, Hispanic, Asian, or any other American citizen.

Go after the American dream.

Then you have black people still falling for the old okeydoke, the same old lie: "We'll do whatever the leader says to do." The leaders are taking advantage of this! As a matter of fact, I even heard somebody say—which I thought was appalling—"Vote blue, no matter who."

Say what?

Now, to me, that is an ignorant view to instill in black people. That "who" could be a socialist who wants to take away your freedom, wants to give you everything for free, as if you can't comprehend and get up off your own ass and get it for yourself.

Mm-hmm. And you know, for decades we voted blue, no matter who, and we see where that got us.

That's right.

See, when people allow other people to indoctrinate them, they lose their ability to think for themselves. Somebody always has to be leading them. Well, we don't have to be led. We are blessed to have our own minds to think for ourselves. That's why Diamond and Silk choose to think outside of the box—which I call the black box.

That's right.

What is it with the Democrats wanting to keep anything regarding slavery in front of our eyes, in front of our children's and grandchildren's eyes, be it on TV, radio, pictures, anything that displays slavery? As long as they can keep black people living in the pain of their ancestors, then they'll keep them stuck there as if they are slaves themselves.

That's why it was so good to hear a billionaire telling us, "I hope you've monetized this." Donald Trump's message was just the opposite of the Democrats' invitation to a permanent pity party. It let us know that he wanted us to make money—and lots of it.

That's right. There's nothing wrong with making money or having money.

Then he asked us to do a little routine. Now, some people got offended by that. We didn't. Even though we are authentic when we speak on our YouTube videos, we do possess a certain flavor when delivering our message.

Mm-hmm. Yes.

So we got onstage, and we did our thing. Candidate Trump didn't know us from Adam or Eve, but he stepped back and he had enough confidence to know we weren't going to say anything to disappoint him in any kind of way.

You know, I would even go as far as to say that he entrusted us with his microphone, knowing that we supported him, period.

That's right.

He put that trust in us, and that was that.

That's right. He knew he could trust us; he went with his gut instinct.

Mm-hmm.

So, once he gave us that mic, we let the world know—because there were hundreds of cameras back there from all over the world.

Mm-hmm, all over the country and the world.

We declared it boldly right there to all of them that he was going to be the forty-fifth President of these United States.

When Diamond walked onto that stage and told the world that Donald Trump was going to be the forty-fifth President of these United States, that's when Diamond and Silk became famous. That was on December 4, 2015.

That's right. Now everybody, all over the world, knew who we were. We didn't even realize what had happened.

Hahaha. We didn't.

As a matter of fact, after the rally, we stayed over to talk to some Trump fans who wanted to snap photos of us with their cell phones. We didn't think there was a security issue or anything unusual about it.

George finally came to us and said, "Listen, girls, you don't know how famous you are. You can't just be down here like this."

That's right.

We had no idea. So George had to get us back in the car and back to the hotel instead of standing around talking to people.

That's right.

I didn't realize how famous we were until the very next day when it hit the media. I mean, it was all over the media that Diamond and Silk met candidate Trump for the very first time and joined him onstage.

When it got to the black media . . .

Whoa.

Black media let their ignorance show. They were so upset that it stunned the heck out of me. Now, remember, I've been bullied, I've been abused, but I have never before received this type of harassment, all because I told the world that Donald J. Trump was going to be the forty-fifth President of these United States.

If we wanted to back down, Daddy had the words of wisdom we needed. He said, "Listen, you can't fold and go cold now. Y'all have to stand up. Now that you've got their attention, you can talk."

Mm-hmm. That's right. And that's what we did.

That was big. Some black people weren't paying attention, but when they saw two black women go onstage and say, "Donald J. Trump is going to be the forty-fifth President of these United States," woah, they had a problem with that.

That's right.

Some of the media outlets were even disparaging and demeaning us because of the power and influence of our words.

Mm-hmm.

We are living proof of what happens to someone when they dare to disagree with the Left. They set a deliberate plan in motion to demonize us before the public so that other Americans, especially black Americans, wouldn't be persuaded by us.

Keep in mind, we didn't even know we had the power to sway others. We weren't trying to sway people at all.

That's right.

We were just on the man's stage sharing our hearts. We had already heard his message: he wanted to kill NAFTA the same way it killed our jobs. We agreed that it just made sense that controlling illegal immigration would be easier if a wall was in place along our southern border. And why should other countries charge us top dollar to bring our goods to their nations while they send their goods here all day long for free?

When we endorsed Donald J. Trump that night, we were simply speaking our minds. Everything we'd seen and heard so far brought us to the conclusion that Donald J. Trump was the better candidate, and we were confident that he was going to win.

That's right. We had no idea that we were going to become famous. We had no idea that a lot of hate was going to be coming from the left-wing media and especially from some black people. We had no earthly idea.

We refused to be bullied into silence, though. I said Donald J. Trump was going to be our forty-fifth president, and I said it boldly. I stood behind that statement as the hate started pouring in because I meant it. If I said it, I meant it.

Well, they sure tried to bully us into silence. The next day, incoming hate surrounded us. I wouldn't say that we second-guessed ourselves, but we had to decide what was really important when this happened. We knew that we could not allow anybody to silence our voices any longer.

We had just gone onstage with a presidential nominee, and straight hate was coming at us. There was so much hate assailing us that we had to do something to fight back. So Diamond came up with another great idea: the Wall of Shame.

The Wall of Shame is a place on our website where people who make disparaging, despicable, disturbing comments are highlighted for all to see. Even people who are prominent, famous, verified, or have a blue checkmark by their name are put on this particular wall. Then we tweet or send out the link on Facebook for all to see who made disparaging comments. They made the comments public; why can't we?

We also have a Wall of Fame for folks that thank us, love us, and support us.

I thought it was very important that America see what true racism really looks like. Oftentimes, white Americans get accused of racism, and it's like all of the bad things that have ever happened or will happen to black people are rolled into this word. No one thinks about what it really means or if they're guilty of it. They just believe whites are the sole cause of it.

Well, that's just not true. Racism can go both ways, and true racism—the belief that all members of each race possess characteristics or abilities specific to that race, especially so as to distinguish it as inferior or superior to another race—was what was happening to us.

To our shock, it came mostly from our black brothers and sisters, and I still call them my brothers and sisters because they didn't know any better. They were being racist toward their black sisters.

That's right.

Sometimes it's hard for some black people to understand change. If anything looks out of the norm, they're going to talk about it, ostracize it, criticize it, and demonize it. So two black girls getting up on a political stage to endorse a very powerful white Republican who happens to be a billionaire businessman was just too much for them. To make matters worse, their skewed thinking was being reinforced by the left-wing media, blogs, social media posts, and so much more.

Again, we faced a moment of deciding what was really important. Diamond and Silk started off strong. We were strong through this whole process, and we were going to continue being strong. The more they spewed hate, the more we let them because—guess what?—our haters made us greater.

Our haters made us greater, and the more they hate, the more we educate. We use those slogans because, like our father said, if they're hating you that means you've got their attention. Now you need to speak. Now is not the time to fold and go cold.

That's right.

And guess what? We got even louder.

That's exactly what we did.

Now, if you think just meeting him was something, we've got a lot more to tell. Wait until you hear the rest of the story.

Now, we don't want you to think it's all bad out there. We couldn't do what we do without some amazing people that come around us with pure hearts to help.

It's the truth, y'all.

Chapter 10

Giving without Expecting Anything in Return

L *ife was still somewhat normal on January 1, 2016. The whole fam-* *ily had come over for New Year's dinner. Delicious aromas filled the air, and there was hope for a great new year.*

The nation seemed to be thawing from the depression put upon us during the Obama years. The prospect of candidate Trump's sure win in November 2016 had me feeling so positive that I renamed my menu and cooked Slap-Your-Mama Southern Fried Chicken, Money-Drawing Collard Greens and Ham Hocks, Extremely Lucky Black-Eyed Peas with Fatback, Magnificently Prosperous Mac and Cheese, and Wealthy Golden Corn-Bread-and-Banana Pudding. Hahaha.

Hahaha. Yes, indeed.

After dinner, we slowly made our way to the living room to watch a movie. Now, as we were sitting there, y'all, I could just feel this chill full of energy and excitement, maybe even a warning in my gut. I turned to Diamond out of nowhere and said, "Something huge is about to happen. Life is about to change; I just want you to know that."

Right. Silk knew something big was about to happen.

That's right. It was midday, I want to say around two or three o'clock.

Yes. And the one thing about Silk and me—I think we both have this intuition—when we say something, it's surely going to happen.

Oh, yes.

We don't know when, but it is going to happen, especially if we start feeling the chill with it.

Oh, yes. It's going to happen. So I felt it, I spoke it out, and we let it go. That was the end of it. You didn't even ask me to expound on it or anything. You just said, "Okay."

That was the end of it.

So maybe an hour later, my cell phone rang. It was George, the facilitator for all of the Trump campaign and rally events.

Mm-hmm. He was the gentleman who had greeted us at the 2015 rally in Raleigh, North Carolina.

So he wanted to know if we wanted to come to the rally in Biloxi, Mississippi, to speak and pump up the crowd, pretty much.

I remember, we were so happy when we got that phone call. You had just said to me, "Our lives are about to change." And it wasn't an hour or so later that we received this call. Well, guess what? Our lives really were about to change because that was the start of us speaking at different rally events.

That's right.

Biloxi, Mississippi: Mississippi Coast Coliseum and Convention Center, January 2, 2016

So we went to the rally in Biloxi, Mississippi. That was the night we met Eric and Lara Trump.

Mm-hmm. They were kind and gracious, y'all, and so enthusiastic about our support for candidate Trump.

Yes, they were. I remember the roaring of the crowd when we got onstage and said, "Are we all stumping for Trump?" They went nuts, y'all. It was a phenomenal event. The room was full of energy, and people were there waiting to see candidate Donald J. Trump.

Yes. What I remember especially about that particular night was they made sure we were placed with the family. We stood down there with Lara and Eric, just the four of us. It was like we were two more of the kids.

So, that night, candidate Donald Trump called us onstage with him again, to say a few words, and this was the beginning of our participation in rallies.

Mm-hmm.

Des Moines, Iowa: Iowa Events Center, Veterans' Fundraiser, January 28, 2016

So I don't know if people can remember, but candidate Trump skipped the January 28, 2016, Republican debate.

That's right.

He went to Iowa to raise money for veterans instead.

Mm-hmm. And it was like we just felt something in our craw, an urgency in our sense of intuition, if you will. We had to be there.

Right. In Iowa.

We were at Diamond's house, making some videos, and we made a decision that night that we were going to Iowa.

If he wasn't going to be on the debate stage, we were going to support him where he was.

That's right.

So we made a phone call to George, booked our tickets, and we went directly to the Iowa Events Center, in Des Moines. I can't remember a more frigid city than Des Moines, Iowa.

It was very cold in Iowa. I do remember that.

When we arrived at the events center, we were taken backstage. We had the privilege of meeting our veterans, some of whom had been maimed, lost limbs, or been disfigured. I remember feeling so humbled and respectful of the fact that these people fought for us to be able to be free in this country. I was so honored to even share the same space as them.

Yes. It was a phenomenal event and a valuable experience.

A valuable experience that I'll never forget.

Yes.

After greeting the veterans, George took us to the stage for our speech. The crowd was pumped, y'all, and candidate Trump hadn't even gotten there yet. I can't explain that kind of contagious energy.

It was contagious and powerful.

So after our time on the stage, we were brought to our seats. Remember those seats in the nosebleed section? Well, this time we were escorted to the very front row of the auditorium, on the left side.

Mm-hmm.

I remember sitting by Tana Goertz, who used to play on *The Apprentice* and was also part of the 2016 Trump campaign.

That's right. Yes.

In the front row, on the right side of the auditorium, sat candidate Trump's family: Ivanka Trump, Don Jr., and Eric Trump. When they looked over and saw it was Diamond and Silk, they came over to greet us, to hug us, and say hello to us.

Yes. They were humble and gracious. They were nothing like the media try to make them out to be.

Right. Say what you want, they were down to earth then, and they're still down to earth today.

They sure are.

They were not bougie; they were not stuck-up; and they didn't know us from Adam or Eve. They were just so kind to us and so grateful that we were stumping for Trump. Their demeanor was not standoffish at all. They thanked us, and we really felt appreciated.

That's a very good description of how it was. Now, keep in mind that we had already met Eric in Biloxi, Mississippi.

Mike Huckabee and Sarah Sanders were also there at this time.

Mike Huckabee had just dropped out of the race.

Mm-hmm. So candidate Trump was speaking and suddenly says, "I see two of my friends in the audience, and they've become very famous and very rich."

We looked around like, who is he talking about? So then he says, "Diamond and Silk, get up here for a second."

I was so tickled by that. I remember turning to Tana and saying, "We're not rich. Maybe he's calling those things that are not as though they are."

Just as we're getting up on the stage, protesters started shouting. His response to them says a lot about him: "You know, I really believe if we took them into a room and just talked to them, it would be fine. They'd understand. We want strength; we want good healthcare, we want good protection, we want borders; we want the wall."

All of these were reasonable things; why was the media making him out to be a monster? We had to wonder.

So he says, "Say hello."

He stood there, y'all, like a father. It was like family, like this man had known us for years.

That's exactly how it felt.

He was so pleasant and genuinely nice that we knew the evil things the media were saying about him were just lies.

Those were lies. Donald Trump is a down-to-earth person. He fights for the little man—that's the truth.

It's the truth; yes, it is.

After the veterans' fundraiser, we went backstage, and that's when we were able to meet Melania Trump.

Yes. When we made eye contact, she was just excited to meet us and speak to us. She was so pleasant.

Yes, she was. She was the most humble, gracious person you ever wanted to meet.

She wasn't standoffish either.

Not at all.

Shortly after we met the future First Lady, George drove us back to our hotel so we could get back to North Carolina the next day.

Charleston, South Carolina: Charleston Convention Center, February 19, 2016

The next rally we attended was the following month, in Charleston, South Carolina. Gurl, that's when we got so sick.

Mm-hmm.

See, we were not used to traveling like that. We were around people who we didn't know, and we were hugging and loving on them, so we got sick.

Well, see, we had stopped for something to eat, and while we were sitting there, our fans, people who loved us, came over and began talking to us.

Yes.

And one particular guy was sick and told us he was sick.

He told us he was sick and then started coughing and sneezing hysterically all over the place while we were trying to eat our food.

Yes. We finally left without eating, it was so horrific.

After that, sure enough, we got sick.

We got sick, sick, sick.

I don't recall ever having a common cold that made me so sick. First, Silk came down with a sore throat that was so bad that she lost her voice. Then, of course, whatever Silk had, I picked it up.

Don't blame it on me. It seemed like that guy might've been a rally hopper.

Yes. I remember seeing him so many times and realizing every time he was around us, we would get sick.

Hahaha. We really would. I don't know what type of cold he may have had, but whenever he showed up, we got sick. The last time we saw him, we told our assistant to keep him away, and they kept him away.

11:21 a.m., April 2016: Time to Pray

So just switching gears, I remember during this time, back in April 2016, the media was trying to throw shade at candidate Donald Trump by calling him all of these different names. And the Left seemed to be changing rules to cheat him.

So candidate Trump was running up against Ted Cruz. Well, I remember sitting at my desk, and I'm like, "You know what? It's time for us to fast and pray."

I knew in my heart of hearts that Donald Trump was supposed to be the president. So it was during one of our Table Talk shows on social media that I said I thought it was time for us to have prayer every day, at 11:21 a.m. EST.

That's right.

And so, let me tell you where I got the time from: I was sitting in my office, thinking we needed to have prayer. What is a significant time to remember? Well, it just so happened that I was looking back at a video of when candidate Trump was announcing that he was going to run for president. The video had the timestamps on it of the different time zones as Donald Trump was appearing in them. So it was on June 16, 2015, at 11:21 a.m., EST, when he announced he was running for President of the United States. I wrote that time down and said, "That will be the time that we will have prayer."

That's exactly what you said.

A lot of people wanted us to change the time. Do you remember that?

Yes, I do. But once you have something written in stone, stick with it. You can't be like everybody else; do what you do, and do it your way.

That time was chosen for a specific reason because that time in history can never be changed.

Mm-hmm.

Okay, so we put that video out on April 12, 2016. Y'all, I remember the next day, on April 13, 2016, Megyn Kelly actually went to Trump Tower to clear the air with candidate Trump. Then, a week or so later,

Ted Cruz dropped out of the race, and Donald J. Trump became the presidential nominee.

That lets you know, prayer changes things.

Yes, it does.

I don't care what anybody tries to tell you, prayer will change some things. Sometimes it just changes us and strengthens us to handle our situation. However, prayer can also make the power company personnel have compassion and allow you to keep heat and lights on in the cold winter months.

That's right.

Prayer can cause the mechanic who fixed your car to extend a payment plan until the end of the month when you can pay for it.

Mm-hmm. I recall saying, "We believe in the power of prayer."

That's how we were raised. We believed in the power of prayer; we believed from the very beginning that Donald J. Trump was going to be President of the United States; we believed he was called to reverse the curse of past leaders who didn't have the people's interests at heart.

Yes. We had faith.

We felt so sure, it was like it had already happened. F-A-I-T-H: "Feel As If the Thing Has Happened."

That's right. Feel as if it's already happened. That's exactly what we did.

Lessons Learned

As were travelling around in 2016, openly promoting Donald Trump, an interesting media buzz dominated the headlines—you know how the media likes to spin their narrative; they're so nasty. Apparently, candidate Donald Trump did not have women who were going to vote for him; he had no support from American women.

Mm-hmm.

And we looked at one another and said, "Well, that's a lie because we're women."

Mm-hmm.

How could they say women didn't want to vote for Donald Trump, when women were showing up at the rallies?

So people started writing us about starting a Women for Trump movement, but we really couldn't manage it at that time due to our full schedule. So when we finally said we would try to start something, we received an email from a lady who wanted to do something just like that.

Right. We received an email from a lady who also wanted to do something when it came to women who support Trump. The event was taking place in Virginia.

Right. She already had the event and location, so she just wanted us to show up and speak at the event.

You live and you learn is all I'll say. Everything, always, is a lesson that God wants you to learn.

That's right. Oh, what a lesson we learned.

Now, in 2016, we made a lot of appearances for free, so we weren't charging for this particular event. We drove to Virginia and got a hotel room, and then we went to a meeting at the facilitator's home.

The same lady who emailed us.

Right. So when we got there, she really insisted that we stay in her home.

That's right. She wanted us to stay at her house.

We said, "Oh, no; we'll stay at the hotel."

She responded sincerely with something like, "No, you don't need to be in that nasty, dusty hotel; you need to stay right here at my house with me."

Mm-hmm.

So I'm like, well, okay, maybe it wouldn't be all that bad because it was a beautiful home.

It was a beautiful home.

She even called the hotel to let them know we were going to cancel our room because we were staying with her.

She was very pushy; this was what she was going to do.

Right. No worries, though. We went back to the hotel, we packed up our things, and we returned to her house because we were going to stay with her for the next couple of days.

Right.

Well, she got us settled in, and she put Silk and me in a room that had its own bathroom.

That's right. We were comfortable because it felt like we were sharing a hotel room.

When we got downstairs, she had fixed us breakfast. Now, breakfast to Diamond and Silk, y'all, is scrambled eggs with cheese, bacon, grits, biscuits and gravy, pancakes, etc. Y'all, it's one of our three favorite meals of the day.

Hahaha. Yes, and don't forget the crispy toast with extra butter.

There on the table, staring back at me, was one, big, Polish sausage and a runny, sunny-side up egg. Now, y'all, Diamond does not like her eggs runny. I like my eggs scrambled to cook out any possible salmonella.

So when she set that plate down, I knew it was food, but I wasn't going to eat it.

Hahaha.

Of course, she noticed that I didn't eat it. So what she did was wrap my plate up and put it in the refrigerator, just in case I wanted to eat it later. Now, I don't care how many times you wrap it up—you can wrap it up and put it in a gift box with a bow on top—I'm still not going to eat it.

Hahaha. Yes.

So that's breakfast. Now, I'm noticing that daylight is turning into darkness. It's becoming night, and there's no sign of dinner. Now, you have to understand, Diamond and Silk are used to eating breakfast, lunch, dinner, and snacks too. We don't miss meals.

Hell, no, we don't.

And back in 2016, we were big.

Huge.

We didn't miss a meal.

We don't have a problem with eating.

Now, it's time to leave for the event, and we still haven't eaten. Thankfully, they had little hors d'oeuvres, so we grabbed us some little mini bites, and that was the only meal we had.

A lot of times, a dinner is scheduled for after the event, so we thought maybe this event was planned that way and we'd go out for a meal afterwards.

Nope. We went back to her house, we got showered, and I had to pray myself to sleep because I was so hungry. You know how people cry themselves to sleep? I had to pray myself to sleep because my stomach was making so much noise, growling for food. I was hoping prayer would shut it up so it wouldn't wake Silk.

Well, hell, I was hoping my growling belly wouldn't wake you up either.

I had never gone to bed hungry.

So I'm thinking, "It's a fresh start, a new day, a new morning. We're going to get us a nice breakfast." In my mind, I was thinking about pancakes, bacon, cheesy eggs, a little syrup on the side, and maybe a glass of juice and a glass of ice water.

When we got up, our hostess was down in the basement, giving a course on dancing, and there was nothing but coffee. She eventually bopped up the steps with a SlimFast. There was no breakfast. I looked at Silk and said, "If we don't get something to eat, we're going to die of starvation." Hahaha.

Hahaha. We'll be like dry bones in the valley.

You cannot invite two black women who have weight on them to stay in a house without having any food available.

That's right.

When I have guests, I like to have fruits, snacks, and a variety of food.

Well, especially when guests are going to be staying with you, I'm thinking it's pretty standard to at least have dinner.

At the very least. When I politely inquired about some breakfast, y'all know what she told me?

What did she tell you?

That the egg and sausage from the day before was still in the refrigerator. Like I wanted to eat that.

She had the nerve to say some mess like that.

Well, we got out of there as fast as we could and headed to the nearest Cracker Barrel.

Hahaha. We sure did.

I had pancakes, meatloaf, ordered it up.

Yes. We had breakfast, lunch, and dinner.

And we tried to eat as much as we could, just in case we couldn't eat again that day.

Then we went by the Family Dollar store and got chips and snacks, hahaha.

Yes. Just in case. She may starve herself, but we weren't going to starve with her. So that was our lesson on not staying with people. Stay in a hotel. A lot of times, our fans—and we love them—they may want us to stay with them and cook us up a meal, make us comfortable. The thing is everybody may not have the same routine, or they may drink nothing but SlimFast, and it's more comfortable for everyone to have their own freedom with those things.

So we ended up doing the event, and the event was very successful. As a matter of fact, the same lady called us to do another event or two.

That's right.

We went and did those events, but we stayed in a hotel.

Hahaha. It only took us that one time to learn that lesson.

We had to be careful during that time because there seemed to be people all around us with hidden agendas.

Yes. Lots of hidden agendas.

It was like this lady was trying to get candidate Trump's attention, and we didn't operate like that. The one thing that we weren't going to do was exploit candidate Trump.

Yes. Remember, we had several experiences with the opportunists trying to exploit us to get next to candidate Trump. This felt the exact same way.

Yes. This lady started acting as if she spoke for us. I remember Silk had to get her straight, that she wasn't to speak on our behalf.

Yes, I sure did.

Somebody wanted us at an event, and she made it her business to call them to tell them what we like, what we don't like, and how they should handle their event.

Right. Now, this was after we had removed ourselves from her.

Right. She wanted to prance us around as if we were some type of sideshow.

Mm-hmm.

And when she got in front of her friends, she was like, "Y'all do this; y'all do that." I had to stop her one day, and I basically said, "We're not doing any of that. Stop telling us what to do." Y'all, I was at my breaking point.

Right. It seemed like she was trying to act as if she was our agent or manager, and she was not. That's when I basically told her, "You don't own us."

Right. The hair started standing up on our necks, y'all, and we got as far away from her as we could. She was not our manager, and she wasn't going to use us to get to candidate Trump.

That's right. We weren't going to exploit him, and we weren't going to let anybody exploit us to get to him. That was the bottom line.

So it didn't surprise us when we received an email informing us that she claimed to have discovered us and that we had lived in her home for weeks. That was a damn lie. If we had lived in her home for weeks, we would have died of starvation.

Bradenton, Florida: Women United 4 Trump, June 25, 2016

We finally decided to do our own event. We pondered the name, as we always do; Silk investigated, and we eventually named our event Women United 4 Trump.

Mm-hmm.

The slogan "Women for Trump" was already taken, so we wanted something that would stand out, something specific, something unique.

Right.

Now, I have to add this: Some people are always trying to see what they can get from you. There are those so skilled at latching on that, if you're not paying attention, they've done it to you and you don't even know what happened.

You can be unaware that it's even happening.

So we posted on social media that the event would be in Bradenton, Florida, and people from that area started contacting us, asking what they could do to help us with getting this event together.

Exactly.

Well, what happened was, two young ladies hijacked the event. They wanted to act as if they were our agents; they said they were going to make us famous. We were like, "Well, wait a minute, we're already famous. We became famous back in December 2015 when we went on candidate Trump's stage."

And the stuff that they were talking about, we weren't interested in. They were supposed to be helping us put together an event.

Right. We weren't interested in becoming more famous. We weren't interested in them doing anything to make us bigger. We wanted to put on this event, Women United 4 Trump.

Sometimes it's hard to relinquish control, and these are some of the reasons why we're all in the mix as to what's going on.

Yes. So we needed a location, a time, programs, and to advertise it to those who were likely to be interested in it.

Well, it was getting close to the date, and we were thinking we had all of it in order. All of a sudden, there's some rift going on.

This was in May 2016.

Then people started saying that they'd heard the event was canceled. Y'all, they had deliberately spread rumors that the event was no longer going to be held.

Right. They tried to sabotage it because we wouldn't go along with their plan. They wanted their people to provide food and drinks to our guests, but they didn't want to give us a cut of the profit.

That's exactly what they tried to do. They tried to make us pay for everything while they made a profit off of the event.

During all of this, Rose Tennent, a conservative talk radio host, had an event that we were invited to speak at. It was a beautiful event, and it was packed out, so we did what we do.

Yes, we did.

After the event, we were gathering our things, getting ready to go, saying our goodbyes, and we couldn't help but notice a young woman who was there at the back table, selling our merchandise.

Right.

That's when we met Tressie Ham. We were taken a bit off guard at our first introduction, but she came to be a true angel in our lives.

First, she mentioned that she was an event planner.

Mm-hmm.

When she said that, Diamond and I were like, wow. Then she basically said, "What do you need? Tell me; I can get it done; I can make it happen. I feel like I'm supposed to be here to help you."

Yes.

So we spilled everything out to her, and she told us in so many words, "Don't worry about anything; I've got this."

Mm-hmm. We told her about how the event had been hijacked and how the people involved had tried to undermine our endeavors.

But we told her that we still wanted to go on with the event.

By the way, don't let anyone rain on your parade and mess up what you have going on. I've said this before, and I'll say it again: when people do that, it's because of their own ignorance or because they may be envious or just greedy.

That's right.

Move right on, and allow it to backfire in their faces. It sure did in our case, because whereas our two young facilitators tried to tell us how to play, Tressie Ham listened. Lord knows, when you can't figure it out, it may be time to step back and let somebody else figure it out.

And that's exactly what we did.

So we stepped back and we allowed this event planner named Tressie Ham to work her magic.

She had the event space within two days.

Yes. She also added two more events to our schedule: a coffee and conversation and a little dance party with cake and wine at night. There was a charge if folks wanted to be a part of that, but the main rally was free.

She had everything lined up, and she said, "Girls, don't worry. We're going to have a nice event."

That's right.

So when we got to Bradenton, y'all, just like she promised, she had everything lined up professionally. Everything looked beautiful. Now, I can't tell y'all that we had thousands; I can't even tell y'all that we had five hundred people. We may have had a hundred people there that day, but it was a wonderful time, and the people who came out were happy to be there.

The media was declaring that Donald Trump had no support from women. This just wasn't true.

To be able to be at that event, especially as a woman—even though some men were there and welcomed—but to be there as a woman declaring, "I'm supporting Donald Trump," that was a magnificent event.

It was a magnificent evening. We did our coffee and conversation that morning. After the rally, we were able to dance, eat cake, and drink wine. We had a great time.

Yes.

We went in the hole because we had to pay for everything.

We were under the hole, hahaha, but we weren't bitter.

No, not at all. We were excited about it.

So we paid for everything, and we asked Tressie how much her bill would be. Y'all, her bill to us was zero.

She wouldn't charge us anything.

She essentially said, "I can't charge you; I feel like I'd be wrong before God if I did. I can't charge you anything."

She just wanted to help us. Out of everybody that has come along in our lives and crossed our path, Tressie Ham is still in our lives. She's still our event planner; she runs the store for Diamond and Silk; she is like a jewel. She was what we needed when we needed it.

Yes. She stepped in, and she wasn't looking for anything. She was just happy that she was able to get it done.

Tressie Ham has never used or exploited us, and she always tries to see how she can make things better.

Mm-hmm. People ask us how we put our events together and how to do this and that, and we can't even tell them because we don't have anything to do with it. We just show up, and Tressie has everything set up. You have to go through Tressie if you want to know what's going on with the events.

You know, by her being a giver she has become a part of us, it seems like for life, because she has been with us ever since.

Ever since 2016.

And here it is, 2020.

Exactly. She's right there with us, along with her husband Bill.

Yes. Now, Bill started coming along on our Chit Chat tours to sell the merchandise, and he just became a permanent fixture.

That's right.

So on all of our Chit Chat tours, the guy that you see back there selling the merchandise is Bill Ham.

Now, I want my black brothers and sisters to understand this: You can't call everybody racist. These people are white people, and they go to bat for us. They make sure everything is done correctly and beautifully.

That's right. They show up before we get there to make sure every-thing is in place.

That's right. So, y'all want to tell me black lives matter? We know our black lives matter.

Yes, we do.

So do these white lives that really look out for us, and that is the truth.

That's the truth. All lives matter.

So Tressie and Bill are just like part of the family. They're loved. We'll never find another like Tressie.

And she makes the best crawfish and gumbo, y'all.

Yes, she certainly does.

Chapter 11

Rejection Is God's Protection—and Redirection

In June 2016, we received an email from someone who offered us money to stop stumping for Donald Trump. Y'all, they wanted us to publicly switch our support to a different candidate and stop stumping for him.

Mm-hmm.

So when I saw that, I was flabbergasted.

When people want to make a contribution to us, that's an investment that they're making to donate to our cause. This wasn't a contribution to invest in our cause; this was a fee being offered to stop us from talking about Donald Trump. The payback for the money would have been for us to shut up.

That's right.

So it wasn't somebody trying to invest in us.

No, no, no.

They were trying to create a deal with us. The deal was, I'll pay you—bam—you shut up.

And what they wanted to pay us was $150,000. They thought that we were that needy and lacking in integrity that $150,000 would make *us publicly switch our support from Donald J. Trump. I could not believe I was actually looking at what I was looking at.*

Well, see, they thought we were token blacks.

They thought wrong.

Token blacks do what they're told to do. We're Diamond and Silk. We're not token blacks, and we don't owe anybody anything.

You got that right.

We can vote and stump for whoever we want to vote for, and that's exactly what we did and continue to do.

No amount of money would have stopped us from stumping for Donald J. Trump.

That's right. We were with him from the beginning, and we will be with him to the end.

To the very end. That's right. We're absolutely not going anywhere. After looking at everything that has gone on within our country, Donald Trump had the solutions to the issues that had been plaguing America, especially black America. For us, it wasn't about the party—and we've said this before—it was about the person, and we wanted him to be president.

Well, you know, during that time, especially back in 2016, you would have black people talking about how they were still in chains. They actually felt like they were enchained.

Yeah. I remember seeing one guy actually in chains.

They didn't realize that the more you stay chained to the system, the more you miss out on opportunities, blessings, and freedoms that exist around you. It's time for black people to wake up. We should not be the poster children for lack and limitation.

That's right. So that was really a manipulative tactic. First came the email talking about how they loved our enthusiasm for the political race, how they loved us on social media, and how they tried to build us up. Then, in the next sentence, they asked us to denounce our beliefs. They couldn't understand why we were supporting Donald Trump.

It's the stereotype that if a black person is doing something, they must be getting paid for it.

What they didn't realize is that we knew what the Democrats were about. We knew how the Left operated. We weren't accepting any of it.

None of it. We didn't tell anybody about this. We didn't make it public. We're talking about it right now in our book so that y'all will know what Diamond and Silk have gone through and all of the different things that have come our way—but we continue to stand strong.

Raleigh, North Carolina, Rally: Duke Energy Center, July 5, 2016

Candidate Trump came to Raleigh, North Carolina, again in July 2016. We were due to speak at the rally. Trump's North Carolina campaign director at the time was Earl. He greeted us and seated us in the audience. We were surrounded by a lot of doting fans; the crowd was excited, and everyone wanted to take pictures.

We were finally called up to speak, and afterwards, y'all, he sat us back in the audience.

Yes, he did.

So we're getting bombarded with people taking pictures and saying hello. Finally, you can tell there's some movement going on, something was happening, and, all of a sudden, Earl comes and says, "You two, come with me."

Mm-hmm.

"They want y'all backstage."

So we went backstage, and we're just standing there. We saw some of the Trump team come in, and we waved at them and spoke to them. Out of the blue, in walked candidate Trump, and when he looked around the corner and saw that it was us, we all just started laughing.

We were like kids at the playground.

When he greeted us, we were standing next to Pastor Mark Barnes. I'll never forget this: First, candidate Trump turned to Pastor Mark

Barnes and said that he wanted him to speak at the convention. Then, Trump turned to us, Diamond and Silk, directly. He had a seriousness in his eyes and said that he wanted us to speak at the Republican National Convention.

That's right. He wanted us to speak.

We were so excited. We didn't know what to do with ourselves because this would be the first time we had ever done something this huge.

Somebody that we'd basically come to genuinely love looked at us specifically and asked us to do this.

That's exactly what he did.

So I remember going home, and I really wasn't able to sleep because I just couldn't believe it. There was no doubt we were going to do this.

Cleveland, Ohio: Republican National Convention, Quicken Loans Arena, July 18–21, 2016

So a few days later, some of the names of the speakers for the convention came out. Well, I was a little disappointed because Pastor Mark Barnes's name was on the list, but ours were not. Even though candidate Trump had requested our appearance and asked us to speak, for some reason our names were left off the roster.

Right.

But even though we didn't know what was supposed to be happening or where, we knew that we were supposed to speak. Before we got to the RNC, we reached out to a gentleman named Rick to see what day we were speaking on. I think he gave us a day, like either that Monday or Tuesday.

That's right. We asked because we needed to know when we were expected to be there, etc.

Right. Because this was the first time we had ever been to a convention.

Right. And this was like three full days; it was a long event. This wasn't something that happened in a day.

That's right. So Rick told us he would get back with us and let us know exactly when we were supposed to speak.

Now, a lady by the name of Ann Stone was going to be our point person at the convention because we really were brand new to this environment. Ann was a lovely lady whom we'd met previously when she picked us up at the airport for another Women for Trump event.

Ann was so helpful and patient. We had a lot of questions because this was our first time really in the political arena, and we didn't know a whole lot about the convention process.

Exactly. She was always respectful and considerate as she explained things to us.

But before we got to the convention, there was a rumor going around that Diamond and Silk wouldn't be attending the event. The false media had hyped it up that people were going to be out there protesting, and it was going to be so bad that Diamond and Silk had canceled their plans to attend.

Mm-hmm.

Alex Jones's people put that out.

That's right.

Now, let me just say this: I don't have anything against Alex Jones, but somebody in his camp used Twitter to make it appear as though we were not going to be at the Republican National Convention because we were receiving threats. That was a flat-out lie.

A flat-out lie.

We hadn't received one threat, and I don't know where Alex Jones's camp got that story from or why they were spreading it around.

Mm-hmm.

So this was just another example of media lies. We said nothing; we knew we were still going to this convention, and we booked our hotel.

That's right.

When we got to the particular hotel, though, we didn't like some of the key features. Luckily, they had a room left at another hotel. Although it was pricey, we decided to switch. When we got to the new hotel, people were loving on us. They knew us, and they were happy we were staying at the same hotel as them.

Now, even though Ann Stone was our handler, there were certain things that we had to navigate ourselves. And, really, I'll tell you, we just didn't know.

That's right. It was a little unorganized.

So the first thing Ann Stone did, the night before the Republican National Convention, was take us to a media party, where we met media personalities.

At this media event for the Republican National Convention, I was so tickled because there we were greeting people in the media that we had been talking about and going off on just days before.

Hahaha.

But this was like an everyday thing for them, and they were all very friendly and pleasant.

They seemed excited about meeting us and wanted to take pictures and the whole deal.

Mm-hmm. And that was the first night, y'all, that we met Omarosa.

Oh . . . Omarosa.

I was interested in meeting Omarosa because she was on *The Apprentice*. She was one of the first reality TV stars. It didn't surprise me when she turned out to be a snake. I found her to be sneaky, envious, and cunning; we learned later on that night that she was allegedly upset that Ann Stone was showing us around and not her. Even though we had some good times, some exciting times, I felt from the first that I couldn't fully trust her.

Mm-hmm. For me, I was honored to meet Omarosa because I'd heard a lot about her. So meeting her was, like, "Wow, this is Omarosa".

We took pictures, and she acted like she was excited to meet us. It was a celebration moment. We just met briefly, and that was it.

There was a young lady who came up to us, and she was supposed to be our go-to person for the speech. Because, remember, candidate Donald J. Trump wanted us to speak.

That's right. He wanted us to speak.

She wanted us to call her the next day at a specific time.

Mm-hmm.

But when we called her the next day at that specific time, we could not get in contact with her.

No answer.

We called and called and called.

We could not get in contact with her or any other person.

We knew we were getting the runaround. Now, when we first got to this party, it was like, "Okay, ya'll are going to be speaking; I'm going to be your go-to girl; I'm so excited for y'all."

Then, the very next day, we do exactly what she tells us to do, and she's nowhere to be found.

Yes. She disappeared like a thief in the night.

So were we disappointed? Absolutely.

Hell, yes.

We were disappointed because candidate Trump wanted us to speak.

And another thing, we're prompt. If we're asked to do something, we want to know when, where, how, and why so that we can be there on time and be present. We're women of our word.

Right.

We wanted to be present and honor our word. So if we're supposed to be somewhere on Monday at eleven o'clock, we want to be there at ten o'clock to make sure we are where we're supposed to be and doing what we said we were going to do.

Nobody could tell us what was going on, and I was not only disappointed, but I was pissed off because I don't like to be in the dark.

Yes. I felt like we were being given the runaround, and these people were acting like cowards. They knew what was going on, but they wouldn't tell us.

Right. And these were people with the RNC in 2016.

That's right. So the next day, we went on media row, which is a big room filled with tables where the different media outlets are positioned. They conduct interview after interview. All major television, cable news, and radio stations are present.

It was like a domino effect. Once we got on media row and did the first interview, somebody wanted the second, then somebody wanted the third and fourth and so on.

Yes.

We spent two days on media row, doing interviews.

Yes, that's how it happened.

We came to really understand the power of the media: we were sitting in this huge room, talking to all of these media personalities one by one, but the whole world was hearing us.

Yes.

I think we had garnered about fifty thousand new fans and followers on social media, just from doing all of those interviews.

That's right. Just imagine sitting in that one room, but we're all over the world at the same time.

Mm-hmm. That's just how it was.

So, finally, we realized we weren't going to speak at the convention. Our names weren't on the programs; they had given us the runaround. Nobody answered our calls; nobody could tell us anything.

Mm-hmm. We were very disappointed.

So we reached out to George, one of our contact people, to ask him what was going on.

Mm-hmm.

He didn't have the answers. He couldn't get involved with what the RNC people were doing.

Right.

However, he made sure that we sat with family and friends.

Yes, he sure did.

So it was like we were home once we got up there. We were able to mingle; we were able to hear; it was comfortable. One day of the convention, they put us in the high-profile section, where you have to rotate, and we were able to sit there for a little bit before going back to the skybox.

Mm-hmm. I remember a lot of people taking pictures.

We had left the skybox and were sitting in the audience directly in front of the skybox when Ted Cruz went onstage to give his speech. That night he refused to endorse Donald Trump, and he was booed offstage.

Right. It wasn't good at all.

Soon candidate Trump was going to be coming onstage. He came out of the skybox, through the door, and all of a sudden the crowd noticed him. They went nuts.

Yes. While Ted Cruz was talking, Donald Trump went ahead and stood there with his presence. All focus was now on Donald Trump. This literally cut Ted Cruz's ass off because he was really throwing shade without the lemonade.

Right. So Trump walked down those stairs, and he saw Diamond and Silk.

Yes.

He turned to the left and saw us and said, "Oh, my God. You made it. My girls." He leaned over and gave both of us the biggest hug and kiss.

And then he got back into his stance and kept on walking down the stairs.

Everybody around us wanted to know, "Who are you? How do you know him? Who are you girls?"

We were right where we were supposed to be. You know, he was about to come down the steps and everyone was looking at him, and he's got his game face on. Then he steps down and looks to the left and sees us, and he didn't care about the cameras; he didn't care about security; he didn't care about anyone else. He was like, "My girls. You made it."

Mm-hmm.

And he rushed up to hug and kiss us both.

Yes, he did. And people around us were like, "Who are you?" We were no one but Diamond and Silk, two black girls from North Carolina that this man happened to admire.

You could say, "Two black chicks that were down with politics."

That's right.

So, y'all, the convention ended up being a phenomenal experience, even though we were disappointed.

Yes.

People asked us what happened, why we didn't speak. We still aren't sure. You'd have to ask whoever was the head of the Republican National Convention at the time.

That'd be your answer. You have to also understand, y'all, that there were a lot of what we called "Deep State snakes" around candidate Donald J. Trump.

Mm-hmm.

They wanted things done their way. So when he became the nominee, the RNC took over a lot of aspects, and the campaign didn't have control over them.

That's exactly right. But when candidate Donald J. Trump separated himself to come and greet us, that was our moment.

Yes, it was.

In the end, when Donald Trump became president, the person who we believe kept us from speaking at the convention was fired shortly into the administration.

Yes. It felt like people were trying to be seen, and they were trying to keep us from being seen. They were riding on Donald Trump's coattails. It was like they wanted to dim our light in order for their light to shine brighter. What they failed to realize is that we were just being our true selves.

Mm-hmm. And all of the ones who have tried to dim our light for their lights to shine have either been fired, or the media has bashed them mercilessly, or they're nowhere in the spotlight. And guess what? Diamond and Silk are still here because we only had one agenda, and that was to stump for our candidate, Donald J. Trump.

Yes. We wanted to make sure he got elected.

Yes. But don't worry about us; others' rejection is always God's protection.

Trump-Pence Women's Empowerment Tour, Trump National Golf Club Charlotte, 2016

So then, about a week or two later, Earl called us. They were putting an event together in Charlotte, North Carolina. There was a group of women that he wanted to be part of this event, and it was called the Trump-Pence Women's Empowerment Tour.

Well, it just so happened that we had other things scheduled right at that same time, but those things fell through, and we were able to attend the Charlotte, North Carolina, event.

Yes, we were. The featured speakers were going to be Diamond and Silk, Omarosa, Katrina Pierson, and Lara Trump.

Mm-hmm.

So we're at this particular event, and they had us go onstage first. Well, you know, Diamond and Silk do what Diamond and Silk do.

That's right.

We went ahead and shut that whole place down.

Yes. In a good way.

Mm-hmm. We gave them a lot of laughter, a lot of energy, a lot of "Yes, we're on the Trump train." We gave them that style.

That's right, baby.

Everybody else had to go behind us. It was good; it just wasn't good for them.

That's right. The audience was able to ask some questions. Everybody was giving their answers, and everybody was able to talk. Well, I remember answering one of the questions with, "Our president is strategic."

Mm-hmm.

He is strategic whenever he does things. And I said, "It's not about ovaries in the Oval Office, it's about who has the balls to build a wall."

That's right.

That whole room went ballistic.

They went ballistic because you were speaking truth.

It was straight truth.

The thing I loved about the crowd is this: they were excited about us saying what they were thinking, even though they were afraid to say it.

It was to the point that when it was time to end, Katrina Pierson brought us back up to close it out.

After that, they changed the program so that Diamond and Silk were the last speakers, hahaha.

Hahaha. We can be energizing. It's this type of connection that generates throughout the audience when we're speaking. It's a particular energy that we've been infused with, and it all goes back to God.

Right. Not everybody has that.

Not everybody has it, but we've been blessed with it, and we are humbly grateful for it. We don't use it to take advantage of people, and we don't take advantage of that gift.

Right.

We use it, really, for what we were put here to use it for, and that's to educate.

Republican Luncheon,
Trump National Golf Club Charlotte, 2016

That summer we attended a luncheon with the Black Republicans. There were about eight of us, including Earl, who chatted with us for a moment before lunch.

The food was outstanding, y'all: shrimp and grits, fresh veggies, fresh fruit, desserts. They had anything that your heart desired to eat. Even the person serving us was a Diamond and Silk fan.

Yes, she was.

After lunch, we went to the other side of the room to talk about issues. Everyone in the room had an opportunity to introduce themselves. One woman, who was a leader within the Republican Party, was particularly disagreeable. She seemed a little perplexed, and I got the distinct feeling that she had a problem with us.

The one thing that bothered me about Earl was that he agreed with her to try to avoid confrontation. She had a problem with the way we delivered our message. Little did she know, we were Diamond and Silk, and we would deliver our message the way we wanted to deliver it.

Yes, we would.

The nerve of some people to tell us how to act, how to be, how to speak, how to think.

Mm-hmm.

So we are all in the same meeting, and we're participating as we should, when she nods toward us and says, "If you think that telling people to get off the Democrat Plantation is going to get the black vote, that's not going to happen."

She said that.

Silk was so upset, I had to calm her down. I said, "Silk, you've got to respect your elders."

Mm-hmm. I can respect my elders, but I can also tell her in a respectful manner that we know who we are and what we need to say. We're not out here just to get the black votes, we're out here to get all the votes.

That's right.

And I said that—in a respectful manner.

She was probably thinking, "Who do they think they are? I've been in this party for years."

What some Republicans still fail to understand is that you may have been in this party for years, but you've acted so timidly that the Democrats walked all over you.

Yes.

The one thing about Diamond and Silk, we opened up our mouths, and we spoke out.

Mm-hmm. That's right.

We spoke out about how people were calling Republicans racist; we weren't racist.

Mm-hmm.

We spoke out about how people were calling Republicans white supremacists; we weren't white supremacists.

We had to get people straight.

That's right.

And we did it openly.

We sure did. Now, at the time this woman made that remark, Omarosa was out of the room.

There was some good and some bad with Omarosa. This was good.

Yes. Omarosa was in the back, so she didn't hear what this lady had just said about us.

We didn't want to disrespect her, but when Omarosa came in that room . . .

She felt the tension, and she just knew something had been said that wasn't right.

Mm-hmm.

Omarosa shut it down.

Yes, she did. She basically told them Diamond and Silk aren't going anywhere. This is a movement, and this is because of Diamond and Silk. So if you're expecting them to be replaced, that's just not going to happen.

She basically broke it down just like that.

Yes. And that lady shut her mouth.

Yes, she sure did.

I don't know what even happened to that lady . . .

We never saw her again.

I'll tell you what, though, Diamond and Silk are still here, still stumping for Trump, and still speaking out, telling people to get off that Democrat Plantation.

Where is she at?

Never let anyone silence you because of their own envy or because they don't think you're good enough. As long as you think you're good, it doesn't matter what they think.

That's right.

That lady was jealous of us because we had something that she didn't.

She couldn't get up there and hold the crowd's attention because her delivery didn't resonate.

She was too politically correct.

Mm-hmm.

People didn't want that at that time. They wanted someone who was going to tell them the naked, nasty truth. Why do you think they loved candidate Trump?

That's right.

The established leaders couldn't understand that we were popular because we weren't robotic talking heads; we were truth-tellers, and we still are. We're like this every day, all day.

That's right. Like you say, "We don't have to get ready; we stay ready."

Mm-hmm. So the tours were exciting, but what really sticks with me are the Americans that came up to us. They would cry on our shoulders because they were so afraid: They were paying astronomical premiums for healthcare and couldn't even go to the doctor, but Democrats wanted to give free healthcare to illegal aliens. Their small businesses were so crippled by regulations that they could barely survive. Their kids were being taught foreign religions in school without the balance of Christianity or basic American values.

And we always comforted them and let them know, "He's going to win."

Yes. We would say, "Don't worry. He's going to win. What we need you to do is to make sure you get out and vote."

That's right. Get out and vote.

We were everywhere, and when we left the poll numbers were going up.

I remember there were some low numbers in one particular state, and they wanted us to go to that state.

Yes.

They wanted us to go to that state, but we weren't able to go because of our schedule.

Women for Trump Tour 2016

So time continues on, we're staying busy, doing our thing, when we receive a group email about a Women for Trump tour. Well, because it was a group email, we didn't know if they were reaching out or if we had received the email by mistake. So we contacted Lara Trump to see if that email was intended for us.

And she said, "Of course. Yes."

Mm-hmm.

So the Women for Trump tour was about to be born, and Diamond and Silk were about to go on tour with Women for Trump.

Yes.

Now, we were so excited about this. They had a wrapped bus; it was one of the buses that the late Aretha Franklin had toured on!

Yes. Aretha Franklin toured on that bus. I felt really honored to be able to use the same space as the late Aretha Franklin.

The tour included Diamond and Silk, Katrina Pierson, Lara Trump, Lynne Patton, and Omarosa.

Yes, that's right.

Y'all, everywhere we went, Donald Trump's poll numbers went up. We went to campaign stops and rallied up people; people were so motivated, people were energized.

Yes, they were.

People were ready to get out there, hit the streets running, and get this candidate elected.

People would actually stand to the side of the road clapping their hands when we were leaving an event. If we pulled the bus over for just a stop, people would gather around the bus.

That's right. We would throw out hats and T-shirts to all of the voters that loved Donald Trump.

Yes.

Around that time, there was a hurricane in North Carolina. What many don't know is that candidate Trump sent truckloads of supplies for us to pass out to people in need.

Yes, he sure did.

And people started having some hope again.

Remember that time candidate Trump was backstage, and he blew us a kiss?

Oh, my God, I believe that was just after we had passed out the hurricane relief because we still had our pink Women for Trump jackets and T-shirts on.

Mm-hmm.

Whenever Donald Trump was speaking at a rally and we were there, we always stood there and paid attention because we were so interested in it all. We're still pinching ourselves because we can't believe that all of this is happening to us.

Right.

So at this particular event, we went backstage and found a nice, quiet spot to wait for candidate Trump to come offstage.

Right. We weren't trying to be seen.

That comes with maturity.

So, after this particular rally, we just stood off to the side. Finally, candidate Trump was coming through the doors, offstage. As he walked down, he looked over, and the first people he noticed were Diamond and Silk.

Out of all of the people that were there, y'all, he noticed Diamond and Silk first. He looked over at us, and he blew us a kiss.

I want y'all to understand something: There were some prestigious and high-profile people there who looked through us or passed us because of their own disdain. That was their issue, though, not ours.

Even Omarosa saw what was happening, and she said to us something like, "Out of all of these people, all of these prestigious people here, he wasn't thinking about any of them, but he sure acknowledged you."

Yes, that's exactly what she said.

I think he acknowledged us because we weren't trying to be seen. We fully, truly supported him, and that's what it was about.

That's exactly what it was about.

The tour was phenomenal. Even though Omarosa started her little spats here and there, we still had a good time on that tour.

Mm-hmm.

We went to some places in Pennsylvania that were terrible. At one place, there was a casket sitting in the middle of the road to remind people of how much death had happened in that community.

Yes. It was very disturbing.

So we actually talked to people, witnessed things, and faced reality head-on. We weren't just riding around on a bus looking cute. What we heard over and over and over again was that people wanted things to change, and they saw the change with candidate Trump.

Also, the people who were attending these rallies were not just white people; they were white, black, there were all kinds of people.

Right.

We were out there, finding out what was going on in some of these communities.

Mm-hmm.

I remember, after one event, the organizers brought everybody out. There were people who wanted to take pictures and hug us.

We were all outside.

Remember, back then the Black Lives Matter movement was very huge. They were going in and disrupting events. At this particular event, we were hugging people, and a black girl came up to me and whispered into my ear, "Black lives matter."

I pushed her away, and I said, "All lives matter."

So that was a little protest. They took out their signs and started yelling, "Black lives matter; black lives matter!"

And I was yelling back, "All lives matter!"

"All lives matter." We had everybody else that was out there with us joining in, so we drowned them out.

It got so bad, though, that they had to grab us and get us back on the bus because they didn't want us to get into a confrontation. For me, "Don't start none, won't be none." Because I will stand my ground if I believe in something.

That's right. And that day, we stood our ground.

After that, a handler by the name of Karen looked out for us. We didn't always understand when the noise meant things were becoming dangerous, but Karen understood it. She would immediately grab our hands and put us back on the bus.

She sure would. She would come and grab us up like we were two little girls playing on the playground in a sandbox.

Lara Trump noticed our popularity. She looked at us one day and said something to the effect of, "Listen, girls, you are famous. You're going to take one of my security, and I'll take the other, so you can be safe out here."

Mm-hmm.

And for the rest of the leg of that tour, we had security.

She even made sure we had security to fly with us.

That's right. We were so popular, she did not want anyone with bad intentions to get to us. I'll always be grateful to Lara Trump for seeing it. We were getting converged upon; people used to kiss me like I was a chocolate bar.

Yes, they sure did.

Raleigh, North Carolina, Rally: J. S. Dorton Arena, November 7, 2016

The last rally we participated in before the election was in Raleigh, North Carolina, where Lara Trump introduced us. I was so excited because I felt we were going to win this.

Yes. We were going to win it.

After we spoke, they let us go down in the crowd, and we were able to pass out hats and memorabilia. I remember grabbing some people at that rally, and they grabbed on to me, and we just started yelling, "We are going to win this!"

I got so excited because I felt it: We were going to win. We had stumped for Trump all over the country; we had done everything that we could to enlighten people and tell them, "If you don't like the Republican Party, then don't vote for the party—vote for the person."

That's right.

And so, by golly, we expected the results to be on our side because we had done our part. We felt as if it was going to happen. We put in the work, and now we wanted it to pay off.

That's right. And it seemed like every time the Left tried to throw something at the president to knock him down, he'd get right back up again after a few days.

That's right. Every time they would try to crucify Donald J. Trump, he'd rise back up bigger, better, and stronger.

Yes. That's right.

That was the last rally we attended, right before Election Day.

Chapter 12

If You Believe It, You Will Achieve It

Election Day

*W*e had never been thrust into the middle of a presidential election, and we didn't know the proper protocol for one. One thing is for sure, things were not highly organized.

People became a part of the campaign and began working wherever they fit in. For Diamond and Silk, our true intent and what we really wanted to see at the end of the day was Donald Trump as the President of the United States. That was our bottom line.

Right.

So the night before Election Day, we had just finished the last rally in Raleigh, North Carolina, and we flew to New York and stayed at the Trump International Hotel.

We were so glad to be safe, sound, and comfortable because it had been a long, exciting, and exhausting day. One thing I appreciated was that security flew with us to New York. For some reason our popularity had grown, being out there on the tour.

Mm-hmm.

So we were at the Trump International Hotel, in New York City, on Election Day, November 8, 2016. I woke up so giddy, I was almost beside myself. It felt like Christmas morning, where I knew something was going to be under the tree, and I just didn't know what it was. I felt like I could not contain myself, but Silk was calm.

Yes. I was eating my breakfast and watching the news. I was focused on the tone of the news, and we were switching back and forth between the news stations. I could tell that a lot of people on the Left were on edge. For me, I was calm, cool, and collected. Diamond was just excited.

I didn't know what to do with my emotions. We had ordered a nice breakfast, and I probably didn't eat any of it.

You didn't eat a lot of it, no.

So CNN—which is fake news in my mind—had Bill and Hillary Clinton on, and they were going to the polls to vote. It was a camera shot of them going in, and she had a crowd outside of the polling place. Well, I wondered, how did the crowd know she was going to be out there?

Right.

When she came out, she started taking photographs. I said to Silk, "That doesn't look real."

It all looked fake, like people were just staged to be there so she could have a photo shoot.

When I saw that, I just knew . . . she was going to lose the election that night. I got a phone call from somebody in Virginia, and I asked how things were going down there. He said people were lined up, and some of the lines were out the door and around the block.

I said to Silk, "Well, why aren't they reporting that?"

Mm-hmm. The mainstream media didn't report on the masses of supporters Donald Trump had. They did not want the American people to see the enthusiasm of Americans who wanted Donald Trump in office. They were out there, and they were voting. But the media tried to keep that from the public, as if it wasn't happening.

Finally, it was becoming afternoon, and we had to get ready to go to the actual election night event.

Mm-hmm.

I'm still giddy; I'm still all over the place, but I managed to get my hair done and pull myself together.

Yes, you did.

Now, most of the time, Diamond and Silk take an Uber or a cab, but we very seldom walk anywhere. Now, we're in New York City, we get an Uber, and the driver drops us off about a block away from where the event was being held.

As we're walking up to the venue, people notice us and want to take photos with us. Well, we love our fans, so we stopped to take some photos with them.

Mm-hmm.

We got to the New York Hilton Midtown, and we went where we were supposed to go, but our names were not on the guest list.

Mm-hmm.

So they let us go to the next section to see if our names were on that list. Well, when we got to the next level, we had to wait because our names weren't on that list either. Finally, in walked Lynne Patton.

Yes. By that time, Lynne Patton had arrived. We were all glad to see each other, and she asked if everything was okay.

We told her our names weren't on the list.

So Lynne Patton quickly handled that.

She made sure we got to where we were supposed to go because we were supposed to be with family and friends. What I can remember is standing there, waiting to see where we were supposed to go, and in walks Donald Trump's brother.

Yes, and he was so excited to see us and meet us.

He gave us a big hug, and we chatted and laughed. Y'all, just walking into the venue, there was so much excitement in the air.

Nobody was on edge; everybody was just excited.

Right. The only bad thing that happened that night was a girl's high-heeled shoe got caught in the escalator while she was going up.

Yes, I remember that.

I'm like, oh, my God, we don't need media to see this. We don't want them to report on anything like this because they will take things and blow them way out of proportion, and something innocent will become a mess.

Mm-hmm.

Thank God, she ended up being okay. We went into the room where the celebration was going on. As we were walking in, along the entire left side of the walkway was media.

Yes. Station after station after station were snapping pictures, filming, doing whatever they had to do to capture a unique piece of this event and history.

I remember one reporter asked us something like, "What are you going to do if Donald Trump doesn't win?"

We basically responded with, "It's not over until God says it's over."

That's right. We stood on that and stayed the course. We had no doubts that he was going to win. So we got where we needed to be, we settled in, and, as we usually do, we got in the zone. We are never all over the place; we found a spot and rode out the event right from there.

Mm-hmm.

So we stayed in our spot and started watching state after state after state called for Donald Trump.

We met a lot of wonderful people that night as we were waiting on the states to come in.

I particularly remember the state of Virginia. First, they called Virginia for Trump, and we celebrated that Virginia went red. Mind you, we already had an inkling this would be true because our contact in Virginia was telling me how long the lines were.

All of a sudden, they took it back. Virginia didn't go red; it was still blue. You know, today, I think something wasn't quite right with that.

Right. Something was fishy.

Other than that, we watched all the states come in red, one right after another. The media kept showing Hillary's crowd, looking sick and devastated.

Yes, hahaha.

Then, they would show our crowd, and you saw people with their Make America Great Again hats on smiling and jumping with excitement. It was exhilarating, motivating, and full of energy. If something is going to actually happen, the energy has to be right.

That's right; and there was a great atmosphere in the room. It was a room filled with winners and filled with winning; that's the best way I can explain it.

When they called Wisconsin for Donald Trump, I looked at Lynne Patton's face. She could not believe that they had called Wisconsin for Donald Trump. A state that hadn't voted for a Republican presidential candidate in more than thirty years had just turned red. Lynne Patton started yelling and hollering. She was excited and shocked all at the same time.

Then, when they called North Carolina for Trump—wow— excitement went to a whole new level because now it was just about reality.

Remember, we had just been in North Carolina the night before and had the opportunity to hand out hats and meet the people. I felt a chill all over my body. I knew we were going to win, and I knew we were going to win North Carolina.

That's right. So as the states for Trump started coming in, the concern was whether he would claim the 270 electoral votes needed to actually win the election. Donald Trump surpassed all of that, winning 304 electoral votes to Hillary's 227.

Right. They said he would never reach a certain number, but he didn't just reach that number, he went way over it.

Yes. He left Hillary Clinton in the dust with her bottle of hot sauce.

When Pennsylvania came in red, we all knew it was over, but Hillary's camp did not want to concede.

That's right.

At that point, it was about 1:30 a.m., and we were heading to the dining area.

Mm-hmm. As we were going, Sarah Palin's team came up to us, and they were telling us that she wanted to meet us. We were like, "Where is she?"

We'd never met her in person before, but we had interviewed with her by video. It felt like we were getting together with an old friend. We grabbed her, hugged her, and got to take photos with her.

Yes. When we had our interview with Sarah Palin, I was so honored. I almost couldn't wrap my head around doing an interview with someone who had run for the vice presidency of the United States not that long ago.

Right.

We were able to see her through the monitor. She's a beautiful lady, really down to earth. I thought that interview was really nice and went really well.

Y'all, Sarah Palin is so beautiful, meek, and humble. She was so excited to meet us, and we were even more excited to meet her.

We sure were.

So Sarah Palin, Katrina Pierson, Lynne Patton, Omarosa, Silk, and I went into the dining room to get something to eat. We were waiting for Hillary Clinton to go ahead and concede.

Yeah. Seemed like it was going to be an all-nighter. Finally, at about 2:00 a.m., someone got a call that Hillary had conceded.

When she conceded, however, she didn't have enough decency to come out onstage.

Right; she left her supporters standing there cold.

When we heard that Hillary had finally conceded, we rushed back out there because Donald Trump was about to be announced as the forty-fifth President of the United States. We wanted to be onstage because Diamond and Silk had worked just as hard as anybody else.

Mm-hmm.

We never got paid for anything, and the one thing we wanted was to be right onstage with our president because he won it fair and square.

Right.

So we moved ourselves into the vicinity of where his team would be.

Right. Everybody that was due to go out onstage with the president was gathering in one area, so we got into that area.

It appeared that we were being given the runaround. We were given directions, but when we followed them, the aisle was blocked. We ended up downstairs in the crowd.

So it was Omarosa, Katrina Pierson, Silk, and myself.

Right. So Omarosa was looking for another entryway so that we could be with the family and the rest of the team. Well, we kept getting blocked and told no.

Every avenue that Omarosa would try, they kept blocking her and telling her she couldn't go.

That's right.

It was such a mess. Omarosa was getting upset and started going off. Now, the one thing that I've learned when it comes to security, if you start running off your mouth, you won't get anywhere.

Right.

If you want something, you can't get it with a nasty disposition or a nasty attitude. So Silk and I did what we were asked to do.

That's right.

We weren't going to act like fools or try to throw our weight around with security.

We stood there on the floor with everybody else, and that's when it was announced that Donald Trump was now the forty-fifth President of the United States. I looked over at Omarosa, and she started crying. I mean, she couldn't hold it in, she couldn't contain it; she started crying uncontrollably. Then, of course, we all started tearing up.

That's why we were so surprised at the antics and the tactics that Omarosa used later, disparaging the President of the United States.

Yeah. Omarosa was genuine in her feelings that night. She wasn't crying because she didn't want to be there. She was crying because she was happy that he won—that we had all won.

Right.

The way that Omarosa portrayed herself about a year after this was absolutely not the Omarosa we knew.

Finally, they introduced Donald Trump and his team to the stage. Now, we had been called derogatory names and been told that we were crazy for supporting Donald Trump. After everything that we'd gone through, especially as black supporters, seeing him there felt like a sense of liberation.

Yes, it did.

And the first thought in my mind was Hillary Clinton had Beyoncé and Jay-Z, but Trump had Diamond and Silk. That's how I saw it.

Right.

So as they were coming out onto the stage, we looked to the side of us and saw these little bitty stairs to get up on the stage.

Right.

So we told Omarosa, and, gurl, when she saw those stairs, nobody was stopping her. She was willing to climb on that stage if she had to. She got up there and turned around and helped the next woman up; then that woman helped the next and so forth. We all got onstage and walked right in with everybody else.

Yes, we did.

Even though we were not part of the Trump campaign, we were doing what we were doing as avid supporters, and we weren't going to miss the opportunity to be onstage for his win.

While the president was thanking everybody, we were standing right there onstage with him. It was such an exciting night, y'all. We will never, ever forget that. I was standing right behind Brad Parscale. He was so tall, I had to keep looking around him on my tiptoes.

Hahaha.

So after it was said and done, President Trump walked off the stage and started shaking hands with his supporters. Everybody that was onstage with him then followed him into the garage elevator. He looked at all of us, and he thanked us all for our support.

Mm-hmm. I remember us blowing kisses at Melania, and she blew a kiss back.

Once everybody got into their respective cars, we called an Uber, and we headed back to the Trump International Hotel.

Mm-hmm.

Our intention had been to get a few hours of sleep and be up early for interviews, but it didn't work like that. Thanks to Hillary Clinton, we had to find a Starbucks and get some coffee before a driver had to drive us to an interview. I was sitting there half asleep, remember?

Yes, I do.

We had interviews lined up all day, but after that first one, I was so under the weather, Silk had to do all of those interviews while I drank juice and slept.

Yeah. We are women of our word, so we did not leave anybody hanging. When one of us couldn't do the interview, the other did it.

We traveled in silence the next day because we knew that the other side was upset. They had adamantly said he wasn't going to win. They were petrified, mortified, and horrified. We didn't want to smear it in anybody's face, so we traveled in silence.

I remember making a video, and we restrained our excitement because we didn't want anyone to be upset.

After a while of respecting everyone else, though, for me, it kind of turned into a restriction, like we weren't allowed to celebrate. That's when we went on The Russ Parr Morning Show *and told them they had to eat crow. We told them to make sure they put seasoning salt and barbecue sauce on it. It was time to eat up!*

Hahaha.

See, the backlash that we got on the back end of everything was ruthless. To be standing as the winner after all that the Left had said and tried to do, it was really freaking liberating. When Donald Trump won, Diamond and Silk won too. We won against all of the doubt, slander, and mistrust, especially from some in the black community. I won't lie about it, it felt good to just tell them all to eat crow.

That's right; they had to eat a little crow.

So after all of that, y'all, we thought we would just kind of come down off of this and glide back into our old lives. It didn't turn out like that. All of a sudden, we started hearing about Russia hacking the election. Even Obama was talking about it.

Right.

The Left wanted Russia to be the reason why Donald Trump won the election. When they said that, they basically tried to remove the validity of every American citizen's vote. They were saying that we didn't really vote for Donald Trump; it was Russia that hacked the election and influenced American voters to vote for Donald Trump.

Well, y'all, we had to do a rant video about this. On December 30, 2016, we put out the video, basically saying something wasn't right. Something was going on. I believe that was the start of letting people know that some peeping and hiding and slipping and sliding was going on. What were they trying to deflect from?

In our minds, we knew Donald Trump won this fair and square. Throughout the past year, we had watched wave after wave after wave of American people not only support Donald Trump but support him enthusiastically. Why was the Left saying the reason for his win was because Russia helped him? We, the American people, voted for him, and he won the correct way.

Mm-hmm.

So then 2017 came along . . .

The Inauguration

Just before Inauguration Day, people started jockeying for positions at the White House. We had no interest in this; we didn't stump for Trump in order to get a position. We used our time and our voices to get this president elected. We did it because we wanted him to be president.

The jealousy got so bad that we heard one of our sister-friends was bad-mouthing us and referring to us as hood rats. She assumed that we would be getting some job that we were never offered. She was angry because she wanted a position that she couldn't get.

Diamond and Silk weren't even interested in a position.

No. We always said that we're too big to fit into the cabinet, hahaha.

That's right. Never let people get under your skin when they slander you and call you out of your name. We had someone with a criminal record saying, "Well, who do they think they are? They're uneducated."

Well, we were educated enough to leave her there in the dust while we continued propelling forward.

That sister is probably still jockeying for that same position that she didn't get, but Diamond and Silk moved on.

So the inauguration was a formal event, y'all, and we had to go pick out our dresses. Remember, we did not wear dresses.

Right. If y'all look on the campaign trail, you always saw Diamond and Silk in pants, nice blouses, and a pair of flats. Hell, we stopped liking dresses when we had to wear them throughout high school.

That's right.

Well, we had to go pick out dresses, and, y'all . . . oh, my God . . . first of all, I had gained all of this weight. So I'm trying to pick out a dress, but I didn't want my arms to show, I wanted to be modest, and I needed something slimming.

Hahaha. You got that right.

So we finally found dresses, but the best part of the whole experience was when we walked into the store where we finally found them, the people in the shop knew us.

They were excited because they knew we were getting ready for the inauguration, and they wanted us to look stunning. For me, not having purchased a dress in years, it felt a little strange and out of the ordinary, but it was fun. I felt like Cinderella going to get a beautiful dress for this beautiful ball.

Right. It was an incredible moment.

It really was.

We made our hotel reservations and, y'all, everything was so expensive. This is why you have to have good credit and a nice credit card. Visa and Mastercard will be your best friends. Get you some good credit.

Hahaha. Sometimes your best friend may be plastic.

The Trump International Hotel was sold out, so we weren't able to stay there, but the Trump team had arranged for our information packets and tickets to be held there. We went there first because we wanted to have those things in hand. Our packet and tickets clearly designated us as friends of the president, and we were supposed to be in that family and friends section throughout the inaugural event.

Yes. Then we went back to our hotel so that we could grab a bite to eat. As soon as we walked into the hotel that we were staying at, all of these people rushed us.

We love our fans so much, but it becomes a safety issue when crowds close in. Security had to get us out of there and up to our room, quick.

Mm-hmm. Thank God for security and executive protection.

Right.

The next day, it was time for the festivities. We had to meet at the Trump Hotel so that we could all get into the specific vehicle assigned for us.

Right. They were loading people into these buses, and it was like the left hand didn't know what the right hand was doing.

It was very unorganized, yes.

We were in the family and friends group, and many of us had to figure out what was going on. The organizers were just loading us along with the rest of the guests.

Once we finally got there and got seated, we were ecstatic about the number of people out there for our president. The crowd literally roared behind us. It was so powerful. There was strength behind the voices.

After the ceremony, we had to get in position for the parade.

Mm-hmm. Nobody knew where we were supposed to be. I don't know who put this together, but I felt it was intentionally set up to be a mess, especially for family and friends.

I'm going to be honest: the ones who didn't have a hand in electing Donald Trump were the ones who got the best seats, the best of everything. Anybody that had a hand in electing him, they got the worst of everything.

That's right. So that let me know that those running it were not true Trump supporters.

We had tickets to the parade, and we couldn't even get there because the bus that brought us to the inauguration left. People were just walking in the streets; they didn't know where to go. It was horrific.

I'm so glad we had our executive protection. They took care of us and got us back to the hotel and out of that traffic.

Yes. We heard that people were protesting in the streets; we never saw any of it because of how professional our protection was.

After that, we went on back to the hotel and waited for the inaugural ball that night.

Right. Now, the inaugural ball was a little bit better organized, and the food was so good.

Mm-hmm. And food-tasting is my specialty.

So we walked into the ball, and we're with family and friends, so it should be a smooth-sailing, amazing night. Well, as soon as we walked in—bam—everybody wanted pictures. We had to start a whole photo line because that many folks wanted pictures.

During the inaugural ball, I looked up, and Omarosa's fiancé, who is now her husband, was rolling her out in a wheelchair because she had done something to her foot.

Mm-hmm.

Now, y'all, I'm going to be honest with you . . . Omarosa had gotten on my last nerve. I didn't have another nerve for her to get on. I'm not trying to throw anyone under the bus, but if she wasn't going off about one thing, she was being irritated by something else.

She was a drama queen, dramatizing all over the place.

Diamond and Silk don't roll like that. If we're in something together, we're not going to put one against the other. It's just not how we act.

So I remember one day Diamond leaned over to me and said that if Omarosa kept jumping and hopping around like that, she was going to end up breaking her leg.

The reason I said that is because she would be all over the place. We would go to an event, and she'd have to get up and walk all around to be seen. Somebody would be standing up talking, and she'd be in the audience taking selfies.

Creating commotion.

I don't like those kinds of things. I think that's rude and arrogant, and it shows ignorance and disrespect. I would see her do that, and I would cringe because it would bother me so much.

Right.

So, I wasn't shocked when her fiancé at the time was rolling her out of the ball in a wheelchair because she had hurt her foot. She probably jumped up out of nowhere to be seen and—bam—now she's in a wheelchair.

Probably from hopping around like a bunny rabbit.

Then, after that, our president and First Lady had their first dance.

Oh, that was really nice.

Not everybody gets the opportunity to be at an event like that, and we felt so blessed and humbly grateful to have that experience.

That's right. We're sure President Trump didn't even know about the disorganization. You have to remember who was running the RNC at that time if you want to get to the bottom of that.

That's right.

So after the inaugural celebration, we went back to the hotel to get ready to leave D.C. the next day. That's when the atmosphere really started to smell swampy.

It looked like a swamp: dingy and dirty. I looked at Silk and said, "Something is not right about D.C. I'm ready to go home."

Mm-hmm.

I said, "Our president is going to need much prayer. There are forces here that are not for him, but against him." I was so ready to go home.

Yes. When we did our next show, we told the people about the inauguration and how something was not right; our president needed prayer.

It turned out to be just the way we said it.

Next we were invited to the White House for the Christmas party, in 2017. We have to thank Omarosa, once again, for extending the invitation.

We were excited and honored all at the same time. We flew into D.C. and stayed at the Trump International Hotel. We had invited our personal assistant Tressie and her husband Bill to the event. As we were leaving for the party, we were introduced to Scott Baio.

Yes, we were. Now, if you don't know who Scott Baio is, let me help jog your memory. He played Chachi on Happy Days. *Do you remember now? He still looks the same, and, between you and me, I had a small childhood crush on him.*

While we were standing there in the lobby, he and his wife wanted to take a photo with us. He mentioned that they were on their way to the same Christmas party. We invited him and his wife to ride with us.

While in the SUV, he mentioned his respect for Donald Trump and that all he wanted to do was shake the president's hand. We told him just what we've been telling y'all: keep believing it will happen, and it will happen.

We made it to the White House grounds, and, after going through the security checkpoints, we walked through the opened doors to the White House. I remember seeing huge Christmas trees with big bulbs.

Everything was white as you walked in. The trees were white, the lights were white. Everything was bright. The First Lady had outdone herself. It was unbelievable.

Yes, it was, Silk; the orchestra was playing Christmas carols . . .

We even stopped and sang the last line to one of the songs.

We sure did. We walked through different rooms that all had a special significance. The tables were heavily decorated and filled with cookies, cakes, candy, and delicious food. We saw a lot of familiar faces that we hadn't seen since the 2016 campaign.

It was like a family reunion. Remember, the swamp didn't allow a lot of President Trump's allies around him.

Tressie, our personal assistant, had already figured out where the president would be giving his speech so we would be in the vicinity when the time came.

All of a sudden, a distinguished gentleman approached us. He looked like he was in the military. He walked up to us, grabbed our hands, walked us up to the ropes, and told us to stand there.

The area did not open up until he placed us at the red rope directly in front of the podium. Then it was time. Music began to play, and the forty-fifth President of the United States and First Lady Melania began walking down the stairs.

As he came around to face the podium, he spotted us, and his face lit up like a Christmas bulb. There was feeling in his smile, like happiness took him over. The very first thing he did was point directly at us, Diamond and Silk. It was like no one else was in the room. He saw his long-lost friends out of all of those prestigious people in that room, and he was overjoyed to see us. He broke all protocol and called us up onstage with him and First Lady Melania Trump.

Somebody had to come hold the rope up so that we could get on the stage. We hugged and kissed them both, and then he asked us to say a few words.

I remember saying how there was a time when our black ancestors used to be slaves and they worked in the White House. Now, look at us; we are standing here with the President of the United States, guests at the White House.

The feeling of euphoria that filled that room was unexplainable. Then we walked offstage and continued to listen to the president.

Y'all won't believe what happened next: President Trump looked across the audience, and, out of all of the people standing there, he spotted Scott Baio. He invited Scott Baio to the stage.

He sure did. I think we may have been more excited than Scott was. He was probably in total shock. Remember, he had just told us about an hour earlier that all he wanted to do was shake President Trump's hand—and it happened, just like that.

President Trump looked over at me and Diamond and mentioned how excited we were. You see, President Trump didn't know that Scott Baio had ridden to the Christmas party with us, hahaha. He didn't know what Scott had said to us in confidence.

Whenever you want something, you get what you think and what you feel. So any time you want something, you have to feel like you already have it or like it already happened. That's the way faith works.

That's the way God is. Think it and believe it; feel it and know it; it will happen. Now, for us, here's the most amazing part of this already extraordinary evening: after it was all over and the president began to go upstairs, he looked back and told his people that he wanted Diamond and Silk, along with a few others, to come with them.

We were speechless. The President of the United States had just invited us to his home. Once we were all upstairs, he gave us a small tour of his residence, along with some of the history behind everything. We spoke briefly. He was so happy to see familiar faces. Of course, we had to take a photo with him.

Yes, we did. We found out later that out of all of the previous Christmas party gatherings that he had had the days before, he had never called anyone on the stage, nor had he asked anyone to speak. We were the first. Not everyone gets an opportunity like that. Just to be able to be in the presence of the most powerful man in the world was an opportunity that we were humbly grateful for, and we will cherish that special moment forever.

Chapter 13

Media Antics

I f you've ever wondered whether labeling the mainstream media "fake news" is fair or accurate, we'd like to offer a few real-life examples for you to consider.

If the media doesn't like you, they will smear you. If they don't like what you're saying, they'll try making you seem insignificant. When that doesn't work, they'll try to categorize you into one of the "evil categories" they've created.

In our case, the media tried to label us and tie us to white supremacy, of all things. Now, the purpose of this was to discredit us and anything that we had to say.

That's exactly what the Democrats were trying to do. Here are a few of our earlier interview experiences.

Newsmax

So the first time we got thrust into the media was when we interviewed with Newsmax.

Mm-hmm.

When we did that interview, we thought millions and millions and millions of people were going to see it.

Right. I remember that. I was worried about finding something to wear on TV. Then I realized that all the viewers would see was my blouse, so I just chose a pretty blouse to wear.

Right. Because we did it over Skype, at home, all we needed was a pretty blouse to wear. We did our hair and makeup, and we went on to do the Newsmax interview with J. D. Hayworth.

Mm-hmm. Okay.

That was our first friendly interview on TV.

Keep in mind, we were new to all of this, so there was a learning curve for us.

Mm-hmm. Then, CNN reached out to us. Don Lemon wanted to have us on his show.

Don Lemon

So before we go further, let me tell about my experience when it came to CNN. I remember when we first got the request to be on with Don Lemon. We were excited about it because it was a major station with a popular news personality.

Yes. We were excited.

It was nothing like it is now. You have to remember, this was back in 2015. They even sent us a big black car to pick us up.

Mm-hmm.

We had to travel about an hour and a half to the studio in Raleigh, and it was evening by the time we arrived.

Yes. Six or seven o'clock.

I was really excited, almost giddy.

When Diamond and Silk go on an interview, we do an interview like we're having a conversation with someone at dinner or sitting in the living room.

That's right.

All of the extra stuff that everybody else is all nervous about, we just play it calm, cool, and collected. We look at it as if we're having a conversation.

The studio wasn't what I expected. It was just a plain room with their cameras and equipment set up. Nevertheless, it was fascinating to see the technical side of TV. It's not as complicated as I thought it would be. It actually looked pretty simple to me.

So they gave us a seat, and we were expecting to meet Don Lemon. We never saw him; we just saw the black hole where we were supposed to look.

Right. But we heard him in our earpiece.

We were new to this; we didn't know anything about it. So we sat there and looked into the lens of the camera and just talked. Whatever the host asked us, we answered the questions the best we could.

Yes. And we were honest with our answers.

We were very honest with him.

The one thing I didn't like about CNN is that they had us looking different, not like ourselves.

Hahaha.

No, they really did. We did not look like ourselves, and the quality of television was not up to par. When I look at the fake news now, after having experiences like these, it was probably deliberately set up to have us look unattractive and appear uneducated.

Mm-hmm.

That's what they do with people who don't agree with their narrative. After I went on CNN, I didn't want to go back on another television interview, and I believe that was their goal, to keep us quiet.

Looking back at myself on that interview, I remember going to the mall to try to find a makeup artist because I thought that's what I needed for future interviews. Come to find out, I didn't need any of it. CNN created that image for us.

Furthermore, we didn't need anyone spoon-feeding us a narrative. I remember telling Don Lemon, "You know, you can either give somebody a fish, or you can teach them how to fish."

The reasonableness of that saying went right over his head. He seemed uninterested in showing Americans that they could rise up.

Oh, absolutely. It seemed like it did go over his head.

People may ask, "Well, why did you go on CNN?"

Well, back in August 2015, when we interviewed with Don Lemon, CNN was not known as fake news.

Exactly.

We didn't deny anyone an interview. If you wanted an interview and wanted to hear what we thought or what we were thinking, we granted an interview. We're disgusted with CNN and Don Lemon now. The disparaging comments that he's made about our president show a disrespect for the office of the president and a pandering to the liberal narrative. I never watch him anymore because journalism isn't about being biased; it's about being impartial.

That's right.

Well, Don Lemon wasn't being fair that night, but he restrained himself just enough so that we couldn't quite pinpoint the real intent, the stunt, the games he was playing with us.

That's right.

After we did that interview, y'all, the hate ramped up again.

Yes, it did.

We got so much flak on social media; people were asking why they had us on television. They were giving their spiel about not liking what we were talking about.

I call that the Mob. Whenever they see something on TV saying something that they disagree with, the Mob comes in and has to demonstrate their outrage. What we basically heard was, "Why do you have them on your station? They're this; they're that. We don't want to hear them. Blah, blah, blah . . ."

The way I saw it, the troll farm came out, and they started bashing Diamond and Silk because we were thinking another way. We were telling it to you from a different perspective, different from the way the fake news media had been spinning the narrative.

Mm-hmm. And it wasn't just CNN, it was all of the left-leaning liberal media.

I felt they were coming at us like, "Who do you think you are?"

Mm-hmm. Another thing to remember, too, is with us being black and still Democrats in 2015, our stumping for Trump really looked odd to them.

We were unique.

They called us "the Stump for Trump Girls."

Yes, they did.

My distinct impression was that they were trying to make us seem like we didn't know what, or who, we were talking about—like we were just in this fog.

Mm-hmm. They were going to try to show us up, but we showed them up because I remember letting Don Lemon know before the show began that we could no longer vote for a system that kept handing us crumbs. We have our own minds; we can think for ourselves; we don't need anyone spoon-feeding us a narrative.

That's right. I can feed my own self.

That's a popular phrase today, but Diamond and Silk said it first. "We have our own minds; we can think for ourselves."

And after that particular interview, that was that. We continued stumping for Trump.

Roland Martin

Remember when we first had to go on with Roland Martin?

Yes, I remember.

We weren't afraid of Roland Martin. Evidently, he must've been afraid of us.

Mm-hmm.

He must've been afraid of our power, our blackness, and our realness.

Right. We were asked to be on with Roland Martin, and we didn't have a problem with being on his show.

Mm-hmm.

Come to find out, the first thing that the Left, especially black people on the Left, wanted to do was try to make us look unknowledgeable and try to make themselves appear to be more intelligent, enlightened, and politically correct.

Mm-hmm.

He tried hard to make us look ignorant and unlearned.

Right. So what we did was make him look ignorant and unlearned. Let me just say this: You know, the interviews with Roland Martin were very challenging for me. When I heard the foolishness coming out of his mouth about how all black folks are supposed to vote one way, I wanted to cuss him out.

Mm-hmm. Me too.

He reminded me of a black man who's still trying to hold on to a bag of beans and a slab of fatback meat. That type of man doesn't want to give up the bag of beans and slab of fatback meat for something bigger and better. He was disparaging two black women because we didn't want to hold on to past Democrat promises they never intended to fulfill. We knew we could have more than just fatback; we could have a whole prime rib.

That's right. Why wait on the Democrat crumbs to make a crumb cake when we can have all the ingredients to make our own cake?

Roland Martin didn't like that. It seems as though people like Roland Martin want to follow Willie Lynch's example of dividing black people: you put the light-skinned people in the house; you work the darker-skinned people in the fields; and you incite them to dishonesty and distrust for each other.

Right.

See, Roland Martin was just upset because he was "in the house"—on television—and Diamond and Silk were supposed to be in the damn field, but because of our influence in politics, we were surpassing him.

It felt like he was trying to keep us in our place or dim our light.

That's exactly what he was trying to do. What I don't understand is how, as a black man, you can disrespect black women. You're married to a black woman, or your mother is a black woman . . . I didn't understand that.

That's right. I don't understand it either.

The real problem was that we were able to grow our platform faster than Roland Martin could grow his. A lot of his antics and the disparaging talk that came out of his mouth stemmed from pure envy and jealousy, in my opinion.

That's right, it was. It really was. His technique was to talk over us, ask questions without allowing us the opportunity to answer them, then put us in a category. He mentioned something about someone on the Trump team giving an interview to a white supremacist.

Let me tell you what happened with that: one of the Trump team members unknowingly snapped a photo with or made a comment to someone that the left-wing media put into one of their evil categories. This was all part of the media's game. Remember, we still thought journalism was a profession of integrity and that our words would be conveyed accurately.

We weren't looking at where you grew up, your age, your background, what your religious orientation was; we didn't ask the people who interviewed us those questions. You want to do an interview about the election? Let me tell you about Donald J. Trump. That's what our position was and still is.

Mm-hmm.

As far as, "Oh, we better not do this interview; we better not do that interview," how is it that we've got to be cautious about who we do an interview with, but other people can do an interview with whomever they choose to and not be condemned for it?

That's right.

Anytime we would go on with Roland Martin, his ratings would go up.

And the videos would go viral. He actually kept our first interview with him pinned to the top of his page, and it's probably the most views that he's ever had on one of his videos.

Yes. When we noticed how Roland Martin was trying to use us, we stopped doing interviews with him because I didn't want to lose my cool. I remember when we were at the Republican National Convention and we had to do an interview with Roland Martin, and I went the hell off on him.

Mm-hmm. Yes, you sure did.

And I think that was the last interview because I refuse to allow anyone to intentionally agitate me to the point that I just want to go off. I mean, I was all up in his face.

"In his face" is an understatement.

How dare he, as a black man, tell me I can't think outside the box? Just because he feels like he's the one in the big house doesn't mean we've got to be out here with the field Negroes doing what the gatekeepers want us to do.

Hell to the no.

Tom Joyner and Russ Parr

When we interviewed with Tom Joyner and Russ Parr, it felt like they wanted us to remain Democrats and were trying to scold us for thinking outside of the box, for seeing things from a different perspective.

That's right.

It's like they were the trap setters, trying to keep the black communities trapped in the same box that the Democrats built for them.

That's right.

Well, we did *The Russ Parr Morning Show* several times. At first, he seemed like he just wanted to play. Well, if you want to play, I'm going to show you how it's done. We were relentless in declaring the great things that Donald J. Trump was going to do for this country.

Mm-hmm.

We stopped doing interviews with Russ Parr because he was acting passive-aggressive with us.

That's right. What they try to do is degrade you and make you seem as though you're ignorant. He would nicely invite us on, then try to verbally attack us in the end.

In a very condescending way.

But it doesn't take somebody with a Ph.D. to know that something was not going right in this country: We had just had a biracial man, who identified as a black man, running this country for eight years. He ran it into the ground, and nothing significant happened for black folks.

That's right. We weren't afraid to call it out. When we went on *Tom Joyner*, we gave him his accolades—because we'd listened to him for years—then we went ahead and shut that show down.

Hahaha. That's what we did.

Tom Joyner and Jacque Reid tried to lay traps for us, trying to get us to criticize Trump and asking us whether we were going to stay in the public eye if Donald Trump lost the election—which they were sure he would. But we had an answer for everything, and there was nothing else that they could say. See, when they knew that we were very powerful in what we were saying and that they couldn't shut us down, they didn't know how to take us.

Right.

Blog Wars

So what the media bloggers would do, y'all, was write the most salacious, nasty, disparaging, disrespectful-style stories about Diamond and Silk.

It was disgusting.

It was deliberate too. They wanted black viewers, especially, to see us as tainted so they wouldn't regard us as valid. See, some black people will follow whatever the leaders say, even if the leader's message is, "We're still down in a box; ain't got a pot to piss in or window to throw it out of."

Right.

Back in the day when they set up programs to give away free cheese, the main group of people that showed up were black folks. You have to remember that people were conditioned to think that they needed the slave master to take care of them.

That's right.

Well, Diamond and Silk were changing minds, and we knew how to change minds by getting people to see the facts.

Let's get out of a fantasy; let's look at the facts here.

Here are the facts: Until Donald J. Trump, nothing had changed for black America. If you want to talk about Obamacare—okay—what we got was a lot of Obama without any of the care. He didn't move the needle. It felt like he stuck us in the eye with the needle, trying to blind us from his true agenda of how he was going to fundamentally transform America.

That's right. I recall interviews with people calling Donald Trump a liar. One time, Diamond said, "Oh, let me get you straight. My president is not a liar."

That's right.

And the way they edit those videos . . . you may speak to someone for twenty minutes, and they chop up the video and put a negative spin around the interview to fit their narrative, then publish it. So the listeners don't really get to hear the comeback from any negative questions that they may have asked.

Don't you worry, though, Diamond and Silk always shut it down.

That's right. We weren't afraid, and when they saw we weren't afraid, there was nothing that they could do. When they can't intimidate you, they actually become fearful of you. Then, of course, they smear you because they fear you.

That's right.

We notice when some black bloggers from the Left write about us, they typically call us derogatory names.

People tell us, "Your ancestors are rolling and turning over in their graves."

Our ancestors are rolling and turning over in their graves when they see people like Roland Martin calling black women out of their names. (In case you're not familiar with that expression, it means that a lot of black male celebrities were calling us insulting and racist slurs instead of having the basic decency and respect to refer to us by our names.)

Yes. We had Montel Williams, D. L. Hughley, Rickey Smiley, and, of course, Roland Martin, all of whom are black men, bashing us and calling us out of our names. I'm like, what's up with these black men calling black women out of their names?

Some of these men we used to look up to because we grew up watching them on television, especially when it came to Montel Williams. You know, I was shocked when we got the first tweet from him, and he said we were just wanna-be reality TV stars.

Montel Williams said that, right.

How dare he think that the only thing black women can be are reality television stars.

That's right.

As a black man, he didn't think we could be better than reality TV stars running around, beating up on each other, and drinking alcohol until we're stupid? It didn't occur to him that maybe we were two black women speaking change and causing something great to happen in our communities and in this country? All he saw were reality TV stars?

Well, shame on him, but it ain't no shame on us. They tried to bash us, to smother our opinion, to make us feel and seem less than. They thought that was going to stop us, and they were dead wrong about it.

It only revved us up even more. When I see any man trying to stop a woman's progress, it lets me know he's weak. Besides, we weren't going to allow any man, especially our black brothers, to think it was okay to disrespect us.

You got that right.

We had no problem with getting them straight and keeping them straight.

Just to know what people's true intentions were made us even wiser to the game.

Absolutely. You are right, Silk; it made us wiser to the game.

Listen, we get interview requests all the time where people want to follow us around to see what we're doing. Most of them we don't even respond to. If we do respond to them, it's a "Hell, no."

Because we already know they're not going to talk about the facts, and they're not going to air what we talk about. They want to cut pieces and segments and put them together to make us look bad and fit their own narrative. That's not journalism; that's defamation.

Right. They love to slice and dice.

So this is how the left-wing media treats those with powerful voices that don't fit their narrative. If we didn't have powerful voices, they wouldn't have gone to such effort to cut up our words in order to make us look undesirable.

Right. They love to dredge up the past and make it appear like it's happening right now, especially if there's any type of indiscretion or something that can be spun as indiscreet. Then they use that against you to make it appear like that is who you are right now. They have a habit of doing that to Donald Trump, to us, and to anyone who openly supports him.

So it was like being asleep but awakening to this game that the media loves to play. They deliberately mislead to make it appear that things are one way when it's really a flat-out lie.

That's the truth. All a lie.

They love to hoodwink and do what's called a fifty-two fake out.

Right.

So when Donald Trump started calling them "the fake news," I turned around and called them "the very fake news." They were fake as hell because they tried to make things appear a particular way to fit the narrative that they were trying to spew out on the American people.

That's right. Not only are they fake news, but they are the enemy of people and the enemy of the truth. Don't believe the hype when you see some of these interviews. A lot of the detail is cut.

Dissected, cut, and edited. I'm the editor when it comes down to chopping up our videos and getting everything out there correctly, so I can tell when something has been edited. They can take your head and put it on someone else's body. They can make it seem like you're speaking from someone else's voice. There are a lot of alterations that can be done when it comes to editing in these different programs.

Mm-hmm.

They edited our interviews to continue their plot because we went against the grain.

Chapter 14

Unsafe to the Community

On December 4, 2015, when we first met candidate Donald Trump, he stated that we had become an Internet sensation. Thereafter, we were known as "Internet Sensations Diamond and Silk." We had taken the Internet by storm. Even though we didn't know much about what we were doing, we did the best with the little knowledge we had.

After doing several media hits, we realized that no matter how often we went on TV, the left-wing media's main agenda was to oppose us. They spun a different adverse narrative every day, and they tried to pigeonhole us into whatever negativity was popular at the time of our interview.

Mm-hmm.

We paid close attention and replied back quickly with answers that blew their stereotypical narrative slam out of the water. We stayed ready, so we wouldn't have to get ready.

When they tried to trick us or ask us a dumb question, they got an in-your-face response. We didn't play with the media. We called it how we saw it, without sugarcoating it. A lot of our interviews would garner millions of views. We were able to sway people by our way of resonating with the viewer, and the media did not like that. We were taken out of the media because we were successful in making them all look foolish. No one could outtalk Diamond and Silk, no matter how many journalistic degrees they had.

We used social media to get our message across. Not only did we use it, we mastered it. The platforms began to grow expeditiously. There were more than a thousand people a day following us on Facebook and Twitter. YouTube was much, much slower building followers. We found out why later on.

People were hearing our message, and they would complain when we didn't drop content within the next week's time frame. We pushed the Ditch and Switch Now campaign and later found out that thousands upon thousands were paying attention. They were ditching and switching.

Yes, they were. People wanted us to do a video every single day. They thanked us for being their voices. Because of prior obligations, we were unable to do a video every day, but we made sure that one was out every week.

We sure did.

Once the president won the election and was inaugurated in 2017, we only had our social media accounts to rely on in order to speak our truth. We even updated our camera and lighting so that our production could look more professional. We started calling out the Russia hoax and the surveillance of the Trump campaign. We were onto something, and people were agreeing with our opinions. Silk would do deep research on the topics that we were discussing, and the information was gut-wrenching.

Yes, I did; and, yes, it was. I couldn't just do research from one source. I had to go through multiple sources in order to form my opinions about what I thought was the truth. We were able to break down some of the most complicated theories coming from the Left by using good old common sense. Our base grew even faster, and people were awaking from the lie.

Yes. We told it how we saw it, and it was nothing for us to call it out. Of course, just like we attracted people who loved us and were waking up to the truth, we also attracted a few trolls. They would say some mean-spirited things within the comments sections. They would thumbs-down our videos and type nasty replies to our loyal supporters. We had to literally filter out words and stop people from posting pictures within the comments sections.

We began to notice how our live broadcast began dragging and messing up to the point that it would make us look distorted. We could be talking, and, out of the blue, we would start getting complaints about the audio sounding choppy.

At times, we would have over twenty-three thousand people watching at one time, with over five hundred thousand views once our one-hour live broadcast was completed. We averaged anywhere from five million to over eight million views in a week. Our video uploads would go viral within a twenty-four-hour period. As soon as we posted anything on our platform, people would immediately begin viewing our content. Our base had grown to over a million followers, and our brand was getting much bigger.

Then, on August 9, 2017, we received an email from YouTube with eight of our videos listed, along with this statement: "The following videos are running limited or no ads, due to content that has been identified as not suitable for all advertisers."

Mm-hmm; that's what they said. I had to go in and investigate to see what was going on. Here it was, August 2017, and they were flagging us for videos dating back to August 2015! I dug a little further, and that's when I realized that over 95 percent of our videos were "demonetized."

So let me explain: YouTube originally played ads around our videos, and we had received a percentage of the revenue from each ad played. This is the way people are able to make a real living off of posting their original content. But now YouTube had stopped the ads from playing around a very large number of our videos.

That's right. We suffered a great loss because this was part of our income to keep our brand going. Then, on September 7, 2017, I received a phone call from Diamond . . .

Yes, I remember. I woke up that morning and discovered that Facebook had actually placed a red notification at the top of our Diamond and Silk page. The notification stated, "Limits have been placed on Diamond and Silk. Your page has been blocked from including advertisements in Facebook videos." I couldn't believe it. I felt like someone had kicked me in the gut.

Mind you, a few months before, Facebook had started letting ads play within our live Facebook videos. Now, all of a sudden, Facebook had demonetized our videos, and they also restricted our reach. There was an option for us to appeal, so you know I did just that: appealed their decision.

What did we do wrong? We hadn't been warned about violating any of Facebook's terms. What was the issue? On October 26, 2017, Facebook shut down all of the posts to our page. No one could see, view, or comment on any of our posts. The chat-support mechanism that allowed me to speak to a live tech-support person was removed, along with the email-support mechanism that allowed me to email Facebook.

After about ten hours of being down, our posts mysteriously appeared back on the page. When they finally came back online, a number of comments had been removed. Our posts' views drastically dropped, from reaching thirty thousand views in forty-five minutes to five thousand views in one hour.

We were getting notifications and messages from people who were no longer able to see our posts on their feed. They were no longer getting notifications when we dropped content. They had to search for our page just to find it.

People tried to like and follow our page, but Facebook had removed the "like" and "follow" options; people tried to comment on our posts, but Facebook would not let them; people even tried to share our posts and page, but Facebook had removed the "share" button.

This was very unfair, especially since the people who liked and followed our page really wanted to see our content. I have emails, chat records, and screenshots of all conversations. I even have the lie from October 13, 2017, when Facebook told me that all blocks on my page had been removed.

No one could give us a reason why limitations had been placed on our Facebook page. We had around 1.2 million followers when they first placed that notice on our page, but hardly anyone was seeing our posts or getting notifications that we had posted any content. Our live views went from over 23,000 viewers down to around 1,200 viewers on a live video. Our views on YouTube went down as well.

Someone from the Left could actually upload one of our videos, or a video with our faces in it, make derogatory statements about us, and have fewer than 18,000 followers yet garner millions of views. If we uploaded the same video, even with 1.2 million followers, we were lucky if we got 20,000 views in one day.

For six months, twenty-nine days, five hours, forty minutes, and forty-three seconds, we chatted and emailed Facebook back and forth about the same issue. We were patronized by being told that our issue would be escalated to the Facebook team, the spam team, the technical team, the appeal team, the internal team, and the policy team.

On January 8, 2018, at 12:57 p.m., we were informed that none of our complaints had ever been sent to any of these teams to begin with. They never started looking into a resolution to any of our issues. It was as if we didn't matter. Facebook couldn't have cared less about our complaints. I would send an email or message every hour, on the hour, to all of the Facebook portals. We worked hard to build this page to over a million authentic likes and followers. For it to be deliberately taken away was deplorable. They weren't going to get rid of us that easily. They messed with the wrong two black women!

That's right. We built our platform one follower at a time. Just imagine using the same tools as everyone else, building something that the average person was unable to build, only for the rug to be pulled from under your feet. It was as if these social media platforms wanted us to go away.

After that, Twitter began "shadow banning" us. Whenever we dropped content, they kept it hidden from a lot of our followers, even though we were able to see it on our platform. It was just another way to limit our reach and censor us.

It almost reminded me of a modern-day lynching; back in the day, they used nooses, today they're using algorithms. Our platforms were choked out by biased man-written algorithms. They did not want people to see our content. They literally tried to make it appear like no one wanted to see us.

Then, on March 14, 2018, at 5:34 p.m., I received an email from a Facebook representative named Jason. He said that he had been able to take a closer look at the page but he could not see any blocks, and he was going to reach out to the appropriate team manager.

I thanked him and sent him back screenshots of the limitation notice that Facebook had placed at the top of our page, along with the analytical to show how our page had deteriorated. It must have been horrific because he emailed us back and said that he was passing the screenshots over to the technical team.

No worries. I continued to remain patient because I refused to fold, go cold, and give up.

Yes. One thing about Silk, she will stay on top of the issue for as long as it takes. She doesn't play.

No, ma'am, I don't. You see, we had just started the Chit Chat tour (ChitChatTour.com), where we traveled from state to state doing grassroots work. Because social media platforms had started their censorship campaign against us, we had to find another avenue to reach the people. We were advertising the tour dates to our followers, and they were shadow banning and censoring that. I can even remember when we began to mail out postcards. We spent thousands of dollars in postage, and people wouldn't get their postcards until after the event was over.

Yep. They tried to stop us at every turn. We used to be able to advertise our store, DiamondandSilkStore.com, but the algorithms must have picked up on key words and shadow banned that too.

That's right. To keep this in simple terms, without sounding geeky, algorithms are written as codes. These codes are step-by-step instructions that tell the computer what to do.

So, on April 5, 2018, at 3:40 p.m., we got a response. I didn't see it until very late that night, but when I did get to it, I was crushed. My sister had been back and forth with these people for nearly seven months. She was adamant about getting to the bottom of this issue.

When I woke up the morning of Friday, April 6, 2018, I picked up the phone and called Silk. Y'all, I wanted to scream. Did these MOFOs really send this to us? Oh, Lord, how was I going to break this to Silk? When she picked up the phone, I let her know that Facebook had sent back a reply.

I asked Diamond what the email said, and this is what she read to me:

> Hi Rochelle, I hope your week has been going well. I wanted to reach out to you because I was able to determine what is going on. The policy team has come to the conclusion that your content and your brand has been determined unsafe to the community. This decision is based on multiple violations of the Community Standards and Content Guidelines for Monetization. This decision is final, and it is not appeal-able in any way.

I asked her to read it again to make sure I had heard her correctly. I wanted to make sure that I didn't have wax built up in my ears, but for some reason, it felt like my ears were clogged because I couldn't believe what she was saying. So she read it again.

I sure did. I read it slower, louder, and, hopefully, clearer.

Yes, you did, Diamond. I discovered that it wasn't wax at all. It was the BS that she was reading from that email. So I had her forward it over to me so that I could see it with my own eyes. I was hoping that maybe she had the wrong glasses on at the time she was reading it. Nope. Every word, every insult was there.

Y'all, I was fuming. If you had put me in the middle of a ten-foot snowstorm, I would have melted all of the snow into running water with enough heat left over to heat every house at the North Pole.

Gurl, you were hot . . .

Yes, I was. That excuse didn't sit well with me. You mean to tell me that for six months, twenty-nine days, five hours, forty minutes, and forty-three seconds, I went back and forth with these people? After investing my time and energy into following the proper protocol, going through the proper channels, and patiently allowing the process to play out, the only thing they could muster up was that our content and brand were "unsafe to the community"?

Yes. We didn't know what to think. How was our brand unsafe? What community were they referring to? It seemed like they were saying that we were a menace to society. In my opinion, a menace to society would be someone selling drugs, committing crimes against innocent people, or hurting a child. We've never done any of that, so how were we unsafe? How is this one entity able to dominate and control the entire world by censoring what others can and cannot see? How is our brand unsafe? We are the brand. We are two black chicks down with politics.

Yes, it was offensive. They took our freedom of speech, limited who could hear our voices on the platform, then labeled us "unsafe."

If Facebook doesn't get it together, they'll be the face without the book and the book without the pages.

And if Twitter doesn't get it together, they'll be the bird without the tweet and the tweet without the bird.

What were Facebook, YouTube, and Twitter afraid of? They were petrified that two average black women who decided to think outside of the box had figured out the schemes of the Left. They didn't want us to reach people. We are a triple threat because we're black, women, and conservative. We challenge the liberal orthodoxy. We don't toe the liberal line and ideology.

President Trump won the election because we the people heard truth—not from the mainstream media, but from social media. Diamond and Silk used this platform to deliver our message about our president, and they didn't like it. They were acting like the KKK, intimidating black people who wanted prosperity, who got above our predetermined station in life.

So, that day, I began writing a reply back. But our hands were tied because Facebook had clearly stated that their decision was final and not appealable. I still continued to write. For over six months we dealt with Facebook and this issue in private. I then decided to make a public post and share what had been happening to us, along with a list of questions for Mark Zuckerberg himself.

Later on that night, I was still working on this post. I wanted to make sure that people understood what we were trying to convey so that no one, not even the fake news media, would get anything twisted.

We had to fly out early the next morning to Pittsburgh, Pennsylvania. I told Silk to just wait until the next day to publish the post. She said no; she had to get it posted that night. There was something in her gut telling her to do it that night.

That's right. Diamond begged me to just go to bed, but I couldn't. It was a must that I got it posted that night. I told my sister that I would be ready to go the next morning, but I wouldn't be able to sleep until this was posted. When you get this unexplainable prompting in the pit of your stomach, you have to follow it. So, on Friday, April 6, 2018, at 9:55 p.m., I tweeted this post:

Diamond and Silk have been corresponding since September 7, 2017, with Facebook (owned by Mark Zuckerberg), about their bias, censorship and discrimination against D&S brand page. Finally, after several emails, chats, phone calls, appeals, beating around the bush, lies, and giving us the runaround, Facebook gave us another bogus reason why millions of people who have liked and/or followed our page no longer receive notification and why our page, posts and video reach was reduced by a very large percentage.

Here is the reply from Facebook. Thu, Apr 5, 2018, at 3:40 PM: "The policy team has come to the conclusion that your content and your brand has been determined unsafe to the community." Yep, this was FB's conclusion after 6 months, 29 days, 5 hours, 40 minutes and 43 seconds.

Oh, and guess what else Facebook said: "This decision is final and it is not appeal-able in any way." (Note: This is the exact wording that FB emailed to us.)

So our questions to Facebook (Mark Zuckerberg) are:

1. What is unsafe about two Blk-women supporting the President, Donald J. Trump?

2. Our FB page has been created since December 2014; when exactly did the content and the brand become unsafe to the community?

3. When you say "community" are you referring to the millions who liked and followed our page?

4. What content on our page was in violation?

5. If our content and brand was so unsafe to the community, why is the option for us to boost our content and spend money with FB to enhance our brand page still available? Maybe FB should give us a refund since FB censored our reach.

6. Lastly, didn't FB violate their own policy when FB stopped sending notifications to the millions of people who liked and followed our brand page?

This is deliberate bias, censorship and discrimination.
These tactics are unacceptable, and we want answers!
~Diamond and Silk

I then followed up and posted the same message on Facebook at 10:06 p.m. that same night. I finished packing, then I went to bed.

The next day when we woke up, the posts on Facebook and Twitter were both going viral. People were furious to know what Facebook had said about us. We love our fans. You all Facebooked and tweeted Mark Zuckerberg like crazy. You advocated for our voices that were being censored. We had President Trump's back, and y'all had our backs.

On April 8, around 5:00 a.m., I woke up to an interview request from Fox & Friends. *They wanted to know if we were available to come on their show to discuss the Facebook post. Our assistant set everything up, and we did our hit at 9:30 that morning.*

After that interview, the mainstream media and bloggers started calling the censorship a hoax, like we had made it all up. What the media didn't know was that we had proof. The next day, while we were flying back home, Laura Ingraham wanted us for an interview, and we granted her and many more people interviews.

We later found out that Mark Zuckerberg was going to be testifying on Capitol Hill for something that had nothing to do with censorship.

On Tuesday, April 10, 2018, we were booked with interviews all day. People wanted to know what had happened, and they were out-raged that we had been labeled as unsafe to the community. We talked censorship, censorship, censorship.

Then, while we were at the end of an interview with Larry O'Connor, Diamond received a text message saying that Senator Ted Cruz had just name-dropped us. Say what? We couldn't scream. We had to act normal and remain attentive, as if nothing was happening. Our hearts were about to burst with joy.

We couldn't believe it. It was April 10, 2018, at 4:18 p.m., EST. Senator Ted Cruz spoke about us in Congress, on Capitol Hill, during the

Senate Judiciary and Commerce Committees Joint Hearing, featuring billionaire Facebook CEO, Mark Zuckerberg. We weren't expecting any of this to happen. We could not have been more shocked.

No, we couldn't. When I put that post on social media a few days earlier, I was not aware that Mark Zuckerberg was going to be testifying on the Hill that following week. I was following that unexplainable sense that we get when we have to get something done right then and there, or else.

What are the odds of going back and forth for over six months with Facebook, only to have our content and brand labeled "unsafe to the community"; then I post the situation on social media for all to see; the CEO of that company is being questioned three days later on Capitol Hill; and the members of Congress questioning that CEO see our posts and ask questions about our situation? Just chance? No. The credit for all of this goes to God.

They thought they could tell us anything, and we would just go away. God said, "Not so." Facebook was exposed to the whole world for its unfair and biased practices. The number of interview requests we got from this was crazy. Facebook, Twitter, and YouTube may have censored us, but we were still able to tell our truth— even more so.

Just imagine if I hadn't followed my instincts; imagine if I had waited to publish my post; imagine if we had gotten Facebook's email a week later. However, everything had already been designed, and it was up to us to follow through with it.

Then, on April 11, 2018, we found out that more senators, like Joe Barton from Texas and Fred Upton from Michigan, questioned Zuckerberg about us. Tennessee senator Marsha Blackburn asked Zuckerberg whether they manipulated algorithms to censor speech. After he gave his answer, she said, "Let me tell you something right now: Diamond and Silk is not terrorism!"

Even Senator Tim Scott spoke out about the discriminatory censoring practices that Facebook used against our First Amendment rights.

Yes, he sure did. I remember when I first saw the video of Senator Tim Scott defending us. After all the ridicule by a number of black men, it brought tears to my eyes to see this one black man, who is a senator, take up for our voices.

Next came Missouri congressman Billy Long and his team. They held up a giant poster board with our pictures on it. It was one of our popular, funny poses.

Yes. You can actually see the grins on the faces of Mark Zuckerberg and the rest of his team. It was hard for them to keep their composure.

Congressman Long asked Zuckerberg if he recognized us.

Zuckerberg looked and said, "I do."

He then asked, "Who are they?"

Zuckerberg replied, "I believe . . . is that Diamond and Silk?"

Congressman Billy Long said, "That is Diamond and Silk, two biological sisters, from North Carolina."

Y'all, we felt liberated. Out of two billion Facebook users, Mark Zuckerberg knew who Diamond and Silk were. My fellow Republicans were using their voices to speak for our censored voices. They were standing up for Diamond and Silk.

Even the iconic comedian Roseanne Bar tweeted, on April 11, 2018, "Diamond and Silk are comedians. Stop censoring them." When we saw that tweet, we started giggling with joy. It was unbelievable.

At the end of that April 11, 2018, hearing, Zuckerberg's new excuse was that his team had made an enforcement error, and that they'd already gotten in touch with us to reverse it.

That was a flat-out lie. No one from Facebook contacted us about fixing the problem until Thursday, April 12, 2018, via Twitter. Until that day, which was the day *after* Zuckerberg was grilled by the senators at the hearing, all that Facebook did was stonewall us and give us the runaround—for over six months.

All of a sudden, on April 12, 2018, the day after Zuckerberg testified, we began to feel the restrictions being removed. People were saying that they hadn't seen us in a while. When we dropped a video, it would garner thousands upon thousands of views. Facebook had gotten caught with their hands in the cookie jar, and they removed all restrictions. They even removed the restriction label from the top of our page. Well, that was short-lived. After a week the restrictions were back but the restriction label was not. People began to complain about being unfollowed from our page; our analytical graph had a sharp uptick and then it took a turn for the worse. Straight down.

Now, let me back up just a bit: On April 10, we had received an email saying that Iowa congressman Steve King's office was trying to get in contact with us. They were having a congressional hearing about social media censorship, and he wanted to know if we would like to come and testify. After being told by the biggest platform in the world that we were unsafe to the community, there was no way that we were going to say no to that!

We appreciate the fact that Congressman Steve King not only heard our thoughts on censorship, but he also wanted to know our thoughts on illegal immigration. After we told him our concerns, he assisted us in writing a bill in 2019 called the Diamond and Silk Act, H.R.3218. The main purpose of the bill was to prohibit certain federal funds from being made available to sanctuary jurisdictions and for other purposes.

We cringe when we hear some on the Left call Congressman Steve King a racist with no evidence. Yet we have evidence of Joe Biden referring to black people as the n-word, and the Left is silent about that.

So to be able to go on Capitol Hill and tell our story about how Facebook censored our right to free speech was satisfying to my soul. We didn't have to gather up a lot of evidence because we already had all of the evidence organized in a folder.

A few days later, we were confirmed as witnesses for the hearing, scheduled for April 26. We put the date on our calendar, and we showed up ready to go. There wasn't a scared bone in our bodies. In fact, we were motivated about telling our side of the story.

Y'all, we were dressed to impress; our security team was in place; we felt like two bold and empowered lawyers. We really didn't know what to expect, but we were ready to face our accusers. I believe that if we had to conquer the world that day, we would have done it.

We sure would have. After going through security, they took us to a holding room to brief us on what to expect. Then it was time to go into the room where the hearing was about to take place. We walked in and sat on the front row. A lot of Republican senators walked up to us and greeted us. Senator Marsha Blackburn even walked up to us and thanked us for being there.

So the hearing began, and New York congressman Jerry Nadler started talking about us like we weren't there in the room. He was so nasty—he made us feel like our complaint didn't matter and we had no reason to be there, like what we had to say was not worth being heard. People ask if we've experienced racism. On that day, we experienced it with him. As black Americans, he made us feel like we didn't belong there and like we didn't know our place. What he failed to realize is that we weren't brought over on a ship, we didn't cross any borders, we were born on American soil. As a congressman, it was his job to listen to us as American citizens instead of turning a deaf ear to our concerns.

That's right. If he didn't have a problem listening to illegal aliens, then he shouldn't have a problem listening to us as American citizens.

Y'all, I started twitching in my seat when he said, "The central thesis of this hearing doesn't hold up under even the most basic scrutiny. The idea that social media companies are filtering out conservative voices is a hoax, a tired narrative of imagined victimhood as the rest of the country grapples with a feckless president and an out-of-control administration! The majority designed this hearing to perpetuate this hoax."

I looked over at Silk and said, "I know this MOFO didn't just say that."

I tried to calm Diamond down by letting her know that the cameras were focused directly on us. Talking under my breath, without moving my lips, I said, "No, no, no, the cameras are on us." Hahaha, Diamond tried to calm down.

Yes, I tried, but I couldn't. I couldn't believe the way we were being characterized like we were second-class citizens instead of Americans.

Finally, it was time for us to tell our side: how Facebook and Mark Zuckerberg had censored our First Amendment rights.

The Left was saying that censorship was a hoax, but we had plenty of evidence that it wasn't a hoax. We had photos, graphs, emails, chats, posts, and so much more. We showed the biased tactics that were being used against our platform.

We sure did. Then it was time for a round of questions. We were honest and truthful with our answers. Then things took a turn like never before in Congress. There was no more of me acting African American; I had to go ahead and act black.

Sheila Jackson didn't understand that the number 12 comes after 11. We were on Laura Ingraham's show on April 11, and Laura asked us if Facebook had contacted us to reverse or resolve our issues. We answered honestly that they had not contacted us, even though earlier that day Mark Zuckerberg claimed that they did.

On April 12, the day after we said that on Laura Ingraham's show, Facebook contacted us via Twitter.

Sheila Jackson repeatedly asked us if we were lying on Laura Ingraham's show, like she just couldn't understand that at the time of our declaration we hadn't heard from Facebook. We clearly explained that we were completely honest on Laura Ingraham's show: we hadn't been contacted by Facebook to resolve our issues.

She couldn't seem to get that. She kept re-asking the same question—a tactic they use to entrap you—as if we were being intentionally unclear. Truth is, she appeared to be acting intentionally simpleminded. When we tried to tell her that we were honest on April 11 because Facebook hadn't contacted us until April 12, she actually asked, "Have you gotten any communication from Facebook?"

I replied, "On April the 12th, via Twitter."

As if it were critical to her point, she asked, "What mode was that?"

I repeated, "Via Twitter."

Her response makes me question if she has the capacity to be in office at all. She completely ignored the dates we were trying to convey and responded with, "All right. So you got information. So your testimony that you did not, is not—is not truthful."

We were astonished because she was acting like a dirty prosecutor. Even though we were telling the truth, all she was hearing were her own lies.

Hank Johnson was concerned about how much money we were making, not how much Facebook had stopped us from making. He was so condescending with his line of questioning, he even had the nerve to say that he had always heard that diamonds were a girl's best friend.

That's when I had to let him know that they're hard, and if I have to be hard and firm, I will. I refused to let him dismiss us like we didn't have merit.

It would have been funny if he had said he heard that Diamond capsized Guam. Hahaha.

Hakeem Jeffries insisted that Federal Election Commission documents showed payment from the Trump campaign to Diamond and Silk in the amount of $1,274.94. This was one of the fake news' false narratives; we were never paid by the Trump campaign. We explained this was a reimbursement for plane tickets that we had paid for.

Now, keep in mind, when Mark Zuckerberg said Facebook had made an "enforcement error" concerning our platform, members of Congress thought that was perfectly acceptable. However, the idea that the Trump team may have made a similar error was deemed an unbelievable explanation.

We were saddened that these black Democrat leaders were trying to make us feel less than. They couldn't have cared less about our concerns and issues. They wanted a spectacle, and we gave them a spectacle that left them all speechless.

Yes, we sure did. We shut it all the way down. Those Democrats probably still don't know what hit them. We didn't bite our tongues or take a back seat. We spoke our minds, and we spoke our truth—something they were not used to anyone doing.

Afterwards, we were told that there had never been a hearing like that before. They couldn't recall anyone ever taking it to those Democrats like that.

Media was waiting for us to exit the front door, so our security rerouted us to leave a different way. We later found out that media had camped out until after 5:00 p.m. waiting for us to exit.

When we got in the car, I apologized to my sister for not being able to keep my composure. She wasn't mad or sorry. She told me I did a fabulous job.

Yes, I sure did.

After this, the media began writing hit piece after hit piece. The more they wrote, the more people came to see who we were. Their negative hit pieces turned into many followers for us.

People who didn't even like us agreed that no one has the right to censor our voices. There were black people upset with the black Democrat senators and how they tried to railroad us. One gentleman said, "We get out in the streets and march for equality, yet you criticize Diamond and Silk for making money." He couldn't understand their concept.

Then Rickey Smiley wrote one of the vilest and most disgusting articles about us. He called us so many names that other black people were disturbed by it. They told him that what he wrote was not acceptable. His mother is a black woman, and that was no way to describe black women.

We politely Facebooked and tweeted him. Our exact words were: "Rickey Smiley, looks like you didn't get the memo. We see that fake news is real. You got 24 hours to retract that, correct that and update that with the facts. Don't 'F' with us!"

People started counting down the hours and the minutes. It didn't take that long, and Rickey Smiley removed the entire article. Then he blocked us, hahaha. We don't know why; it's not like we were following him anyway.

The Left still wants to say that what Facebook did to us was a hoax, but how can this all be a hoax when Facebook apologized to us twice? Though Mark Zuckerberg said it was an error, it happened to us for over six months, and it's still happening to us now.

We brought light to the censorship issue. We told the world what was happening and why it was happening. Some didn't believe us then, but I bet they believe us now.

We still get complaints daily. Sometimes the option to share a post is gone; people can't comment; if people get a notification, they will click on it only to be taken to an error page or the video won't play. We could gain five followers and lose three followers within the next minute. Facebook, Twitter, and YouTube throttled our reach, and they made it hard for people to see our content.

No worries. If you can't beat them, join them.

And that's exactly what we did. Two years later, on April 26, the same date that we had testified on the Hill, we launched our own social media platform, www.ChatDit.com. This will give us the ability to reach our followers without being censored.

Chapter 15

Who the Hell Said You Can't?

*If you allow God to direct your path, your impossible
will turn into endless possibilities. Our steps were ordered
and ordained by God.*

Remember when we told you that some say our ancestors are turning over in their graves because we choose to support a billionaire businessman? Well, we say that if our ancestors are turning over in their graves, it's because they see how black people are being duped into repeating the same mistakes from the past. Black people are the descendants of black slaves who were whipped and beaten. Though black Americans living today have never experienced slavery, they walk around still feeling the sentiments of being beaten like a slave. As descendants of the slaves who built this country, black people should have access to the American dream before an illegal alien.

Our ancestors weep from the grave when they see some black people disregarding human life and liberty the same way the slave masters did. They grieve when they see some black people not taking pride in themselves and falling prey to the liberal ideology, the same persuasions and tactics used to keep our ancestors enslaved.

You will never become extraordinary if you don't learn to do things out of the ordinary. After all, who the hell said you can't? We literally took nothing and made something on our own, just by using what we were blessed with—our God-given minds. The only thing that we had was the truth, and that's what we spoke: the nasty, low-down, dirty truth. Let us be clear: we're truth-tellers, not robotic talking heads. I don't have a problem with sticking the knife in you, twisting it, and bringing you down with the truth.

And when Diamond starts cutting the lies with the truth, I'm the one who softens the blows with a loving spirit and a golden nugget to give you something to think about.

For Diamond, she couldn't care less about your feelings because her motto is, "The truth may make you feel queasy or uneasy, but the truth and nothing but the naked, nasty, low-down truth will set you free."

While some have characterized us as angry women, tried to put us in a box as talking heads, painted us as unintelligent, stereotyped us as caricatures, and belittled us as a minstrel show, we're the total opposite. We're smart, perceptive, funny, passionate, educational, sassy, and classy; but if you cross us, things can get a little nasty!

Now, what you can't do is think you're going to say something derogatory about us and we're not going to get you straight from the gate. We don't have a problem with giving you the facts, and we will not hold anything back. We don't have a problem giving you the truth with the proof. We know exactly who we are; that's why no one could name us.

They say the truth hurts, so our words may be painful to swallow. At times, it may cut you like a two-edged sword, but it's our truth, and it's our truth to tell. This is what we love about President Donald Trump. His brutal honesty is raw but real. This is what's been missing in the political arena.

There is enough success to go around the table, and we absolutely love seeing people win. A success for my sister is a success for me. When she wins, so do I. When she hurts, I feel the pain. We are each other's courage and shoulders to lean on. We're similar in many ways, yet we are still very unique. We share the same goals, lifestyles, and spotlights, but I'm still Silk, and she's still Diamond.

The definition of Diamond is a precious stone consisting of a clear crystalline form of pure carbon, the hardest naturally occurring substance. She's precious because her words hold great value, and hard because her solidarity with the truth is rock solid. My sister has always had my back, even when she may not have agreed with some of my decisions. She's never left my side. Though she's very blunt and opinionated, she's firm and knows how to articulate her words so that you will know she means business.

As far as I can remember, she has always been an intuitive kind of person with a strong sixth sense. It's a sense of understanding what's going on around her. She typically sees things before I do, even though we both possess the same gift. That understanding is her greatest power of protection. When her gut tells her that something is not right, ten times out of ten she's absolutely right.

Let me be really honest with you all: If my sister had not followed her intuition and started passionately speaking out, then we probably wouldn't be here today. She took the first step of walking through the fear of the unknown. There was no way that I was going to let her walk through the fear of the unknown all alone.

Silk is just as *Webster's Dictionary* defines it: fine and strong. Silk, being the oldest, has always been the one who handled things. I, on the other hand, was the one who ran around like a mouthy, spoiled brat, who always had a way with words. Silk, however, was the quiet and calm one. I would do all the talking and arguing, but you best believe, when it came down to it, Silk would snap, crackle, and pop all over you. She would sit back, quiet as a mouse, but ready to pounce on you if need be.

Silk may be silent, but like the old cliché says, "Silent is violent." I've never had to worry when my sister was around; she's always had my back. She's always been the strong one who looked past obstacles while keeping things in order. Silk is the lighter fluid, and I am the fire. If I came to Silk with an idea, she would always find a way to turn my idea into reality. I know I'm fiery, but one man put it so nicely and said I can use my fire to heat up the house or use it to burn the whole house down, hahaha.

For a while, something was burning inside of me, and I just had to let it out. I used to talk to my sister about my frustration with how the world was changing for the worse. Our country was headed down a dark tunnel, spinning out of control. We began seeing things we've never seen or experienced before. Our reality was becoming that of a new-age slave being controlled by a government that wanted to push anything down our throats and force us to swallow it. This kind of political correctness was causing us to choke.

Our gagging reflexes weren't having it. We were choking on the political agenda of President Obama, who seemed eager to change the trajectory of the United States by transforming America, abandoning our values, and aborting our traditions.

Before we go any further, let's make one thing clear: These are our thoughts and our opinions. The First Amendment gives us the right to have our opinions.

It's like eating from a buffet bar. Eat what you like, and what you don't like, leave on the bar.

Obama gave us Obamacare, but it should have been named ObamaDidn'tCare because he did not care about the mandates that were pushed on Americans who couldn't afford it. He also ran on "Hope and Change." We were hoping that things would change, but we all got short-changed. He made off with a lot of change because now he's filthy rich.

On top of all of that, he was about to sign the Trans-Pacific Partnership (TPP) into law to outsource more of our jobs and leave the American people riding dirty.

In no way are we trying to erase Obama's legacy. High unemployment among blacks, reaching or exceeding 16 percent on eleven different occasions, and the high number of blacks on food stamps is a legacy that he can keep. Giving away Obamaphones—instead of job applications so that people can go to work and buy their own phones—is definitely a legacy that can stay in the history books.

With Obama's name right by it.

We have a responsibility to enlighten you on how history continues to repeat itself when you continue to vote for the same system that keeps handing you empty promises and a pack of lies.

When Donald J. Trump came along, he was the Heimlich maneuver we needed to free our airways so that we could speak and be heard. Let me emphasize this: We've never forgotten where we came from. We just knew we couldn't stay there.

We were lifelong Democrats. We were taught and conditioned to vote for the head of the ticket, no matter what. We were told that we would be able to make it and eat under a Democrat, so vote for one. Then one day we had a lightbulb moment. We started to realize that we've been voting for Democrats for years, and there were a lot of those who voted Democrat who just weren't making it. How could we keep voting for the same party while expecting a different result?

You can't get something different by doing the same old thing. We found that just because you're black, it doesn't mean you have to vote Democrat.

Looking at the Democrat Party today, in our opinions, they've always been the party of division. To divide and conquer are their goals. They divided Americans based on race, gender, sexuality, and class, then put us against each other. A lot of the oppression going on in our country has been created by liberalism and liberal ideology, whose strongest supporters happen to be black.

Black lives have been decimated by liberal Democrat policies that helped deindustrialize communities, which resulted in a substantial number of people without a job or source of income. Liquor stores popped up on every corner and abortion clinics on every other block, all to eliminate black people, especially the black male. The welfare system was implemented with stipulations, one being that the man—the husband, the father—could not live in the same home with the woman if she was receiving welfare. This created a generation of black women that relied on the government instead of their husbands.

Liberalism and liberal policies not only eliminated the black male from the family but damn near destroyed the black man's existence with the crack and heroin epidemic, leaving them with the option to sell it or use it. To top it all off, the Democrats even implemented legislation to have them jailed for damn near the rest of their lives, even if the crime was a nonviolent crime. Remember, Joe Biden pushed the 1994 Crime Bill, and President Bill Clinton signed it into law.

Not to mention being categorized as minorities. Lexico.com defines the word minority as "the smaller in number or part, especially a number that is less than half the whole number." So liberal Democrats actually categorized and labeled the black community as "less than." Just think about that.

Even down to the music that had gotten very raunchy. It promotes sex, murder, and drugs, along with calling women derogatory names. Influencing the young with disrespectful lyrics, it was designed to trick their minds so that they will become trapped into a system designed to house them in a 6' x 8' steel cell for the majority of their lives. This makes them nothing more than a commodity, while someone gets kickbacks off of the back of their criminal act. If black people only knew their power, they wouldn't allow liberalism to destroy their very existence.

During the days of slavery, the slave master separated the black mothers from their black children by selling them off to other plantation owners with no regard. Then, in the 1800s, they further normalized the separation of a child from its mother's body by touting abortion as "just a choice." Today, some black women pay to have their black babies separated from their bodies while being told that it's healthcare.

How are you planning to be a parent if you are killing the baby that's supposed to make you a parent?

Good question, Silk. Sometimes it's hard for people to see the obvious. Let me tell you how this all got started. Margaret Sanger, the founder of Planned Parenthood, said in a letter to Dr. Clarence Gamble in 1939, "We do not want word to get out that we want to exterminate the Negro population, and the minister is the man who can straighten out that idea if it ever occurs to any of their more rebellious members."

See, Margaret Sanger wanted to exterminate black lives, black babies.

Just look at the way the slave owners controlled their slaves. They would beat the strongest black man within an inch of his life in front of all of the other slaves, just to show his weakness. Today, some black men have allowed the liberal ideology to browbeat them down and emasculate them to the point that they appear to be weak instead of strong.

This has nothing to do with white people; this has everything to do with some black people clinging to the very things that keep them stuck and confined to the negativity that controls them and their mindset.

During the '60s, black people marched in the streets for equality. Today, some black people still march in the streets for equality while voting for the same party that equates them to being less than.

Liberalism tells everyone that the statues are the problem; the statues are racist. Instead of people doing research, they attack something made of bricks and stones, something that can't feed them, clothe them, or give them a job. After seeing just how easy it was to control the narrative, liberals told everyone that the American flag was against them as black people. Once again, instead of doing research, people went out of their way to disrespect the very thing that represents the men and women who fought for their freedoms.

Kneeling on the flag is another way for liberals to control the narrative while creating a fog that keeps people from seeing the real truth about what's happening within the black communities.

Black-on-black crimes get swept under the rug. Where are all of the marches against blacks killing other blacks? Everyone is quieter than mice peeing on cotton.

Don't get us wrong, we love our police officers, even though there are a few bad apples in the bunch. But to demonize all police officers, whose job is to protect and serve, is wrong. The people you demonize are the same ones you call when you need help. Like I said before, when you need an officer, you can't pick up the phone and call Black Lives Matter. You can, however, pick up the phone and dial 911.

Then everyone wants to blame the white man. Don't blame the white man; blame liberalism, which consists of Democrats who happen to be white and black. You can even put some of the blame on the media, which depicts black people as thugs and criminals while wondering why there is a divide between black and white or mishandling from the police. The line of trust and respect is deteriorated. It wasn't the white man who made some black people prisoners in their own communities. It was some black people who intimidated, harassed, terrorized, and bullied black people within their communities.

Black people have never had a place in the Democrat Party; they were just tolerated. Democrats have cleverly and strategically created division and oppression within the black community. Just listen to the words of Lyndon B. Johnson, spoken to Democrat senator Richard Russell Jr. of Georgia regarding the Civil Rights Act of 1957:

> These Negroes, they're getting pretty uppity these days, and that's a problem for us since they've got something now they never had before: the political pull to back up their uppityness. Now, we've got to do something about this. We've got to give them a little something, just enough to quiet them down, not enough to make a difference. For if we don't move at all, then their allies will line up against us, and there'll be no way of stopping them. We'll lose the filibuster, and there'll be no way of putting a brake on all sorts of wild legislation. It'll be Reconstruction all over again.

It makes us cringe when we hear black Americans praise Lyndon B. Johnson and talk about how he passed the Civil Rights Act and signed it into law. He was a known racist. The crazy thing is, some sources also attribute this quote to Johnson: "We will have those n*****s voting Democrat for the next 200 years." So while he was signing the Civil

Rights Act into law with one hand, he was unapologetically spewing racist words and trying to control the black vote with the other hand.

If Everyone Had Equal Rights, There Would Have Been No Need for Civil Rights

We often refer to the Democrat Party as the "Democrat Plantation." Some think we are actually talking about a plantation. We're not. We are talking about a mindset that keeps you restricted by beliefs that control you.

The liberal Democrat Party has been pulling the wool over black Americans' eyes and giving conflicting signals for decades. They say one thing and do another; they never uphold any of their promises. Democrats love keeping black people in a fight, causing us to distrust everything. We've been taught not to trust anybody, not even ourselves.

The goal is to keep minorities dependent on Democrats instead of showing them how to depend on themselves.

Democrats attempt to force us into their amoral beliefs through education and indoctrination against traditional right and wrong. They left black Americans wounded while portraying them as the face of victimhood. They stifled freedom of speech and freedom of thought with political correctness. When they're questioned about their actions and intentions, they'll brand and label you with terms like xenophobe, Islamophobe, homophobe, racist, white nationalist, and white supremacist.

The Democrat Party changes the rules in the middle of the game and expects you not to notice. They preach equality, but their goal is to control your quality of life, leaving you destitute and in pieces. They are not concerned with protecting democracy; they are concerned with protecting themselves. They are not concerned about our republic; they are only concerned with demonizing the Republican Party. They're not concerned about the Constitution; they're more concerned about going against the Constitution to create chaos.

They Don't Need to Rewrite the Constitution, They Need to Reread the Constitution

Like many others, we were asleep, in a stupor. The Democrat Party and its stronghold politics were strangling us, our liberties, and our freedoms. We were slowly and methodically being silenced. Once you start becoming conscious of what's going on, there will always be consequences that you will face. When you become a threat to their system, you will become their target.

We recognized this and used our natural abilities to make a step to change it. We were no longer going to allow the narrative that others have written for us to be our truth. That's why we decided to do our own research and start speaking the reality. The reason the Left has a problem with us, as black conservative women, is because they are afraid that what we say might make sense.

When a poll came out giving President Trump more than one-third of the black vote, Ana Navarro, a commentator for CNN, about lost her mind. She even had the nerve to call us out of our names. She claims to be Republican, but to us, she was acting more like a liberal.

Wonder what made her think that it was okay to call us out of our names?

Maybe she thought it was okay to demonize us like white liberals do because she's beige. Hahaha.

Hahaha.

Even down to Tom Arnold making sexist remarks toward us. Maybe he felt that we would tolerate it because, back in the day, black women were abused and sexually exploited by the white slave master and passed around like a cheap two-dollar bill. He soon realized that he had messed with the wrong two black women.

Neither the Me Too nor the Time's Up movements ever came to our rescue. There were even some black people who went along with Tom Arnold's antics.

Black influencers have been trained by their white liberal Democrat counterparts to be the gatekeepers in the black community. When the gatekeeper sees that you are speaking something different, believing something different, or thinking something totally different from what you were taught to think, they come out like the bloodhounds that were used back in the day to hunt down the runaway slaves.

They act as if they own you, like you are their property. It offends them if you have a rational thought, so they attack you by calling you derogatory names. They only want you to have a plantation mindset.

Just like Spike Lee referring to us as "house slaves." He couldn't stomach the fact that we were afforded the opportunity to be at the White House with President Trump. While there, everyone in the room was able to pray with the president.

What we couldn't understand was how he was upset about black people being at the White House when black people lived at the White House for eight years.

We've allowed the gatekeepers to exploit, use, and profit off the pain and agony of black Americans. The gatekeepers have enriched themselves while petting black people on the head, manipulating them into a sense of helplessness and saying, "We shall overcome."

We've heard the talk about the Jim Crow days and the KKK. All of this was designed and implemented by the Democrat Party to intimidate and manipulate in order to dominate—a tactic used to control the masses. Democrats have cleverly and strategically created a divide within the black community by conditioning some to believe that they are in the plantation house with the slave master, while the others are outside tending the fields.

The Democrat goal is to segregate, separate, and decimate the black community.

The Democrat Party Thrives on Low Standards and Underhanded Principles

The Democrat Party has gone so far to the left that they don't require you to have any morals or standards. Anything goes, and if you don't go along with it, they label you a white supremacist.

Lexico.com defines white supremacy as "the belief that white people constitute a superior race and should therefore dominate society, typically to the exclusion or detriment of other racial and ethnic groups, in particular black or Jewish people."

Hell, they've even labeled us, Diamond and Silk, as white supremacists, and we're two black women.

There isn't only white supremacy but also black supremacy. Supremacy is not just one color; it can come in all colors.

Places like Chicago, Detroit, and Baltimore are all being run by liberal Democrats. A lot of these Democrat politicians have been running these cities into the ground, leaving people in rat-infested places to figure it out for themselves. You have those who are skimming from the top while leaving citizens at the bottom suffering. This creates inequality within communities that should be thriving.

What Democrats try to do is hide their hands while coercing you to blame white people, conservatives, and Republicans. A lot of the cruelty and atrocities that our ancestors had to deal with were put in place by the Democrat Party. Remember, the Democrat Party wanted to protect their slaveholders' interests; they didn't want slavery to end.

That's right. Then, decades later, they came out with another con game named "reparations." Lyndon B. Johnson 2.0, all over again. They figure that they can make it look like they're apologizing to black people about how they enslaved their ancestors. It's really a bribe for you to keep your mouth closed about their past, their history, and their nastiness. Unfortunately, some black people still fall for the banana in the tailpipe every single time.

Black People Don't Need Reparations, They Need Liberation from the Democrat Plantation

Don't allow the Left to trick you into going along with reparations. Guess who pays for it? Is it fair to make everyone pay for something that is not their fault? All white people were not slave owners. Slavery started in Africa, where an African sold black people into slavery. So should black people pay reparations to themselves for enslaving themselves? Stop blaming all white people for slavery. We were all dealt the same hand of history when we got here.

So the question is, why do you keep voting Democrat? They promise you everything but deliver nothing.

Sometimes you have to grow through what you go through. We can honestly say that we've grown. Because we don't dance to the beat of everybody's drum, we've heard many say that we're just token blacks, which is a lie.

That's right. We have our own flavor, intertwined with our own melody. We can do it our way, without anyone's permission.

We don't want reparations, we want an equal playing field.

Our Ancestors Built the American Dream, Now It's Time for Their Descendants to Obtain It

As we've said, in our opinion the Democrat Party is the party of slavery; it's just a modern-day slavery. Now Democrats are advocating for open borders. They are thirsty for an influx of poor people to our country so that they can be taken advantage of and used for slave labor. And, please, stop telling us that the Democrat Party changed. It's not true. The Democrat Party is still the same old Democrat Party: Hand everything out for free, like Tic Tacs, and in return they can control your very existence. The party didn't switch. Black people switched to the Democrat party because the Democrat party was giving everything away for free. Little did they know, free stuff doesn't equal freedom!

They deemed black people a project. That's why they didn't have a problem with throwing them in the projects.

The Democrats are concerned with obtaining power. They work for their own greed and not the needs of the people. They advocate for illegal aliens, MS-13 gang members, and terrorists. They talk about saving the earth but never talk about saving babies in the womb. They are so concerned about farting cows, but they don't seem to be concerned about the smell of people defecating on the streets of California.

This is exactly the atmosphere that the Democrats love. They want to keep you oppressed and feeling like a victim. Democrats only care about power and control. We live in a free society with free ideas, not controlled ideas. So all Americans should turn a deaf ear to those pushing these socialist and communist ideas designed to take us back to the dark ages, which are the days of slavery.

That's right. When black people ask us what Republicans have done for us, our answer back to them is, "Before President Trump, absolutely nothing because we didn't vote for Republicans to do anything. We voted for Democrats, and they've done nothing."

If you don't innovate, you will stagnate. We got tired of being stuck in the same old rut. We saw something different in President Trump. That's why we ditched the party and voted for the person. We had to be in control of our own destiny.

Just think about it: Do we want free stuff, or do we want freedom? It was the Republican Party that fought to free the slaves. It was the Democrat Party that fought to keep slaves enslaved to them and their government.

We chose freedom.

The left-wing media's demonization of President Trump is just propaganda, highly politically motivated by their agenda to control and keep power.

President Trump's movement is not a squad, it's more like a battalion. There is an army of men and women—gay, straight, black, white, Hispanic, Asian, Democrat, independent, liberal, Republican, and conservative—from all walks of life who support President Trump and his policies.

President Trump is not talking about taking care of illegal aliens; he is talking about taking care of Americans. He's cutting a lot of regulations to make sure that Americans have opportunities to better their lives. He has managed to create seven million jobs.

Mm-hmm. The same jobs that Obama said would never come back, that you'd have to wave a magic wand for. Well, we waved the magic wand: we got President Trump, and the jobs are coming back.

President Trump signed the Criminal Justice Reform Act and the First Step Act into law, giving formerly incarcerated people a real second chance. He signed the Tax Cuts and Jobs Act, which established opportunity zones to help rebuild inner and urban cities. He has given more money to historically black colleges and universities than any other president in history. Finally, we have someone standing up for black issues and solving black problems.

Not only that, he donates his salary every quarter while working hard for free. One of his goals is to make sure that we, the American people, have more money and can keep more money in our pockets.

President Trump stands up for America, and he doesn't apologize for America's greatness. He's a true champion for all Americans. President Trump has made a commitment to a growing and prosperous economy, and he is delivering.

As we said before, the more you stay chained to the system, the more you miss out on opportunities. It's time for all people, including black people, to stand up and start realizing that they hold the keys to unlock their power.

It's time to get off the sidelines of victimhood and come join us at the front lines of being victorious. You will never grow by staying stuck inside the four corners of a box. Your vote is your voice, and your voice is your power. So use it.

Whatever you are going to do, do it now because if you wait until later you may never do it. Stop allowing the Left to intimidate you into fear. We are not a commodity; we are not slaves; we are voters who make up a powerful voting bloc.

You miss out on your destiny by living in that of your ancestors. It doesn't disrespect their struggle for you to succeed; it makes their struggle worthwhile. You're too busy being downtrodden or enraged to grab hold of the opportunities that are out there for every American. Open up your mind, and go get it for yourself. Stop thinking that everybody, including all white people, is against you.

And who cares if they are against you? If you think you're going to be successful without ever facing down opposition, you're not living in reality, black or white.

That's right.

That's where it starts, really, when you tell yourself that you will succeed, no matter who or what comes against you.

Right. We've long ago passed that era in our history, but there are so many black people who are still stuck right there, thinking it is okay to live in poverty and that nothing else is going to ever happen for them in their life.

Right. They want to blame rich white Republicans for the fact that they live in poverty, yet it's the rich black and white Democrats who are trying to keep you stifled.

When you are called to do something great, people will always hate. That's how you know when you're doing something right. We can't wait until the day that the only demographic that matters in America is American.

Chapter 16

Schemes and Beams

Russia, Russia, Russia

*B*efore any of the news media or bloggers said anything, Diamond and Silk spoke about the Russia hoax in December 2016. We spoke about the atmosphere in Washington, D.C., being hostile toward President Trump, and we started calling out what we felt wasn't right. We have video to prove it. Does ObamaGate ring a bell? During the earlier part of 2017, right after the inauguration, we titled a few of our videos ObamaGate. Nobody gave us any information or told us what to say or how to say it. We used common sense and did our own research to connect all of the dots as we saw it. Our God-given gut intuition was our best friend, and we knew that the Russia witch hunt was all lies created from the top to undo the 2016 election. The censorship on social media began about two months after we started speaking out about what we felt. We were even called conspiracy theorists. After three years and millions of dollars wasted, it looked like the supposed Russia collusion was the real hoax, a clever scheme to take down a duly elected president. We were right about ObamaGate—which may turn out to be worse than Watergate when it's all said and done.*

That's right.

When the Left started pushing the Russia hoax, we knew we needed to be out there with our feet on the ground and our ears open. We needed to hear what was going on so we could counter it with the truth. We knew that Russian collusion was nothing but a made-up lie, and we told the people.

So when the fake news said Russia won the election, we spoke out and said, "No! The American people won the election." When they said a border wall was nonsense, we spoke about how much sense it did make. We wanted to make sure that people knew what President Trump's true agenda was because the mainstream media was straight-up lying.

That's exactly what they were doing—lying.

When candidate Donald Trump came down the escalators with the future First Lady, Melania, we saw a businessman and boss, but the media, the Left, and even Hillary Clinton herself tried to paint him as a racist.

Donald Trump had been a public figure for almost three and a half decades, and no one had said these disparaging things about him. Most men, especially black men, wanted to be just like him. Ballers, shot callers, rappers, and ball players all wanted to be like Donald Trump. Name me one black man who ever wanted to be like Joe Biden.

To add insult to injury, Jesse Jackson and Al Sharpton used to be friends with Donald Trump, but even they became two-faced and chose to throw him under the bus by going along with the racist narrative from the Left. Then, all of a sudden, the Left and the Democrats started bringing up the KKK, as if the Trump administration endorsed the KKK's views. What the media didn't mention was that, according to history, the Democrats are the ones who created the KKK.

The left-wing media knew that using "racist" and "race-baiting" in the same sentence was the ultimate trick to keep black people in line. When the race-baiting didn't stop candidate Trump's momentum, they started pushing Russia . . . Russia . . . Russia . . .

Before President Trump even won the election, the Left started pushing Russian collusion. We knew from the very beginning that it was nothing but fake news propaganda perpetuated by the left-wing media and the Democrats to stop candidate Trump's campaign.

The mainstream media cleverly and methodically used their platforms to strategically push their Russia collusion narrative, just to advance their political agenda and the agenda they wanted for America and the American people. The mainstream media wanted to continue exerting their influence on the American people through lies and persuasion instead of facts and truth. They wanted the same old career politicians to push the same old political tactics, while the rich got richer and the poor got poorer.

They weren't concerned about the voters or protecting their interests; they were only concerned about protecting the career politicians they were trying to elect by abusing the power of the media instead of using the power of the vote. When the media started losing control over the will of the American people, it became evident, like it or not, that they were going to exert their will on the sixty-some million Americans who had voted for President Donald J. Trump in 2016.

Listening to and watching the media push their Russia collusion was a slap in the face to the American people. The whole narrative was based on a made-up lie, orchestrated by the Left and the left-wing media. Neither the Left nor the Democrats cared about the insult they were causing to our democracy and the injury they were causing to our republic. They were mad as hell because Donald J. Trump had become the forty-fifth president, and they knew that his presidency was going to disrupt all of their corrupt tricks and schemes.

People like Congressmen Adam Schiff went on national TV and tried to convince the public that they had evidence that Trump and his campaign had colluded with Russia. Come to find out, it was a lie. Schiff had no problem comfortably lying to the American people because, in our opinion, he knew that the media wouldn't challenge him on the basis of his lie but would protect him from scrutiny.

Millions of American taxpayer dollars were spent on a frivolous Russian collusion investigation that had no evidence from the start. People were investigated and lives and livelihoods were ruined by something that turned out to be a hoax and a malicious deception.

Day in and day out, the left-wing media told us tale after tale, and, when it finally came out that there was no Russian collusion, the media didn't even have enough decency to apologize.

Some of the media outlets are the enemy of the people and the enemy of the truth because they bear a lot of the responsibility for the divisiveness. They couldn't care less about facts. They seem to care more about making their factitious lies stick. Yet we, as Americans, continue to accept and tolerate their foolishness while they continue to dominate.

The Left tends to ignore the fact that Hillary Clinton and the DNC purchased a dossier that was tied to Russia to use against candidate Donald J. Trump. What we couldn't understand was, why would she spend millions of dollars for information that came from Russia when candidate Donald J. Trump didn't live in Russia?

Then there was the FISA abuse, leaks, and unmasking, and the illegal surveillance of Carter Page. We heard no criticism or condemnation of this from the left-wing media. Total silence. You could have heard a safety pin drop on carpet when it came out about how people from the Obama administration schemed and beamed against Michael Flynn. It's like they went and hid their heads in a bucket.

If the media can't hold itself accountable, then we the people have to hold the media accountable. Americans have turned a blind eye and accepted this type of behavior as the norm for far too long. This is why the Left feels like it is okay to throw the stone and hide their hands. They know that there will be no repercussions for their actions.

Never in our lifetimes have we seen such hatred for the President of the United States and straight disrespect for the highest office in the land.

Witch Hunt 2.0

The President of the United States making a phone call and congratulating the President of Ukraine is not a high crime or a misdemeanor. It's a simple phone call.

Wonder why someone wasn't listening to Obama's phone calls when he was the president? Why didn't he, or any other past president, get the same type of scrutiny that was put on President Trump?

What the Democrats and the left-wing media were trying to do to President Trump was clearly an abuse of media power, and it was unjust.

To put the icing on the cake, the Left decided to come up with another scheme that included an imaginary whistleblower who overheard—or should we say "eavesdropped on"—a phone call. If it wasn't eavesdropping, then it was someone's opinion about a phone call, based on what someone else told them.

Sounds like secondhand information to me.

Let's face it, three people can listen to a phone call, and all of them may come out interpreting the phone call in a different way. Just because they may have heard about a call or overheard the call doesn't make their interpretation of the call accurate. Yet Nancy Pelosi, who is the Speaker of the House, launched an impeachment inquiry based on hearsay. Hearsay is inadmissible in court.

If hearsay is inadmissible in court, then why were the Democrat representatives making it admissible in Congress? Imagine being convicted of something where there's no facts or proof.

What the Left failed to realize is that everything they were accusing President Trump of, Joe Biden had already done. Let's not forget that it was Joe Biden who called the Ukraine president and did an undercover shakedown by threatening to withhold foreign aid, which was American tax dollars. Joe Biden is on video talking about how he threatened to withhold one billion dollars if the Ukraine president didn't fire the prosecutor who was investigating the company that his son, Hunter Biden, was working for as a board member. Not only is that quid pro quo; but we call it Quid Pro Joe trying to get that quid pro dough.

This impeachment sham had Americans like me outraged. It got to the point where enough was enough. The back and forth with Congress searching for a crime, trying to make anything stick like glue to paper, was the end of their integrity.

I, for one, was emotionally drained and upset that the President of the United States was being railroaded the same way black people were railroaded back in the day. Congress would not allow President Trump due process.

They wouldn't let him call the witnesses that he wanted to call. Adam Schiff was having meetings in the basement, but he would not allow any of President Trump's legal team access.

The Left, along with the media, started calling Trump guilty even though he hadn't committed a crime. Yet according to our laws, a person is supposed to be innocent until proven guilty.

According to the Left, however, if they say that you are guilty, then it's up to you to prove yourself innocent, even if it bankrupts you.

We watched Adam Schiff get in front of the American people and literally make up words and read them off a sheet of paper as if he were reading the words of President Trump. Every word was a bald-faced lie. If they really had evidence of high crimes and misdemeanors, then why did he have to lie? If it was the truth, it would have been obvious in the transcribed call President Trump made available to all.

I can remember, during the impeachment process, I was watching the trial play out on national TV. I noticed how the media was trying to sway the public. They kept the coverage of the trial on TV all day. It didn't matter to us because people were able to see just how biased the Democrats were being towards President Trump. People actually started questioning the integrity of our Congress. It was all a game to them. They couldn't have cared less about wasting millions of our tax dollars. Hell, they had just wasted over thirty-five million of our tax dollars on their Russia witch hunt. If the media was supposed to hold Congress accountable, why didn't they do their job? It looked like everyone had been bought and paid for. The Left, along with the left-wing media and the Democrats, were all in on another scam, better known as the Witch Hunt 2.0.

I seriously needed a break from it all. I was sitting in my den, watching the news, when my heart started palpitating very fast. I didn't know what was going on, but I did know that oftentimes heart palpitations can be caused by stress. I was stressed-out and numb at the way our U.S. Congress was deliberately trying to hoodwink the American people.

Right. It was disturbing. It made me wonder how many more people they had tried to railroad. It seemed like they were playing a familiar scheme and beam game. They knew all of the little corrupt tricks, and the sad part was that they didn't try to hide it. They didn't care if you knew that they were underhanded, and they didn't care who it hurt.

When the palpitations started getting worse, I ended up in the emergency room and then in the hospital for two days, all because of stress. My heart was fine, but my stress levels were through the roof. I knew if I was feeling this way, others were also feeling the same anxiety. It was time for me to pull back and get still, and that's exactly what I did.

Finally, President Trump was acquitted. Looking at the antics and biased tactics used by the Democrats, we will never vote Democrat, nor will I ever trust the media again. No one should ever want to vote for a party whose members are okay with exerting their will instead of following our constitutional laws.

Over sixty million people voted for President Trump. If the Democrats were okay with taking away his constitutional rights, they wouldn't have a problem taking away the average American's rights.

Millions of Americans voted for Donald Trump because they knew he would stand up for America and Americans. We knew who we were voting for before we voted him into office. We wanted a disrupter, a job creator, and a negotiator.

President Trump has given us all permission to start standing up for ourselves and push back on these false narratives and sources that continue to bamboozle us. Who the hell does the Left think we are? We are not chumps; we are American citizens. We may have taken these shenanigans for decades, but we are not taking them anymore!

Chapter 17

The Invisible Enemy

After the Ukraine hoax, used by the Democrats to impeach President Trump, then came the coronavirus, which originated in Wuhan, China. First Russia, then Ukraine, then China.

Unbelievable. Our president was winning for America and breaking all kinds of records. Then out of nowhere, America was fighting an invisible war. The Wuhan virus shut the country down.

President Trump began calling it the Chinese virus because it originated in China. The Democrats and some in the media began calling the president a racist for stating the obvious. Well, was it racist when Democrats and the mainstream media called their hoax the "Russia" collusion?

It has been widely reported that in January 2020, the United States intelligence community began briefing President Trump on the respiratory disease now known as COVID-19. According to the health experts and their projections, 1.6 to 2.2 million people were going to die. The economy was thriving when President Trump was told, *Sir, we're going to have to close it up until we get rid of this hidden enemy—this terrible scourge.*

President Trump created a task force of scientists and medical professionals to deal with the situation. Americans were told that we had to listen to the scientists. Nothing about this felt right to many Americans. We later found out the projections were flawed.

Despite having the best economy in history, the lowest unemployment, and record-breaking stock market gains, the United States of America came to a screeching halt in a matter of days. The stock market went from hitting an all-time high, 29,551.42, on February 12, 2020, to hitting as low as 18,917.46 on March 18, 2020; Americans lost their jobs; and unemployment claims soared to over three million during the week of March 26, 2020.

The left-wing media seemed excited by the losses. It was like they were celebrating the collapse of America's economy. Anything to hurt President Trump. The way the Democrats politicized each development to manipulate the pain was mind-boggling. Not only were they manipulating the pain, but they were manipulating the public with fear and panic. Yes, there was a virus, but the way the media was politicizing and sensationalizing it was over the top. They only focused on the number of deaths, not the number of recoveries. Seeing what they were doing, I wanted to scream at the top of my lungs. Something wasn't right. I couldn't put my finger on it, so I kept watching, looking, and listening.

It felt like we were looking at a movie where we were all forced to participate in a Deep State experiment. It was one thing to ask us to work together by staying home, but it was another thing for governors to implement limits and stipulations as to how we, as U.S. citizens, could spend our money. This was a clear sign of undercover socialism mixed with a globalist-takeover mentality silently being pushed down Americans' throats.

This whole thing wasn't making sense to me. Something just wasn't sitting well in my spirit, and I had a lot of questions.

If you don't know by now, I'm a strategic thinker; I think outside of the box. I've never lived through or recalled experiencing anything where my freedoms and civil liberties felt violated beyond my control. When something doesn't feel right, keep your eye on the ball because a distraction and a deflection is merely used to divert your attention to focus on presumptions instead of true realities.

We began to watch it from both angles and pay attention to the opposite of what we were being told. Something wasn't adding up, and something wasn't making sense.

On March 24, 2020, during a coronavirus townhall, President Trump stated that he would love to have the country opened by Easter. Seemed reasonable to me. Easter was a little over two weeks away, on April 12, 2020.

All of a sudden, the media began criticizing the president for being optimistic about opening the country back up. Immediately things took a turn for the worse. The number of deaths skyrocketed within a matter of five days.

We started asking questions like, How did one person die from the Wuhan virus within thirty-nine days after the first case was reported in the U.S.A., on January 21, 2020, but more than a thousand people died within a two-week time period after testing began? What accelerated the deaths within two weeks? And why wasn't the number of people recovering from this virus being reported?

Right, Silk. It seemed like the media's goal was only to keep the negative news in front of the viewers. Please note that when you are in panic and fear mode, it's easier to be controlled.

Here's another question: Did people die with *the virus or from the virus? Meaning, did people die from another cause but happened to have the virus, or were they dying because they contracted COVID-19? Where were the statistics, and why weren't those statistics being shown to the American people?*

So we were paying close attention. On April 7, 2020, while listening to the Coronavirus Task Force briefing, we heard Dr. Birx make a revealing statement. She said, "If someone dies with COVID-19, we are counting that as a COVID-19 death."

This statement answered my questions. My gut intuition was confirmed: There's a difference between dying with COVID-19 and dying from COVID-19. This Deep State experiment was about more than COVID-19. I asked myself, is this a virus with an agenda?

Hydroxychloroquine and azithromycin seemed to be working for people who had the virus. Both medicines may have been used for different purposes, but it seemed that when they were combined, the combination was successful for treating the virus. People began thanking President Trump for making everyone aware of the medicine and its possibilities.

People also thanked President Trump for the S.204 Right to Try Act, which he had signed into law on May 30, 2018. Right to Try opened a new pathway for terminally ill patients who had exhausted government-approved options so they would be able to get into clinical trials to access experimental treatments.

For some, this was their only hope. Some people were able to bounce back after several days of the combination of medicines, but some Democrat governors restricted the medicines from being used in their states. This seemed inhumane to me.

Yeah. If there's something that can possibly save someone's life, why not allow them the right to try instead of letting them die? To me, it didn't make sense to wait two years for a vaccine when a combination of already available medicines was working.

By the way, COVID-19 is said to mutate. How the hell are you going to create a vaccine if the virus keeps changing?

So why was there such a big push for a vaccine when it wasn't even a cure? What was so wrong with allowing my immune system to defend my body naturally?

That's right, Diamond. What happened to "Our bodies, our choice"?

Then we have Governor Cuomo of New York on TV begging for ventilators after the Trump administration had already started sending them. Day after day, Cuomo begged for thirty thousand ventilators, anticipating a huge wave of COVID-19 patients. From the way he sounded, you would have thought that patients were coming in droves. That was why they needed these ventilators right then and there.

After a few weeks of this begging, a video surfaced showing Governor Cuomo saying, "We have ventilators in the stockpile, and we haven't sent them to the hospitals yet." He said he was planning for an apex.

Well, why didn't he tell the public that he was stockpiling the ventilators? Why did he make it appear urgent that he have the thirty thousand ventilators or people were going to die? When we saw his actions, we had even more questions. Was the governor claiming to need ventilators in order to make the crisis seem more severe?

I began to observe how a lot of elderly people were having the worst reaction to this plague and were in serious danger of dying from it. I had more questions: How were the elderly in nursing homes, especially in New York, all of a sudden catching this virus when they had not gone out in public, after the nursing homes had been forbidden to have visitors?

Y'all, later on I found out something horrible: According to Breitbart News, Governor Andrew Cuomo and his administration implemented a policy on March 25, 2020, that demanded nursing homes take in active COVID-19 patients. They had just banned family members from visiting the nursing homes a week and a half before, on March 13, 2020.

Not only that, on April 1, 2020, a state law was implemented granting hospitals and nursing homes some immunity from civil and criminal liability.

I wept for the vulnerable. I found myself missing meals, and my blood pressure was elevated, I was so hurt by what I saw, heard, and felt. Elderly people were dying, and nobody seemed to care.

Wow, why would anyone be OK with placing the sick with the vulnerable? Why?

The elderly and our veterans—another group that is often disrespected—know exactly what our freedom means. They can tell of America's greatness. They can explain, from irrefutable experience, why capitalism is the only government for them—and they'll crawl through glass to vote for it. If they were eliminated, who would even know our history or be able to testify about liberty and justice for all?

Now I can only go off of my feelings. Not to downplay the virus and the number of people who were affected by it, but I truly believed that a lot of the Deep State snakes were upset because they no longer had power and because President Trump wasn't afraid to poke the bear and disturb the status quo.

There was a lot of speculation that the virus had been man-made in a lab and bats had been injected with it. There was also speculation that the virus had occurred naturally. Well, according to the patent laws, you cannot patent anything that occurs naturally—and several strands of the coronavirus were already patented.

My thoughts were, if China created this mess, then China should have stopped it at the source. They should not be able to benefit and make millions off of the collapse of America's stock market and economy. If they are responsible, then they should foot the bill, not the American taxpayers. If China concealed this and didn't reveal it, they should be held accountable.

On April 8, 2020, the CDC reported that African Americans were disproportionately affected by the coronavirus because obesity, high blood pressure, and type 2 diabetes are more prevalent in African Americans. Well, we had real problems with that theory. Obesity, high blood pressure, and diabetes are all national issues, not African American issues.

Later on, we had the privilege of interviewing Jerome Adams, the United States surgeon general. His thoughts were that because of close living and shared housing, many minority groups were being disproportionately affected.

But I still had a few nagging questions: Why does it feel like every time something breaks out in this country, black people are the ones disproportionately affected? Why does it feel like black people are always the ones who are more adversely affected than everyone else in a crisis? Black people are human beings, just like every other race of people.

But we were persecuted for asking these questions. We were smeared and slandered by the media for daring to even have an open conversation about a matter that disproportionately affects black people. Y'all know this only caused me to ask more questions. What was the real intent, and why was it okay for liberal blacks and liberal whites to talk about the coronavirus but not Diamond and Silk? Is this a form of systemic racism?

That's right, Silk. They don't cut your tongue out of your mouth to keep you quiet; they cut your tongue out of your mouth to keep you from telling the truth.

Right. I began thinking about this, and the thought that just kept coming to me was, if they think they are about to make black people the guinea pigs for their vaccine experiments, they have another think coming. This reminded us of the Tuskegee experiment all over again!

I felt like the black community would be used like we were part of a science experiment to test their supposed cures. I picked up the phone and called Diamond to tell her what I was feeling . . .

And, y'all, I was having the same thoughts. All of this was going on at the same time that the World Health Organization (WHO) was supposedly developing a vaccination. This did not comfort us at all. It seemed the WHO was pushing handwashing, social distancing, and a vaccine—that's it.

They never mentioned practical health steps like eating right to boost your immune system, vitamins, sunshine and fresh air, and God forbid the use of hydroxychloroquine and azithromycin—drugs that were reported to help people who already had the virus. The only answer for them was to wash your hands and stay away from others until we can develop a vaccine.

Well, when the WHO was looked into, it was discovered that they were not upfront and upright concerning the virus and that they seemed to be protecting the decisions China was making. China wanted their own responsibility for the virus deflected and even went so far as to blame American soldiers for bringing coronavirus to their shores!

That wasn't happening on President Trump's watch.

No, it wasn't. He set them straight on that.

The WHO seemed only too willing to parrot what China said. Then, it came out that America invests about ten times more money annually in the WHO than China does. On top of that, it was reported that they knew about the virus and its catastrophic effects earlier than the information was released.

It didn't help them when the WHO chief made the statement, "We will have many body bags in front of us if we don't behave." Sounded to us like a threat. We began asking questions: Why did the WHO threaten the President of the United States with more body bags? Did they know something we didn't know? Were they the orchestrating this whole pandemic? On April 14, 2020, President Trump halted U.S. funding to the World Health Organization, and we couldn't have been happier with that decision.

The Wuhan virus pandemic opened a lot of people's eyes. We all realized just how many products were being made in China. We even found out that China was making 97 percent of all of our antibiotics, along with 80 percent of the active pharmaceutical ingredients used to make our medicines.

So they fail to warn us of a virus, but we're supposed to rely on them to handle our medicines honestly and fairly? That's a hell no! It was obviously time to bring our manufacturers back home to America. It was time for Americans to start making our own products instead of depending on a foreign country and its cheap labor. You've heard the old saying: you get what you pay for!

You got that right. You also get who you vote for.

There was something very sinister going on, and I'm not referring to the virus. I'm referring to the Democrat anti-Trump governors who were doing more harm to their states than the virus. It felt like some Democrat leaders fell right into a tyrannical strategy. All of a sudden, a communist and socialist agenda was in play, and it was as if we the people shouldn't think it was unusual.

As many states began opening back up, a lot of Democrat-run states were extending their lockdowns. Not only did this flatten the curve, it also flattened small businesses; it flattened people's livelihoods and savings and retirement accounts. People lost their jobs and couldn't provide for their families, and the number of deaths from suicide climbed as the quarantine continued.

They were too blind to see that destroying the economy doesn't kill the virus; it kills the people. They were truly acting like dictators.

Some of the governors, mayors, and judges didn't seem to care about violating people's constitutional rights and civil liberties. They appeared to be hungry for power. The things that Democrats were trying to push through the stimulus bills, like vote by mail, made their intent crystal clear.

There were a lot of Democrat officials complaining about the unemployment numbers being high, yet they were the ones who had extended the lockdowns that were keeping people from working. In the name of providing for the people during this crisis, the Democrats offered the Federal Pandemic Unemployment Compensation program. This program added an additional $600 to each unemployment check provided because of the virus. People were actually getting paid more for being unemployed than what they would have made working on the job. This was another contributing factor to the sky-high unemployment numbers.

Next I began to wonder: How was it that big businesses were able to be open, but small businesses created so much threat to our health that they couldn't be? Why was it safe for abortion clinics to be open, but church gatherings carried too high a risk of contagion? How could criminals be released from jail for their protection, but Americans could be jailed for working to provide for their families? To me, it seemed like the main side effect of the virus was that America was suddenly implementing the Democrats' entire agenda.

Mm-hmm . . . their tactics made it seem more like we were in a "plannedemic" than a pandemic. They just slid right in with their socialist, communist agenda as if this had been the plan all along and we had better just get used to their new normal.

We had to take the bitter with the sweet. We knew that we would come through the storm because we believe Isaiah 54:17, "No weapon formed against thee shall prosper."

We couldn't get discouraged. President Trump declared Sunday, March 15, 2020, a National Day of Prayer. Because we were already praying every day at 11:21 a.m., EST, we posted a picture of where we had prayed for—and with—President Trump during one of our visits at the White House. We posted a message to uplift everyone's spirits. We wanted people to focus on something positive. We encouraged people to learn how to live again: focus on faith, not fear; focus on peace, not panic; focus on love, not hate.

Y'all, even though people had to stay in their homes while President Trump was kicking coronavirus's ass, almost every single day President Trump and his Coronavirus Task Force team held a press briefing. This gave all Americans, including people who didn't vote for President Trump, the opportunity to see him in action without the media's distortion of the truth.

People were also able to see how the media would ask asinine questions filled with hate while ridiculing the president for being optimistic. President Trump's approval rating skyrocketed. People started saying that they had once been anti-Trump but they would be voting for President Trump in 2020 because they saw how he really cared for Americans.

Through it all, President Trump stepped up to the plate with strength and great leadership. While members of Congress were at their homes like cowards, leading from the back, President Trump was at the White House leading from the front.

While President Trump was getting China in hand, the Democrats and their backup media supported the communist nation. Why protect them? Why pander to them? Why did past administrations allow our medicines to be made in China?

Why didn't Joe Biden and the Obama administration propose some type of legislation to stop China from ripping off America instead of running supplies down so low that the Trump administration was left hanging? Why in the hell did they roll over and allow China to become such a menace to the world? Why was Joe Biden, now the leading Democrat presidential candidate, repeating China's propaganda?

After being threatened with more body bags if we didn't conform to the WHO's rules, why did Joe Biden say that he would reverse President's Trump decision to defund the WHO? Sounded like this man was in the tank with China. It seemed like he was part of the problem instead of part of the solution to help get rid of the Wuhan virus.

This country was founded upon biblical principles, and there's no way that we can sit by and let any devil from the pit of hell destroy what God built.

We've never seen a storm that didn't pass, not even with Noah's Ark. It rained for forty days and forty nights, but it did come to an end.

We had to keep telling ourselves and our viewers, "This too shall pass."

In the midst of everything, fake news outlets were acting like provocateurs. Dictionary.com defines a provocateur as "a person who provokes trouble, causes dissension, or the like; agitator." The mainstream media's clickbait headlines about Diamond and Silk were straight slander, bigotry, and hate. It was brutal.

The fake news media had been writing a lot of blogs about Diamond and Silk with false and deceptive information. They took our words out of context; they chopped up some of the content from our Chit Chat videos to make it appear a specific way; they sliced and diced our sentences to make it seem like we were spewing conspiracy theories; and they tied Fox News and Fox Nation to their blogs to make it appear like pieces of the content they had edited and placed in their articles were from the videos that were licensed to Fox Nation. Clearly these people had cast off all restraint. Producing fair journalism was not even a consideration for them.

We started asking ourselves why they were coming after us. We are not conspiracy theorists; we are critical thinkers. Why were they switching up our words to make us sound a specific way?

Please note that when the pandemic began, Fox News used professionals such as doctors and epidemiologists, along with a host of other specialists, to discuss the COVID-19 virus and the pandemic. We didn't have these medical qualifications. It made perfect sense to have the professionals on during this time as they could better assist the public with understanding the pandemic.

Mm-hmm. That's right. Diamond and Silk are two black chicks who are down with politics, not pandemics.

We never lost touch with our viewers. Throughout all of this, we continued to do our Chit Chat Live shows and post them on our social media platforms. Not only that, we continued to do our five-minute videos for Fox Nation as well.

On April 23, 2020, we received an email inquiry from a reporter, who asked why there hadn't been a new episode of our Fox Nation show since April 7, 2020. We were unaware of this, so we confirmed with one of our contacts at Fox that our videos were still being transferred to the appropriate person. After that confirmation, we also received a note that they were dialing back on posting any content that was overly political.

So we asked Fox if they wanted us to do videos that were not political. We were informed that we should keep doing videos as we would normally do them, and they would save them for a time when they could post them all!

I felt like one of the agendas of the fake news was to silence us. We were catching on to too many things too quickly, and we were boldly proclaiming our opinions to our millions of followers. That obviously got some in the media so upset that they became obsessed with trying to tear down Diamond and Silk. Every time they wrote a hit piece about us, the media acted like a jealous ex-boyfriend who stalks and harasses his ex-girlfriend who never gives him the time of day. It's like we were living rent free in their heads!

Yes. Silk, that's a great description. It was sickening. When they would write false things in their articles to try to make us look bad, they would deliberately tie Fox News to the articles.

On March 14, 2019, we flew into New York to do an in-studio interview with the president's daughter-in-law, Lara Trump. The 14:09-minute interview must have been too powerful for the left-wing media to handle. They wrote a blog post that stated that we had appeared in a Trump campaign video. They wrote about the content of the video being highly complimentary towards the president. They felt that cable news company hosts were not supposed to appear in a campaign video. In my mind, I was thinking, who died and made them the cable news campaign patrol?

So a Fox News spokesperson said, "The duo are not employees of the network: Diamond & Silk license short weekly videos to Fox Nation—they are not Fox News contributors or employees. When they appear on FNC and FBN, they do so as guests."

These fake news bloggers knew that we had never been employees of the network, yet they continued to tie Fox News to all of their articles and hit pieces about us as if we were employed by Fox News.

We are loyal supporters of President Trump, and no one—and I do mean no one—is going to stop us from supporting him, not even fake news. Before we sign any contracts or make any deals, we make extra sure that there are no restrictions that will keep us from supporting the president in any way, shape, or form. We are up-front, with no sugar-coating. It's definitely a "no deal" if you try and block us from supporting him.

So we saw that the fake news was trying to drive a wedge to dismantle our friendships and professional relationships. It was a low blow even for them, but we weren't surprised. The Left owns about 90 percent of the media; therefore, they can spread a lie faster than the truth, and that's exactly what they did.

They sure did. On Monday, April 27, 2020, at 4:53 p.m., I received another email from the same reporter who had inquired about not seeing a new episode of our Fox Nation show since April 7, 2020. At the same time, I received a notification that Diamond and Silk were mentioned in an article written by the same person, from The Daily Beast.

So they emailed us and released the article on the same date, at the same time, 4:53 p.m., EST. I was on the phone talking to Diamond. I read the headline to her: "Fox News Cuts Ties with Diamond and Silk, Unofficial Trump 'Advisers' Who Spread Bonkers Coronavirus Claims." I said, "Oh Lord, they are at it again."

I was driving at the time, so I asked Silk to read the article to me. The first line said, "Fox News has cut ties with MAGA vlogging superstars Diamond & Silk."

So the first thing I said was, "Hell, why didn't Fox tell us?"

She continued to read on, and the next paragraph stated that a source with knowledge of the matter had told The Daily Beast that after what we've said and tweeted, we won't be seen on Fox Nation or Fox News anytime soon.

So my next thought was, "Hell, why didn't the source tell us?"

Y'all, the article was full of twisted lies to fit their twisted narrative. This was definitely the beginning of a smear campaign. A few minutes later, Silk received another notification, and another, and another. The headlines were saying that Fox News had fired Diamond and Silk.

My first thought was, Fox can't fire us because they never hired us! You see, we were never hired by Fox. As Fox clearly stated, we only licensed our video content to their streaming platform, Fox Nation. So seeing the headlines didn't make sense to us, but when it's coming from the lamestream media, you're liable to see anything.

That's right. The smear tactics being used were despicable. It was like someone turned on a water spigot in an overflowing pool. There was no regard for the truth. The majority of the articles didn't even allege anything. They wrote the stories to be just as false as they could be, and they deliberately made it appear as truth.

On the same day, April 27, 2020, at 5:56 p.m., EST, we sent an email to our contact at Fox News to make them aware of what was going on and to see how they wanted us to respond. To our surprise, the contact didn't have any knowledge of what was happening but advised us to "Probably ignore it if possible."

We replied with links to a few of the articles and continued to honor our Fox Nation contractual agreement.

Y'all, I'm not going to lie. It was hard for me to just ignore it. Anytime Diamond and Silk are written about, anywhere in the world, we get a notification. Imagine getting inundated with email after email, message after message, interview request after interview request asking for us to respond.

Just when we thought it was over, there was another dump of derogatory articles defaming us, assassinating our characters, and smearing us. It didn't look like the clickbait was going to end.

Keep in mind that anytime the media starts writing stories by "unnamed sources," there's a strong possibility that they made something up.

Not only that, but no one from Fox clarified whether there really was a source or not. That didn't sit well with us. What was really going on?

On April 27, 2020, we trended on Twitter for almost the entire day. Blogs, videos, magazines, radio shows, and even Jimmy Kimmel had something to say about Diamond and Silk. Now, in the midst of all of the hate, we were able to see who our true friends were. It was like we were having an out-of-body experience. We were talked about all over the world, all because of a lie and smear campaign.

We were being put through the wringer all because we had dared to speak against the left-wing narrative. We had dared to ask questions about a huge crisis that was plaguing this country. We had dared to ask questions about the inflation of the number of deaths—something that was later questioned by Dr. Birx herself.

Yeah, Silk, if you questioned the obvious agenda or spoke out against the narrative, you were ridiculed.

By April 29, I was furious. We called another contact at Fox News to see what was going on and why no one at Fox had addressed the lie from The Daily Beast. I was so overwhelmed that it brought me to tears because we had done nothing wrong. Not one time did Fox News inform us or reprimand us for anything. Not one person at Fox News, not top executives, journalists, reporters, or any of our contacts at Fox News called or emailed to inform us of any wrongdoing.

A few days later, the same contact at Fox News that we had called wrote us an email and said, "I want to assure you the stories are not true and executives here feel lies like that should just be ignored. Stay strong and keep fighting!"

Y'all . . . I was so mad. I know that I had damn near gotten on Silk's last nerve. We were being lied about and relentlessly smeared in the media. Silk was cool, calm, and collected. Me, on the other hand . . . I was livid.

Where the hell was Fox? Where was their PR department? Why the hell didn't they correct the lies published by The Daily Beast? Why didn't Fox speak up?

Their silence spoke louder than their words. Fox News was so quiet that you could have heard a bicycle stop for a turtle crossing the road ten miles away.

In the midst of it all, I couldn't panic. I had to get still and be thankful for all of the good that I knew was about to come out of all of this. I focused on the good and strategized. We were Diamond and Silk before Fox, and we would be Diamond and Silk after Fox. Our weekly videos were licensed to Fox, not our brand and definitely not Diamond and Silk.

That's right. So don't get it twisted. We had millions of followers before Fox. Fox didn't make us, so Fox couldn't break us.

How the hell were we supposed to feel? Not one executive from Fox had told us we were spreading misinformation or conspiracy theories, but the left-wing media was spreading misinformation and theories from an unnamed source from Fox.

Here is the crazy thing, y'all: Fox News hosts like Tucker Carlson, Sean Hannity, and Laura Ingraham were questioning the same things we were questioning about the virus and pandemic. The very same questions we had raised were being discussed openly on Fox News.

That led me to ask this question: Why were our Fox Nation videos dialed back because they were deemed overly political, but it was okay for others on the network to talk about politics, even down to asking some of the same questions we had? Why were we such a threat? We only did one video every week, and it was hidden behind a paid subscription wall. When you really think about it, was this part of the systemic racism that everybody was talking about?

Yeah, Silk. How in the hell was it OK for for the white show host to ask the same questions and talk about the same things that we were speaking about, but our video content was dialed back for being overly political? We were all asking the same questions and talking about the same thing.

The first thing I thought was, who in the hell ordered the hit? Was this something that came from the top floor, the higher-ups, or was this bigger? This seemed to be bigger than we knew.

The day before the hit, on April 26, 2020, President Trump had tweeted his displeasure with Fox News and some of its personalities, hosts, and one of the board members. He had criticized them for being politically correct. He let them know that some of their viewers were angry at Fox and that he and those viewers wanted an alternative.

It makes you wonder if this was some type of retaliation against us, especially since it happened the next day. Perhaps that's why we were thrown under the bus. Hell, we don't know. All we do know is that Fox never told the public that they had cut ties with us. As a matter of fact, Fox never even told us that they had cut ties with us.

The day of this writing is May 15, 2020. Our videos are still licensed to Fox Nation. It's totally up to them to post them or shelve them. After we make the videos and send them, they can do what they damn well please with them!

We understand that during an election year one of the tactics from the Left is to silence the voices making the most impact. We're not saying that this is what Fox did, but it damn sure felt like it.

Y'all, here's the funniest thing: The fake news media actually amplified the message that they were trying to suppress and censor. When they wrote those horrible lies about us and tried to label us, people began asking the same questions. Even Diamond and Silk haters started asking questions and agreeing with our opinions.

Over a hundred thousand additional people began following us on our social media platforms. Plus, our weekly Chit Chat Live viewership jumped to the highest it has been since being censored by social media. People were stopping by to see who we were and wondering why they'd never seen us before.

We received lots of encouraging messages, thousands of additional followers, many business offers, and an amazing message from the President of the United States. I had tweeted out, "Haters keep saying they hate Diamond and Silk, but you can't hate what you ain't never loved!"

We were so tickled when President Trump himself replied to the tweet with this message: "But I love Diamond & Silk, and so do millions of people!"

Yes, he did. It was unexpected yet welcomed. We answered back, "We love you more!" We received so much love that it was truly unexplainable. We absolutely love and thank our loyal fans for their support.

We were the first ones to question the inflation of the numbers of deaths, and we were the first ones vilified for questioning it. Diamond and Silk were right once again.

We were the first ones to question the death of elderly people in rest homes and rehabilitation centers. Come to find out, these facilities were being forced to admit COVID-19 patients, and this was one of the factors that contributed to the death of many of the elderly. Even Tucker Carlson interviewed a nurse on June 11, 2020, who video recorded the mishandling of COVID-19 patients who were mixed in with non-COVID-19 patients in the hospital. This was more proof that something sick and sinister was going on!

If the media sensationalizes stories and spews lies, the American people will never trust them or anything they have to say after this.

That saying about your haters making you greater is true. The fake news, hate-filled, lying, disgusting media—which includes The Daily Beast—meant it for evil, but God turned it around for our good.

That's right. We've been with President Trump since the beginning, and we will be with him to the end. There was something sinister happening, and we could see the invisible enemy clear as day. While everyone else was looking at the virus, Diamond and Silk were looking at the real invisible enemy.

Mm-hmm. We could see them with all eight of our eyes. Especially when the Democrats removed their disguises and began to reveal their true colors.

Right. Just look at what they did:

1. At the beginning of this pandemic, the Democrats were too busy screaming "impeachment" to properly focus on the worldwide disaster China was covering up.

Not only did the Democrats handle that impeachment in the most unconstitutional way—the accused (President Trump) was denied the right to face his accuser, one of the foremost rights of any American citizen—but they made certain to keep impeachment in front of the American people instead of focusing on a real, worldwide threat.

2. On January 31, 2020, President Trump imposed travel restrictions to and from China, and the Democrats threw a hissy fit. Later, these same leaders condemned President Trump for not acting soon enough.
3. When President Trump went to Congress for monetary aid for this disaster, the Democrats tried to use the crisis to push their agenda. At a time when the coronavirus pandemic was at the front door of every American household, the Democrats thought it was important to add things like tax credits for solar and wind energy; emissions standards and carbon offset requirements for airlines; policing the racial makeup of corporate boards; retirement plans for community newspaper employees; $300 million for PBS; and, among other nonessential things, climate change studies for civil aviation and the aerospace industry. Luckily, the Senate rejected this.

Democrats seem to be okay with giving millions of American taxpayer dollars to aid foreign countries and refugees living overseas, but they choked when it came down to giving millions of American taxpayer dollars to aid America and Americans!

This is why there need to be term limits. The same people, with the same old ideas and tactics, implementing the same old fears.

4. Right when this pandemic began to get real, the Dems started to push for ballot harvesting and mail-in voting,

even though there are proven inaccuracies with this method.

5. The media (of course) and career politicians like Joe Biden were blaming President Trump for this crisis. He had only been in office for just over three years; Joe Biden had been an active politician for nearly half a century. Name us one thing that he's done to benefit America. This is why we've nicknamed him Jim Crow Joe!

6. During the protest and rioting at the end of May and beginning of June 2020, it seemed like the coronavirus decided to go on a two-week hiatus from the public. We didn't hear the news media talk about it. Then all of a sudden when President Trump made the statement that he was going to be holding a rally, the number of cases for coronavirus decided to spike up. Mm-hmm, they can fool y'all, but they can't fool us!

Now we were able to see that the Democrats didn't care for America or Americans, because they chose to defend China instead of defending America. They spread Chinese propaganda lies instead of the truth about who was responsible for this virus. They were salivating with joy at the fact that the economy was tanking with millions being unemployed. They refused to investigate China for starting the virus, but they wanted to investigate the President of the United States for how he handled the virus.

Clearly, the Democrats were more interested in Americans experiencing socialism, along with the destruction and fall of America, than in the rise and prosperity of Americans.

Fake news media is the invisible enemy of the truth. They lie, lie, lie. They are the true conspiracy theorists who create negative narratives, packed full of misinformation, to deliberately mislead the public. They act like the hall monitors, as if it's their job to police and control freedom of speech and freedom of thought. They smear you, intending to destroy, when you become a threat to their narrative. They seem to think that any lie they create is justified as long as if fits their agenda.

If our First Amendment right is freedom of speech, then who gives any media the right to infringe on that right and censor our speech? Why can't people be allowed to hear all points of view and be free to make their own decisions?

Yeah. Makes me wonder if these reporters went to journalism school or janitorial school because they oftentimes spew a whole lot of trash.

We are standing for things like constitutional rights that go directly against the media, who happen to be in bed with the Democrats. That's why the narrative is one-sided. Anyone who steps outside of the narrative or speaks against the narrative is demonized, branded, and damn near destroyed.

Our country, our lives, and our livelihoods are at stake. If Americans don't get it right in this election, our children will be paying a heavy price. For decades we've done it the way the career politicians wanted us to do it. It has never worked. What has worked, and continues to work, is a businessman who knows how to build an economy.

If you went from poverty to prosperity in the last three years, you achieved that under President Trump. Remember when he asked the question, "What the hell do you have to lose?" Well, if you don't vote RED (Remove Every Democrat), we are all going to have a hell of a lot to lose: our freedoms, our liberties, and our constitutional rights. Our pursuit of happiness and the American dream will be dismantled and destroyed. This election is about capitalism versus socialism. The question is what type of country you want to live in.

This is not the time to debate and wait; now is the time to act with facts. We have the power, and it doesn't matter if you are a Republican or Democrat; it's time for us all to vote red, or our republic as we know it is dead. We are the land of the free and the home of the brave, not slaves. Now is the time to stand and band together as Americans.

This is the United States, not the divided states. United we stand, divided we fall. Uniting together will cause all of us to stand and prosper! God wouldn't have brought us to it if He wasn't going to see us through it.

President Trump built the economy before, and he will do it again, even bigger, better, and stronger. He knows how to use commonsense solutions to solve problems.

And he is the man with the master plan to Make America Great Again.

We were created for such a time as this. In the words of President Donald J. Trump, "The best is yet to come!"

President Trump's Acknowledgments of Diamond and Silk

Introducing Diamond and Silk at
a December 4, 2015, rally:
"I see two of my friends in the audience, and they've become very famous and very rich."

"How great are they? I turn on my television one night, and I see these two on television. I say, they are the greatest. What is it? They became an Internet sensation. I hope you've monetized this."

After Diamond and Silk spoke, he said:
"How good—how good. What people—what great people."

On Fox News, April 26, 2018:

"We have Diamond and Silk, who are warriors, by the way. How about Diamond and Silk? They've become amazing. You know, that started off like—somebody was talking about them on the Internet. There were two women, these two beautiful, wonderful women, and I said, 'Well, let me check it out.' It took me about two seconds to say, 'stardom.'"

February 2020, at a Black Voices for Trump Event:

"My wife, the First Lady, said—it was a long time ago now, it's like four years ago—she said there were two people that she was watching on the Internet, the most incredible two people she's ever seen.

"I said, 'Big deal; what is it?'

"She said, 'You have to see this.'

"Then I saw it. I guess it's been almost five years. And I watched them, and they had such a spirit. They were for me before I was even running. They were so early, and you have been such great fans. I appreciate it."

Introducing Diamond and Silk at a March 2, 2020, rally, in Charlotte, North Carolina:

"Two great people, Diamond and Silk. We love them."

Official White House Photo by Shealah Craighead

Acknowledgments

We would like to thank our parents for raising us to be the women we are today. Mother and Father, you've instilled in us a boldness like no other. You have always encouraged us to reach beyond the sky. To trust and believe in God by stepping out on faith, no matter what anyone says. We love you so much. May God continue to bless you both.

To our children, siblings, and loved ones: We want to thank you for supporting us, for standing in the gap while we travel the world to help save our country, and for believing in us and our endeavors. We love you all.

To the President of the United States, President Donald John Trump. We thank you for your hard work and your love for the people of this country. Your tenacity and persistence have shown us how to keep moving forward, despite the naysayers, and that winning is our only option. Thank you for being a true friend. We love you and First Lady Melania Trump. May God continue to bless you, your family, and the United States of America.

To our fans and followers: Thank you for having our backs. You've been there with us through our journey and have witnessed the evolution of our efforts. We love and appreciate you.

Thanks to our personal consultant and research developer, Christy Stevenson Scott, for assisting us in our efforts to write this book.

Thanks to our literary agent, BMM Worldwide, Suzanne, and Elliot, for their patience and their guidance as we transitioned this book into reality.

Thanks to Regnery Publishing for believing in our vision and goals and for publishing our side of the story.

Now, let me expound on the Chit Chat Tour. We have a beautiful team that plays an important part in making sure that the tour is successful. . . . Tressie Ham handles all of our events. Her husband Bill is in charge of the merchandise sales at our Chit Chat shows. They have been like family to us since 2016.

Our DJ, by the name of Cem, is the one who keeps the crowd bumping and grooving as our photographer, Kevin, snaps pictures from beginning to end. We are so blessed to have a loyal team of people who look out for us. We love you all.

Gene Ho was the original photographer for candidate Trump during the 2016 campaign. Now he is the personal photographer for Diamond and Silk. From time to time he travels with us to snap behind-the-scene photos. We called him Geno. We found out five years later that we've been calling him by the wrong name. His name was Gene Ho. We love you, Gene Ho. But till this day, we still call him "Geno."

Special thank you to Joe Seales and RSBN, the Right Side Broadcasting Network family, for being there since day one. We thank you and your network for supporting our efforts to accelerate our message to the world. We love you and your team from the bottom of our heart.

There are a host of radio stations that have interviewed us. We love them all and thank them for the chance to share our opinions.

We sincerely thank the following newscasters: Sean Hannity, Jesse Watters, Judge Jeanine, Laura Ingraham, Rachel Campos-Duffy, Pete Hegseth, Ainsley Earhardt, Steve Doocy, and Brian Kilmeade, Fox Business with Varney and Co., and our main man, the iconic and legendary Lou Dobbs.

Special thank you to Mark Levin and Mike Lindell for supporting us in our endeavors.

May God bless you all! Love, Diamond and Silk.

Index